THE NEW IMPERIALISM, VOLUME I

Montreal, Quebec, Canada
2010

THE NEW IMPERIALISM VOLUME I

MILITARISM, HUMANISM, AND OCCUPATION

Edited by
Maximilian C. Forte

ALERT

PRESS

Montreal, Quebec, Canada
2010

Library and Archives Canada Cataloguing in Publication

The New Imperialism, Volume 1: Militarism, humanism and occupation
/ edited by Maximilian C. Forte.

(The new imperialism ; v. 1)
Includes bibliographical references and index.

ISBN 978-0-88947-496-3

1. Imperialism. 2. International relations. 3. Militarism.
4. Humanitarianism. I.
Forte, Maximilian C., 1967- II.
Series: New imperialism (Montréal, Québec) ; v. 1

JC359.M55 2010   325'.32   C2010-907350-9

© 2010 Alert Press, Montreal
1455 de Maisonneuve Blvd., W.,
Montreal, Quebec, Canada, H3G-1M8
www.alertpress.net

Printed in the United States of America

CONTENTS

FIGURES

PREFACE

This volume emerges from a recently concluded advanced undergraduate seminar in the Department of Sociology and Anthropology at Concordia University in Montreal, Canada, from which all of the contributions are drawn. The title of the seminar is "The New Imperialism," and this is the first of what is intended to be a (near) annual series of volumes.

The seminar focused on the ideological, political, and military expressions of the "new imperialism," as well as the contemporary justifications for global intervention that have advanced themselves as rationales for a "new imperialism," what others might call "liberal imperialism," "humanitarian interventionism," "military humanism," and so forth, and as we learn, it is not all that "new." While concerned with wars against "terror" and "insurgency," and Canada's own involvement in the war in Afghanistan—indeed, the war in Afghanistan remained one of the constant points of reference in most of the discussions held throughout the 13 weeks of the seminar—the key concern was the contemporary merging of humanitarianism, universalism, diplomacy, peacekeeping/peace-building, development, the production of knowledge in the social sciences, with an ascendant and expansive militarism. We therefore also addressed the militarization of the social sciences, as well as militarism in popular culture, and the militarization of foreign aid and diplomacy.

There were no lectures in this seminar. Instead, seminar participants were invited to develop or advance their own analytical perspectives around research areas of relevance to the seminar and of interest to them, and to engage with one another—quite intensely as it turned out—on a weekly basis, offering their ideas, defending them, and discovering new knowledge. While by no means always perfectly balanced between competing perspectives on a weekly basis, the assigned materials in the seminar, around which most of the discussions were held, emanated from a wide range of views, from those of military officers, political leaders, journalists, media pundits, the "policy wonks" in major think tanks, public intellectuals, to historians, political scientists, and anthropologists within academia, from diverse political standpoints. Most of the textual materials used were written for a general audience, and seminar participants themselves obtained some training in developing and articulating their own ideas in writing for a general audience. The chapters contained herein are also suitable for a general audience. One of the ideas behind the seminar was indeed about how to comprehend and address public debates and contemporary political conditions under which we, as anthropologists and sociologists, all work, and to be conscious of that fact, rather than another instance of training persons to better fold themselves into a discipline, with only academic reading within disciplinary confines. While there are excellent works by anthropologists and sociologists dealing with contemporary warfare and imperialism (or empire-building as some prefer to call it), not all of what anthropologists and sociologists need to know comes from within their disciplines, so that an introverted approach would prove inadvisable.

Each one of the chapters presented in this volume has clearly been carefully built, based on intensive and often extensive research and analysis, presenting ideas and information that most members of the general audience will find both illuminating and compelling. Not only that, they possess these qualities in equal or greater measure to much of the published material for a general audience that addresses these subjects. Having said that, not all of the papers produced by seminar participants made the final cut. The chapters, with the exception of that of the editor, are the product of consultation, review, and revision, often extending well past the end of the seminar. Their strengths are to their credit, and any shortcomings are those of the editor.

The "New" Imperialism of Militarization, Humanitarianism, and Occupation

Maximilian C. Forte

Until the recent shift from empire denial to empire avowal (Johnson, 2004, p. 67) among prominent proponents of an aggressive expansion of the U.S. presence in world affairs as the world's unrivalled military superpower, there has been for at least a few decades great reticence among scholars in North America to use the term "imperialism." Indeed, more often than not, it was bracketed by scare quotes, as I just did, as a term whose use should inspire caution, caginess, treating it as a term that possibly signaled propaganda or hyperbole. This stylistic practice has continued to a significant extent in the mainstream media, even while showing no such concern when writing about "terrorism," which has itself become an expansive, ambiguous, politically motivated catchword that can apply to just about everything from blowing up babies, to counter-terrorism, to attacks on soldiers, to erecting a blockade on a Native reserve in Canada, and to questioning the very use of the word terrorism (implying that only terrorist-sympathizers would do so). So why bother using the word, imperialism, if it presents too many definitional and political challenges to begin with? One reason is that now the leading actors themselves employ the term, and not just the anti-imperialists. Another reason, as Cohen (1973, p. 9) put it, is that the "word is part of the common language and preoccupies a large and growing part of the world's population." As he adds, to "avoid its use would be, in a sense, to avoid the issue itself" (Cohen, 1973, p. 10). What is imperialism, and what is the new imperialism?

The New Imperialism: The First Time

Imperialism has clearly taken on many different meanings, and its uses have been varied. It has referred to political systems under the rule of an emperor, with greatly centralized power (and reappears today in discussions of the "the imperial presidency" in the U.S.); it has also been synonymous with colonialism overseas, with the acquisition of colonies central to building an empire; it has been tied to monopoly capitalism; it has referred to both indirect control through economic and cultural pressures, as well as direct military intervention; it has been implicated in nation-building and internal colonialism in settler states such as the U.S., Canada, and Australia; it has been both nationalistic, and materialistic, driven by either ideology or strict calculations of economic gain, sometimes both. In the midst of this mass proliferation of meanings of imperialism there have been, over the past 150 years, two periods when one encounters references to a "new imperialism."

In the first instance, in late nineteenth and early twentieth century Britain, the term was used by both opponents and adherents to an imperialistic policy. In the 1870s, when use of the term imperialism spread to Britain, "supporters, as well as critics, of Prime Minister Disraeli began to describe his policy of strengthening and expanding the British colonial empire as imperialistic" (Cohen, 1973, p. 10). In the second instance, especially notable in the U.S. since the advent of George W. Bush and liberal interventionists (wrongly yet widely called "neo-conservatives"), the phrase has once again surfaced in the literature. "Imperialism" is neither passé, nor solely the rhetorical possession of one side of a debate.

As best as I can tell, the earliest and most salient use of the phrase in the literature, "New Imperialism" (written with or without capitals, in the same text even), is to be found repeatedly in the 1905 classic, *Imperialism: A Study*, by J. A. Hobson (specifically on pp. 21, 22, 23, 27, 35, 38, 39, 43, 45, 46, 53, 64, 71, 118, 124, 136, 138, 139, 152, 304, 328, 337, 352, 353, 355, 367). It is not even clear that this "new imperialism" was all that new, in the way Hobson handles it. It seems to be his particular way of distinguishing between colonization through white settlement, versus acquiring despotic control over non-European populations: "The new Imperialism has been…chiefly concerned with tropical and sub-tropical countries where large 'lower races' are brought under white control" (Hobson, 1905, p. 136). On the one hand, there does not appear to be anything "new" about that, not even when restricted to Britain alone, since it had multiple forms of colonization from the 1600s onwards. On the other hand, Hobson gives the phrase more specific meaning as he delves further into comparison between past and then (present) imperialism, with some telling parallels (the original spelling is retained): "The new Imperialism differs from the older, first in substituting for the ambition of a single growing empire the theory and the practice of competing empires, each motived by similar lusts of political aggrandisement and commercial gain; secondly, in the dominance of financial or investing over mercantile interests" (1905, p. 304). Most important, it is what we might call a post-crude imperialism—new for being more refined, more indirect, more competitive, and not based on outright slavery and direct political control. There are then, it appears, two new imperialisms in Hobson's work: one being the imperialism that acquires control over populations in tropical zones, the other being dominated by competition between empires and the dominance of the financial sector. These need not be mutually exclusive.

In some instances, pertaining to the late nineteenth century, writers spoke of a "new imperialism" as a means of referring to something that was not so much substantively new, as it was a current phase, a new wave of imperialism, especially with reference to the Scramble for Africa (Bongie, 1991, p. 18). In other cases, with reference to British and American imperialism of the late nineteenth and early twentieth centuries (circa 1880-1915), "the new imperialism" refers to "a new attitude of responsibility and obligation" (Betts, 1968, p. 74), not so unlike the current preoccupation with "humanitarian interventionism" and the "responsibility to protect." As Betts summarized, "many late-nineteenth-century Europeans convinced themselves that they were discharging a significant burden by helping the 'lesser breeds'" (Betts, 1968, p. 74). This was a "new" conception of "Empire as a duty" (Carrington, 1950, p. 663), as a duty to the prestige of the motherland, to world order, and to "civilization" itself.

Other arguments hold that there was something indeed "new" about imperialism in the late nineteenth century, without positing any fundamental break with the past. For August (1985, p. 1) the erection of tariff walls and the rise of the new nationalism contributed to "a new vision of empire" in both Britain and France. Also distinctive was that imperialists in Britain and France "set out to build a mass movement, to win the hearts and minds of their compatriots" (August, 1985, p. 1). The public proponents of imperialism argued that "economic and political rivalry among the leading industrial powers" dictated a "redefinition of the 'national interest' along imperialist lines" (August, 1985, p. 1).

Even at this stage, in the first articulation of "the new imperialism," we see a conjunction of forces and motivations paralleled by the new imperialism of the early twenty-first century. Among these we can list, from the aforementioned arguments: 1) economic competition against other emergent powers; 2) a new phase of expansionism; 3) empire as responsibility and duty; 4) public propaganda to win supporters at home for new adventures abroad. The latter element is today referred to by various terms: public diplomacy, information operations, strategic communications, and soft power.

The New Imperialism: One More Time

In the simplest of terms, the "new imperialism" today (now appearing more often in book and chapter titles—see Connelly, 2006; Harvey, 2003; Heller, 2006; Magdoff, 2003, ch. 2; Mooers, 2006) is not a phrase that is necessarily used to argue that current imperialism is fundamentally new and without historical precedents and foundations. With respect to the temporal dimension—the new—the idea tends to be used more often as a shorthand for contemporary imperialism, that of the U.S., following the end of the Cold War. More substantively, it embraces the confluence and culmination of several trends and factors in the contemporary period, ranging from unilateralism, empire avowal (no shame in being imperialists, let's do a better job of it), increased militarism in popular culture, war corporatism, the extraordinary global spread and multiplication of U.S. military facilities, the militarization of politics and economics, neo-colonial forms of "humanitarianism," full spectrum occupation and the creation of new international protectorates when convenient (notably Bosnia, Kosovo, and Haiti), and the increased interest in the use of "soft power" to acquire some degree of legitimacy that was lost by undermining the UN and its Charter. The chapters in this book explore these various dimensions in the new imperialist cluster, across a range of countries, including Algeria, Afghanistan, Canada, Colombia, Ethiopia, Somalia, Iran, Kosovo, Kuwait, and the U.S. The dominant themes of the chapters prepared by the seminar participants place themselves under certain logical headings, given this cluster: militarism and militarization; humanitarianism and the responsibility to protect; occupation; and, soft power.

Historical Context, Political Economy, and the New Imperialism

In Magdoff's work there is an attempt to retain ties between contemporary imperialism and world capitalism. Magdoff argues that "there are good and sufficient reasons for clearly marking off a new period in the affairs of world capitalism," for which the term "new imperialism" may be used (2003, p. 35). The distinguishing features of the new imperialism that he highlights are: a) that the U.K. is no longer the leading industrial power, and, b) that within each of the leading industrial powers, economic power shifted to a small number of very big integrated industrial and financial firms. However, even this approach appears to be dated, valid perhaps only to the 1980s, since it does not take into account de-industrialization or any of the other features listed in the last paragraph—nor should we attempt to develop a definition for a "new new imperialism" for the obvious abuses to which this lends itself. Indeed, much of his definition of the "new imperialism" seems most applicable to the late nineteenth and early twentieth centuries (Magdoff, 2003, p. 41). Magdoff goes beyond this, to more recent times, and he writes:

> "The imperialism of today has several distinctly new features: These are…1) the shift of the main emphasis from rivalry in carving up the world to the struggle against the contraction of the imperialist system; 2) the new role of the United States as organizer and leader of the world imperialist system; and 3) the rise of a technology which is international in character." (Magdoff, 2003, p. 46)

What is also new, Magdoff later adds, is that the U.S. has become a "have not" nation for a wide range of common and rare minerals, on which giant corporations still rely and which are now almost always "foreign" sources (2003, p. 50). We will return to this point later.

Placing the new imperialism today in historical context, Heller (2006) deals with globalization, neoliberal capitalism, structural adjustment across the "developing world," the decline in multilateral political institutions and the rise of U.S. dominated multilateral economic institutions, and military actions since 11 September 2001 (frequently referred to in this book, as elsewhere, as "9/11"). Discourse also matters, considerably, to the extent that it announces intentions, plays a role in shaping public opinion, and articulates policy. In this vein, Heller notes that since the end of the Cold War around 1990, we see a case where the dominant U.S. discourse of power evolved from, "discussion of American indispensability, unipolarity, and possible unilateralism," to one that was soon enlarged "to frank avowals of American primacy, hegemony, empire, and even imperialism" (Heller, 2006, p. 320). Empire avowal means that "imperialism" no longer needs the scare quotes—imperialism is no longer a dirty word of accusation, when we triumphantly adopt it as the buzzword of our new public credo. Here Heller observes that "key foreign policy experts spoke of the necessity of preventive war to block the emergence of possible rivals to American military power" (2006, p. 320). In addition, "the militarization of American foreign policy was a notable feature of this rhetoric" (Heller, 2006, p. 320). Combined with this was the rise to dominance of a political elite in Washington with close ties to the defense industry, and the rise of a new imperialist elite that frankly championed unilateralism and outright empire, the emergence and inclusion in government of the so-called "neo-conservatives" such as Richard Perle, Paul Wolfowitz, and Douglas Feith, and their Project for a New American Century. Other "neo-con" branches were to be found in private Washington think tanks which frequently provided the talking heads called upon by the mainstream media, as well as neo-cons housed within media outlets themselves, these two facets best represented by Bill Kristol and Charles Krauthammer, and Max Boot, who spans the think tank-media distinction (not divide).

The new imperialist project, singularly American, envisages a coercive refashioning of the world to suit American interests. This call for a new order was first used to justify a massive military buildup, even without a superpower rival to justify it, and the retention of all Cold War military installations, with the creation of hundreds of new ones worldwide. Launching itself in an open-ended and permanent "war on terror," the U.S. cared less and less for multilateral solutions, paid scant attention to domestic and global public opposition, and set about remaking the Middle East and Central Asia, targeting Iraq and Afghanistan, and heightening threats to Iran. With reference to multilateralism, Chomsky quotes former Reagan State Department official Francis Fukuyama who wrote in 1992: "[the UN is] perfectly serviceable as an instrument of American unilateralism and indeed may be the primary mechanism through which that unilateralism will be exercised in the future" (2003, p. 29).

While discourse matters, so do underlying economic conditions for American imperial expansion. As Heller explains:

"This audacious U.S. plan [described above] was born out of overwhelming military strength combined with a growing sense of economic vulnerability. On the latter point, American military power and, if possible, control of Middle East oil would enable it to reassert its waning economic primacy while shoring up the dollar. Massive increases in military and reconstruction expenditure in the form of contracts to American companies would help to reawaken the United States economy out of deep recession." (Heller, 2006, p. 321)

Eric Hobsbawm makes an almost identical point: "Military strength underlines the economic vulnerability of a United States whose enormous trade deficit is maintained by Asian investors, whose economic interest in supporting a falling dollar is rapidly diminishing" (2008, pp. 56-57). In U.S. strength, Hobsbawm finds weakness: "Indeed, may not the very rhetoric of aggression justified by implausible 'threats to America' indicate a basic sense of insecurity about the global future of the United States?" (2008, p. 57).

Again, in historical context, this new imperialism parallels some of the phenomena of the early twentieth century, during "new imperialism, part one." Heller speaks to this question of historical cyclicality:

"Predatory and militaristic behaviour may, in fact, be rooted in factors deeply lodged in an American economy in relative decline, in the predisposition of American politics and society, or, indeed, in the nature of the existing global political economy. If so, the American invasion of Iraq marks the beginning of a new period of unpredictable and destructive international rivalry that harks back to the conflicts of the early twentieth century." (Heller, 2006, p. 325)

This volume focuses on a particular cluster of the current magnification or reconfiguration of power, ambition, intent, and means. The focus is specifically on militarism, the military-industrial-media-academic complex, soft power, humanitarianism, and occupation. Certainly there are other approaches worth considering that shed some light on the new in the new imperialism. David Harvey (2003), using that phrase as the title of his volume, provides one of these approaches, focusing on the contemporary, and in particular on the invasion of Iraq. To those who would scoff at (their caricatured) arguments about a "war for oil," Harvey effectively says: not so fast. There is more to this argument than meets the eye, if one is willing to go beyond simplistic assertions, and equally hasty denials.

What is new about the new imperialism is partly reflected in the deeper and unstated reasons for the U.S. war against Iraq, Harvey argues. One reason for the war that he highlights is the tactic of using foreign military adventures abroad, and the concomitant fear mongering at home, to divert attention away from domestic "difficulties" (Harvey, 2003, p. 12). He admits this is nothing new, but certainly the specific problems motivating leaders to use this tactic are particular to the present. Among the difficulties he lists, are those that have become acute for the past decade, and that continue to worsen: a recession that began in 2001; rising unemployment; corporate scandals; catastrophic corporate accounting failures; lost pensions; health care in a mess; increased domestic indebtedness, and foreign indebtedness, with the U.S. becoming the biggest debtor nation in world history. We can also add to the list a loss of legitimacy of national institutions and mainstream party politics; the growing disgust with influence peddling in Congress; dependency on loans and imports from abroad, and so forth. Any party in power—and specifically the Republican Party on the eve of 11 September 2001, would favour distraction, deflection, and a nationalist revival (Harvey, 2003, p. 13).

A second and related explanation offered by Harvey is that war is a means for the state to increase its power, and for a government to build national solidarity and domestic social cohesion, in a situation that seems to lack both (Harvey, 2003, pp. 15-17). As American society was perceived by some on the right as collapsing into a state of increased disorder, the chaos of competing private interests coupled with "irrational" acts of disaffection (riots, school shootings, militia violence), society "seemed to be fragmenting and flying apart at an alarming rate" (Harvey, 2003, p. 17). The absence of a defined external enemy in the 1990s only aggravated this perceived senseless disorientation. War after 9/11 would help to change that, by inspiring national purpose, national solidarity, and patriotism. Security, the "homeland," flag pins, real Americans. As Harvey argues,

> "The engagement with Iraq was far more than a mere diversion from difficulties at home; it was a grand opportunity to impose a new sense of social order at home and bring the commonwealth to heel. Criticism was silenced as unpatriotic. The evil enemy without became the prime force through which to exorcise or tame the devils lurking within." (Harvey, 2003, p. 17)

A third reason for war with Iraq, that highlights a key aspect of the new imperialism in Harvey's explanation, concerns oil. Harvey, arguing against easy dismissals about the "war for oil" theme, says that "there is no question that oil is crucial. But exactly how and in what sense is not so easy to determine" (2003, p. 18). Harvey does not agree with simplistic assertions that the U.S. intended to simply go into Iraq and take all of its oil for itself. Instead, Harvey argues for a different proposition, that the war was about *controlling access*, as an economic good in itself: "whoever controls the Middle East controls the oil spigot and whoever controls the global oil spigot can control the global economy, at least for the near future" (2003, p. 19). For a U.S. dependent on imports and foreign loans, this is a vital stranglehold, a clever way to use its massive military apparatus to positive economic effect. It is international economic blackmail. China could conceivably cause the collapse of the dollar, and cause the U.S. to implode economically by recalling all of its loans. On the other hand, the U.S. could cause the industrial collapse of China by shutting off access to its most important sources of oil. In the meantime, China continues to lend and export, and therefore the oil continues to flow. The U.S. has thus implicitly negotiated for itself an arrangement with ascending economic powers, as its own power declines, using the best instrument it has at its disposal, to exercise maximum leverage: the military.

Harvey notes that this started to take shape as policy at least as far back as the administration of Jimmy Carter in the late 1970s:

"President Carter enunciated the doctrine that the United States would not under any circumstances allow an interruption of the flow of Gulf oil. This meant a commitment to keeping the Strait of Hormuz open *(for the delivery and distribution systems are every bit as important as the oilfields themselves)* and a permanent military presence in the region, plus the formation of a Rapid Deployment Force to deal with any emergencies [emphasis added]." (Harvey, 2003, p. 21)

Likewise, on 11 September 1990, then President George H. W. Bush in a joint address to Congress about the impending Gulf War made these very telling points (see Appendix B for the full speech):

"Vital economic interests are at risk as well. Iraq itself controls some 10 percent of the world's proven oil reserves. Iraq plus Kuwait controls twice that. An Iraq permitted to swallow Kuwait would have the economic and military power, as well as the arrogance, to intimidate and coerce its neighbors—neighbors who control the lion's share of the world's remaining oil reserves. We cannot permit a resource so vital to be dominated by one so ruthless. And we won't. (¶ 9)

"Our ability to function effectively as a great power abroad depends on how we conduct ourselves at home. Our economy, our Armed Forces, our energy dependence, and our cohesion all determine whether we can help our friends and stand up to our foes. For America to lead, America must remain strong and vital. Our world leadership and domestic strength are mutual and reinforcing; a woven piece, strongly bound as Old Glory. To revitalize our leadership, our leadership capacity, we must address our budget deficit—not after election day, or next year, but now. (¶ 21)

"Higher oil prices slow our growth, and higher defense costs would only make our fiscal deficit problem worse." (Bush, 1990, ¶ 22)

(Bush also said in the same speech, "Americans must never again enter any crisis, economic or military, with an excessive dependence on foreign oil and an excessive burden of Federal debt" [Bush, 1990, ¶ 23]—presumably this is an element of the speech that some American leaders have forgotten or never accepted.)

Harvey concludes his explanation of the root economic basis of the new imperialism thus: "Access to Middle Eastern oil is now…a crucial security issue for the United States, as it is for the global economy as a whole" (2003, pp. 23-24). The issue is so critical given that the rate of exploitation of oil reserves has exceeded the rate of discovery of new reserves for the past 30 years, and oil is thus becoming increasingly scarce (Harvey, 2003, p. 23). Harvey also notes that, "the only fields that look set to last fifty years or more are those in Iran, Iraq, Saudi Arabia, the United Arab Emirates, and Kuwait" (2003, p, 23). Harvey's argument has been reinforced by more recent data about world oil production, increased demand, and reduced supply (see especially Macalister, 2009a, 2009b; Elkington & Kendall, 2009).

The Iraq war may not have been a war *for* oil, but it seems likely to have been a war *about* oil, about U.S. nationalism, and about enhancing the U.S. military presence worldwide, as a strategic means to delay inevitable imperial decline that is already in progress. That is yet another feature of the "new imperialism"—for Britain in the early twentieth century, as for the U.S. in the early twenty-first century, it appears as the empire begins to collapse.

There are also decidedly non-Marxist interpretations of the existence of American empire that choose to focus heavily on military power. One prominent example comes from the works of a former CIA analyst, Chalmers Johnson. Johnson focuses on the global spread of U.S. military bases. Military ubiquity is critical in his analysis, especially as with the end of the Cold War it should have become clear even to the empire-denying part of the American public that America's vast network of military bases abroad was being maintained despite the absence of any external military threat like the USSR (Johnson, 2000, p. 5). He writes of "America's informal empire" as one "based on the projection of military power to every corner of the world and on the use of American capital and markets to force global economic integration on our terms, at whatever costs to others [emphasis added]" (Johnson, 2000, p. 7). Johnson then provides us with his theory of empire:

"In speaking of an 'American empire,' however, I am not using the concept in these traditional senses [those being Marxist-Leninist ones, and those based on historical analogies with Rome, Britain, etc.]. I am not talking about the United States' former colony in the Philippines, or about such dependent territories as Puerto Rico, nor when I use the term 'imperialism'…do I mean the extension of one state's legal dominion over another; nor do I even want to imply that imperialism must have primarily economic causes. The more modern empires I have in mind normally lie concealed beneath some ideological or juridical concept—commonwealth, alliance, free world, the West, the Communist bloc—that disguises the actual relationships among its members." (2000, p. 19)

Also divorcing imperialism from capitalism, somewhat in the same vein as Johnson, is the approach offered by one of the leading "new imperialist" scholars, Niall Ferguson. Ferguson argues that "empire" denotes "the extension of one's civilization, usually by military force, to rule over other peoples" (2004, p. 169).

Catherine Lutz's approach to the "empire of bases" relinks the spread of military bases with other basic features of imperial dominance. Lutz argues that "a country can be called an empire when its policies aim to assert and maintain dominance over other regions," and those policies succeed when "wealth is extracted from peripheral areas and redistributed to the imperial center" (2009b, p. 9). There is a proliferation of military bases when states have imperial ambitions and exercise either direct control of territory or indirect control via political economy, laws, and foreign policy. An empire of bases, Lutz says, "is associated with a growing gap between the wealth and welfare of the powerful center and the regions affiliated with it," and along with this there has often been an "elevated self-regard in the imperial power, or a sense of racial, cultural, or social superiority" (2009b, p. 9).

Most controversial in recent times, perhaps, has been the work of Michael Hardt and Antonio Negri as found in *Empire* (2000). What they call empire is "a new global form of sovereignty", with a "series of national and supranational organisms united under a single logic of rule" (Hardt & Negri, 2000, p. xii). They distinguish "empire" in their sense from "imperialism" (Hardt & Negri, 2000, p. xii). Moreover, they assert that *"The United States does not, and indeed no nation-state can today, form the center of an imperialist project* [their emphasis]. Imperialism is over. No nation will be world leader in the way modern European nations were" (Hardt & Negri, 2000, pp. xiii-xiv). What is critical about Empire (as they capitalize it) is the lack of boundaries: "Empire's rule has no limits" (Hardt & Negri, 2000, p. xiv). Their Empire is all pervasive, and seeks to rule down to the deepest depths of human nature. Its aim is "peace," they think: "although the practice of Empire is continually bathed in blood, the concept of Empire is always dedicated to peace–a perpetual and universal peace outside of history" (Hardt & Negri, 2000, p. xv). The crisis of the nation-state form is what propels the world toward Empire. The new normative global order, as they see it, rules over all:

"what used to be conflict or competition among several imperialist powers has in important respects been replaced by the idea of a single power that overdetermines them all, structures them in a unitary way and treats them under one common notion of right that is decidedly postcolonial and postimperialist. This is really the point of departure for our study of Empire: a new notion of right, or rather, a new inscription of authority and a new design of the production of norms and legal instruments of coercion that guarantee contracts and resolve conflicts." (Hardt & Negri, 2000, p. 9)

Tracing the genealogy of Empire back to Christian Rome, the authors see a "rebirth of the concept of Empire" evidenced by key symptoms (except that this Empire apparently has no Rome):

"One symptom, for example, is the renewed interest in and effectiveness of the concept of bellum justum, or 'just war'....The traditional concept of just war involves the banalization of war and the celebration of it as an ethical instrument, both of which were ideas that modern political thought and the international community of nation-states had resolutely refused. These two traditional characteristics have reappeared in our postmodern world: on the one hand, war is reduced to the status of police action, and on the other, the new power that can legitimately exercise ethical functions through war is sacralized." (Hardt & Negri, 2000, p. 12)

Another key symptom is the development of the "right of intervention" (Hardt & Negri, 2000, p. 18). What stands behind this intervention, on humanitarian and moral grounds, is "a permanent state of emergency and exception justified by *the appeal to essential values of justice* [their emphasis]" (Hardt & Negri, 2000, p. 18). Theirs is an empire without imperialism, and governance without government. A new Rome, but without the Rome.

One wonders then, to borrow Gertrude Stein's phrase: "Is there a *there* there?" Boron (2005) argues there is, and thoroughly dismantles Hardt and Negri's attempt at reformulating empire as a post-modern juridical innovation with no real centre. Taking away the discovery of novelty, historian Eric Hobsbawm reminds us that "Empires have always justified themselves, sometimes quite sincerely, in moral terms—whether they claimed to spread (their version of) civilization or religion to the benighted, or to spread (their version of) freedom to the victims of (someone else's) oppression, or, today, as champions of human rights" (2008, p. 52). Likewise, Bricmont argues that the rhetoric of humanitarian intervention is what links the new imperialism of the late nineteenth century Britain with the new imperialism of the early twenty-first century U.S.: "British liberal imperialists discovered in the late nineteenth century that presenting foreign interventions as moral crusades was particularly effective in whipping up popular support in a parliamentary democracy with a press eager to denounce foreign villainy" (2006, p. 69).

Empire Avowal

As mentioned before, one of the features of the contemporary "new imperialism" is precisely the explicit embrace of imperialism by writers and policy makers tied to the defense establishment, to think tanks, and elite academic institutions. As the New York Times' Emily Eakin observed:

> "Americans are used to being told—typically by resentful foreigners—that they are imperialists. But lately some of the nation's own eminent thinkers are embracing the idea. More astonishing, they are using the term with approval. From the isolationist right to the imperialist-bashing left, a growing number of experts are issuing stirring paeans to American empire." (Eakin, 2002, ¶ 5)

"The label of empire does not bother William Kristol, a neoconservative leader and editor of the *Weekly Standard* magazine," Morgan (2003, ¶ 15) tells us, "'If people want to say we're an imperial power, fine,' he has stated." Harvard University historian Niall Ferguson, author of *Empire: The Rise and Demise of the British World Order and the Lessons for Global Power* says the U.S. should stop denying its imperial role and study the good the British Empire did in spreading prosperity and progressive thought: "The United States is and should be an empire" (Morgan, 2003, ¶ 18). "People are now coming out of the closet on the word 'empire'," said columnist Charles Krauthammer, and with approval he adds: "The fact is no country has been as dominant culturally, economically, technologically and militarily in the history of the world since the Roman Empire" (quoted in Eakin, 2002, ¶ 4). Robert D. Kaplan stated: "There's a positive side to empire. It's in some ways the most benign form of order" (quoted in Eakin, 2002, ¶ 16). Max Boot, of the Council on Foreign Relations and frequent columnist in many of the U.S.' largest circulation newspapers, had a stream of articles with titles such as: "The Case for American Empire" (2001); "American Imperialism? No Need to Run Away from a Label" (2003a); "U.S. Imperialism: A Force for Good" (2003b); "Washington Needs a Colonial Office" (2003c); and, "Enlightened Imperialism Could Save Liberia" (2003d). Boot (2003a, ¶ 5, 6) frankly stated:

> "on the whole, U.S. imperialism has been the greatest force for good in the world during the past century....Yet, while generally successful as imperialists, Americans have been loath to confirm that's what they were doing. That's OK. Given the historical baggage that 'imperialism' carries, there's no need for the U.S. government to embrace the term. But it should definitely embrace the practice."

Elsewhere, Boot has asserted: "Afghanistan and other troubled lands today cry out for the sort of enlightened foreign administration once provided by self-confident Englishmen in jodhpurs and pith helmets," adding later, "unilateral U.S. rule may no longer be an option today" (2001, ¶ 7, 9).

As Chalmers Johnson remarked,

> "not since the jingoists of the Spanish-American War have so many Americans openly called for abandoning even a semblance of constitutional and democratic foreign policy and endorsed imperialism." (Johnson, 2004, p. 67)

Almost as if a cyclical return to the first new imperialism, at the time of the Spanish-American War, two camps have formed: those who call for an unconstrained, unilateral imperialism, and those who seek empire through the pursuit of "humanitarian" objectives (Johnson, 2004, p. 67). Representative of the former are Charles Krauthammer, Robert D. Kaplan, Max Boot, and others. Representative of the latter, heirs to the tradition of Woodrow Wilson, defenders of soft imperialism or humanitarian imperialism, are the globalist liberals who believe in "making the world safe for democracy" such as Sebastian Mallaby and Michael Ignatieff.

Speaking of imperialism, Michael Ignatieff argued for its necessity:

> "Imperialism used to be the white man's burden. This gave it a bad reputation. But imperialism doesn't stop being necessary just because it becomes politically incorrect. Nations sometimes fail, and when they do, only outside help—imperial power—can get them back on their feet.

> "Nation-building is the kind of imperialism you get in a human rights era, a time when great powers believe simultaneously in the right of small nations to govern themselves and in their own right to rule the world. Nation-building lite is supposed to reconcile these principles: to safeguard American interests in Central Asia at the lowest possible cost and to give Afghanistan back a stable government of its own choosing." (Ignatieff, 2002, ¶ 69)

Speaking of the U.S. in particular, Ignatieff asked: "what word but 'empire' describes the awesome thing that America is becoming?" (2003b, ¶ 2). He then answers with obvious admiration and approval: "the 21st century imperium is a new invention in the annals of political science, an empire lite, a global hegemony whose grace notes are free markets, human rights and democracy, enforced by the most awesome military power the world has ever known" (Ignatieff, 2003b, ¶ 5). Elsewhere he adds, "America's entire war on terror is an exercise in imperialism. This may come as a shock to Americans, who don't like to think of their country as an empire. But what else can you call America's legions of soldiers, spooks and Special Forces straddling the globe?" (Ignatieff, 2002, ¶ 4). Ignatieff concludes: "The case for empire is that it has become, in a place like Iraq, the last hope for democracy and stability alike" (2003b, ¶ 23). Iraq has neither—but Ignatieff has yet to revise his "case for empire." Indeed, he has offered the imperialists some helpful advice: "Effective imperial power also requires controlling the subject people's sense of time, convincing them that they will be ruled forever" (2002, ¶ 29). Ignatieff worries: "The question, then, is not whether America is too powerful but whether it is powerful enough" (2003a, ¶ 29).

Ignatieff writes in a rather sober way about the humanitarian imperialists. Having argued for their necessity, it's not clear that his words are meant to be taken as criticizing them. Ignatieff (2002) states, and it is worth quoting at length,

"Wherever the traveling caravan of nation-builders settles, it creates an instant boomtown, living on foreign money and hope (¶ 37).... Kabul is the Klondike of the new century, a place where a young person can make, if not a fortune, then a stellar career riding the tide of international money that is flooding in with every United Nations flight from Islamabad. It's one of the few places where a bright spark just out of college can end up in a job that comes with a servant and a driver. So Kabul has the social attractions of a colonial outpost joined to the feverish excitement of a boomtown (¶ 38).

"Nation-building isn't supposed to be an exercise in colonialism, but the relationship between the locals and the internationals is inherently colonial. The locals do the translating, cleaning and driving while the internationals do the grand imperial planning (¶ 42).

"The UN nation-builders all repeat the mantra that they are here to 'build capacity' and to 'empower local people.' *This is the authentic vocabulary of the new imperialism, only it isn't as new as it sounds.* The British called it 'indirect rule.' Local agents ran the day-to-day administration; local potentates exercised some power, while real decisions were made back in imperial capitals. Indirect rule is the pattern in Afghanistan: the illusion of self-government joined to the reality of imperial tutelage (¶ 48, emphasis added).

"American foreign assistance concentrates on food aid in part because it sops up U.S. farm surpluses. The unpleasant underside of nation-building is that the internationals' first priority is building their own capacity—increasing their budgets and giving themselves good jobs. The last priority is financing the Afghan government." (¶ 50)

Where Ignatieff seems to write with acid about the reality (and remember, necessity) of humanitarian imperialists, he is much brasher about defending pre-emptive war (the most supreme of all international crimes, according to the Nuremberg tribunal [International Criminal Court, 1998, ¶ 9]):

"The dilemmas here are best illustrated by looking closely at pre-emptive war. It is a lesser evil because, according to our traditional understanding of war, the only justified resort to war is a response to actual aggression. But those standards are outdated. They were conceived for wars against states and their armies, not for wars against terrorists and suicide bombers. Against this kind of enemy, everyone can see that instead of waiting for terrorists to hit us, it makes sense to get our retaliation in first." (Ignatieff, 2004, ¶ 44).

Here Ignatieff plays at forgetting that the war in Iraq was first a war against a state and its army, and against a state that never attacked the U.S., nor had the means to do so. Ignatieff went as far as defending torture and targeted assassinations, also crimes under international humanitarian law: "To defeat evil, we may have to traffic in evils: indefinite detention of suspects, coercive interrogations, targeted assassinations, even pre-emptive war....A liberal society cannot be defended by herbivores. We need carnivores to save us, but we had better make sure the meat-eaters hunt only on our orders" (2004, ¶ 11, 52).

Militarism, Militarization, and War Corporatism

Ascendant, and nearly hegemonic militarism is also a critical feature of this new imperialism. Here I wish to quote Johnson at length, given his effective description of the fundamental changes that have occurred in American political economy that demonstrate this militarist ascendance and the dominance of the national security state:

> "As late as 1874, well after the Civil War, our country's standing army had an authorized strength of only 16,000 soldiers, and the military was considerably less important to most Americans than, say, the post office. In those days, an American did not need a passport or governmental permission to travel abroad. When immigrants arrived they were tested only for infectious diseases and did not have to report to anyone. No drugs were prohibited. Tariffs were the main source of revenue for the federal government; there was no income tax.

> "A century and a quarter later the U.S. Army has 480,000 members, the navy 375,000, the air force 359,000, and the marines 175,000, for a total of 1,389,000 men and women on active duty. The payroll for these uniformed personnel in 2003 was $27.1 billion for the active army, $22 billion each for the navy and the air force, and $8.6 billion for the marines. Today, the federal government can tap into and listen to all citizens' phone calls, faxes, and e-mail transmissions if it chooses to. It has begun to incarcerate native-born and naturalized citizens as well as immigrants and travelers in military prisons without bringing charges against them. The president alone decides who is an 'illegal belligerent,' a term the Bush administration introduced, and there is no appeal from his decision. Much of the defense budget and all intelligence agency budgets are secret. These are all signs of militarism and of the creation of the national security state." (Johnson, 2004, pp. 78-79)

The military has become the single largest purchaser of goods and services in the U.S. It is also the world's single largest consumer of petroleum. Almost every imaginable company, and most of the major mainstream media corporations, either has defense contracts, or is owned by a major defense contractor (see Turse, 2008). As anthropologist Catherine Lutz (2009a) described, the American nation-state is one marked by permanent war. Permanent war began in 1947 with the passage of the National Security Act, and the creation of what is effectively a second, shadow state organization that includes the National Security Organization (NSA), the National Security Council (NSC), and the Central Intelligence Agency (CIA), to which we can now add several more. The head of this second state, as Lutz puts it, is an imperial President with ever expanding powers. The U.S. has the largest military budget in recorded history, regardless of the end of the Cold War. This goes beyond published figures, as there is also a "black budget" whose funds are kept secret even from Congress. The Pentagon's black budget reached $32 billion a year under Bush and "billions more in black funds go to the CIA and NSA, whose budgets are completely classified, disguised as seemingly unrelated line items in the budgets of other government departments, which sometimes even Congress does not realize" (Lutz, 2009a, p. 368). In 2009, $1.2 trillion was spent on military matters, including the off-budget costs of the wars in Iraq and Afghanistan, debt payments for past wars, and allocations for veteran care. In terms of global reach, the U.S. now has over 190,000 troops and 115,000 civilian employees in 909 military facilities in 46 countries and territories, with bases located on 795,000 acres of land owned or rented by the U.S., housing over 26,000 buildings and structures, figures that obviously do not include secret and other unacknowledged installations (Lutz, 2009a, p. 368). The U.S. military rents or owns 28 million acres in total (43,750 square miles). The U.S. military has become the single biggest employer in the U.S., paying the wages of 2.3 million soldiers and 700,000 civilians, with even the largest private corporations dwarfed by comparison. This in a country where politicians and public commentators shriek at any hint of "socialism," yet remain largely mute in the face of such massive state expenditures and social regimentation. Having remodeled itself, as Lutz says, after neoliberal business restructuring, the U.S. military now has as many temporary employees as permanent ones: 1.4 million are permanent employees in the regular branches of the military, with another 0.9 million in the Reserves and National Guard. Millions more Americans receive paycheques through defense contracting. Taking all of this into account, Lutz shows that military labour constitutes 5 per cent of the total U.S. workforce (Lutz, 2009a, p. 369). One quarter of scientists and technicians in the U.S. work on military contracts. Now, work that was once done within the military is now contracted out to private firms. To this we can add the fact that the Pentagon has "perhaps the single largest public relations apparatus on earth—spending $4.7 billion on P.R. in 2009 alone and employing 27,000 people, a staff nearly as large as the 30,000-person State Department" (Taibbi, 2010, ¶ 7), and substantial influence in Hollywood (Forte, 2010; Robb, 2004; Stahl, 2010).

Where Lutz points to the U.S. military's consumption of natural resources, we might return to Magdoff who tells us of the interests of the U.S. Defense Department in securing access to strategic raw materials. He informs us that it "operates with a list of strategic and critical raw materials as a guide to the stockpiling program," materials that are "critical to the war potential" (especially because they are used for the production of armaments) and where "supply difficulties can be anticipated" (Magdoff, 2003, pp. 54-55). For more than half of the items that the Pentagon needs, "80 to 100 percent of the supply...depends on imports" (Magdoff, 2003, p. 55). In addition, "For 52 out of the 62 materials, at least 40% have to be supplied from abroad" (Magdoff, 2003, p. 55). Moreover, "three quarters of the imported materials in the stockpile program come from the underdeveloped areas" (Magdoff, 2003, p. 55). As a board reporting to the President stated in the 1950s, "The loss of any of these materials, through aggression, would be the equivalent of a grave military set-back" (Magdoff, 2003, p. 55). When it comes to the production of the jet engine, six critical materials are needed (Tungsten, Chromium, Nickel, Columbium, Molybendum, and Cobalt)—and except for Molybendum, the U.S. is dependent on imports for an adequate supply of all of these items, and totally dependent on imports in the cases of columbium, chromium, and cobalt (Magdoff, 2003, p. 56).

We can also relate the militarization found under the new imperialism to the neoliberalism that has reshaped economies and reformulated the power of the state. Hobsbawm identifies one of the current transformations of the sovereign state given the ascendancy and global spread of "the prevailing theology of the free market," as being the privatization of seemingly everything: "states are actually abandoning many of their most traditional direct activities–postal services, police, prisons, even important parts of their armed forces–to profit-making private contractors. It has been estimated that 100,000 or more such armed 'private contractors' are at present active in Iraq" (2008, p. 43). One of the dominant features of current military interventions by the U.S. is that of war corporatism. This is tied by Hobsbawm into another contemporary feature of politics in the U.S., and that is the unwillingness of the population to serve on war fronts: "I very much doubt whether any state today—not the United States, Russia, or China—could engage in major wars with conscript armies ready to fight and die 'for their country' to the bitter end" (2008, p. 44)—despite the profusion of patriotic jingoism in the U.S., few are actually willing to foot the personal, bloody cost of war. In the imperial state fear of the public is paramount (see Chomsky, 2003, p. 39), and thus we see the vigorous fortification of the national security state: "The extraordinary rise of technological and other means of keeping the citizens under surveillance at all times" (Hobsbawm, 2008, p. 45). Another important feature is the decline in warfare between states (Hobsbawm, 2008, p. 48). Moreover, we also witness with reference to, "noninterference in one another's' internal affairs, and...a sharp distinction between war and peace," that "neither are any longer valid today" (Hobsbawm, 2008, p. 51). What is not a crucial dimension, contra Johnson above, is an emphasis on military superiority.

In this volume, Cameron Fenton, Corey Anhorn, Ricky Curotte, and Mark Shapiro consider militarism and militarization from diverse angles. Fenton focuses on cultural militarism, and the militarization of public discourse stemming from the "support the troops" slogan, which has gained strength in Canada, with obvious American inspiration. Interestingly, some of the critical questioning of the glorification of the Canadian military is offered by Anhorn as well, the seminar's only serving member of the Canadian Forces. Anhorn's chapter offers a very provocative, sometimes shocking look at the militarization of the Boy Scouts, the role of the JROTC in schools, the Pentagon's relationship with Hollywood, and military counter-blogging. Both Fenton and Anhorn speak to the rise of "the new military normal." This can be witnessed in Canada through governments' endorsing more aggressive forms of foreign intervention; the lower role of Canada in international peacekeeping; the scandal involving Canada's Afghan detainees who were transferred into Afghan hands, reportedly knowing they could or would be tortured (with such a transfer being a crime under international law), and the Harper government's bullying of the senior diplomat behind the disclosures. Also of concern was the rise to prominence of a brash military commander, such as now retired General Rick Hillier, former chief of staff for the Canadian Forces, who once stated: "we're not the public service of Canada, we're not just another department. We are the Canadian Forces, and our job is to be able to kill people" (Leblanc, 2005). This flies in the face of most Canadians' support for peacekeeping, not counterinsurgency missions.

Cameron Fenton argues that "to be pro-troop but anti-war is hypocrisy." His reason for this daring argument is that "armies are the physical force extension of state power, and in a nation such as Canada, where the values of democracy are trumpeted, that should make the military a tool of the people." This also means, he says, "that as long as these soldiers march with the flags of our nations stitched to their sleeves, we are culpable for their actions." Fenton also argues that "soldiers of all levels need to be held accountable for their actions, regardless of the number of stripes on their arms, or if their uniform is a Tory blue suit, because from order givers to order takers, to the tax payers who fund the destruction, we are all responsible for what our governments and militaries do in our name." Cameron Fenton, an anthropologist, was also the seminar's only journalist.

Corey Anhorn, writing as an anthropologist and a member of the Canadian Forces, begins by suggesting, quite reasonably, that "as the militarization of culture and society becomes increasingly more apparent both in Canada and the U.S., the need for an honest discussion of the potential ramifications of…militarization is needed more than ever." In his discussion he examines the Boy Scouts, the JROTC, and the fact that "nearly every major military film recorded in the U.S. over the past 40 years has either been asked to change portions of their content to show the U.S. military in a better light or has agreed to in exchange for the benefits it entails in production." This is a phenomenon now known as militainment. Anhorn is not necessarily enchanted with the ways in which young children are taught to glorify the military, and to some extent his discursive angle is an auto-biographic one.

Ricky Curotte's extensive chapter produces another view of militarization, this time the militarization of foreign policy, aid, and development. He does so by looking specifically at the stated reason for being of the new U.S. Army Africa Command (AFRICOM). As Curotte argues, "the desire of the U.S. to establish a permanent AFRICOM signals the growing strategic, political and economic importance of Africa in the post-Cold War world."

The militarization of academia, and anthropology in particular, became the concern of three seminar participants at one point, and the only chapter here on this topic is that by Mark Shapiro, dealing with the U.S. Army's Human Terrain System. Shapiro's terse chapter "addresses two fundamental ethical questions pertaining to Human Terrain Teams: whether team members practice anthropology in accordance with the Code of Ethics of the American Anthropological Association and whether the Human Terrain System contributes to a devaluation of the professional integrity of all anthropologists."

Humanitarianism, Human Rights, and the Responsibility to Protect

During the course of the seminar several discussions revolved around what has been varyingly labeled as "military humanism," "humanitarian imperialism," "humanitarian interventionism," and the new international doctrine of the "responsibility to protect." Chapters in this volume by Elizabeth Vezina, Thomas Prince, Justin De Genova, and Nageen Siddiqui, each weigh the value and place of human rights discourse in the new imperialism that has taken shape since the end of the Cold War, and especially during this so-called "war on terror." The chapters are very much related to those discussed and listed under the Occupation heading in this volume, with those in the latter group separated out mostly because they chose to focus squarely on current interventions that, to some extent, have leaned on humanitarian discourse as sources of justification.

In this section the authors examine the role of non-government organizations (NGOs), multilateral financial institutions, the UN, NATO, and the U.S. military as central among the key actors in drawing "humanitarianism" to an interventionist point. Vezina focuses on the NATO intervention in Kosovo, which although ostensibly committed to protecting the civilians of Kosovo, it was carried under a relentless wave of aerial bombardment that severely deteriorated the humanitarian situation for everyone concerned on the ground. Vezina notes that "U.S. officials admitted that the goal of demolishing civilian targets ('Phase Three' in military terms) was to make life miserable for the people and to put pressure on Milošević to surrender." Chomsky (1999, ¶ 2) aptly described this humanism applied by military means: "the bombing had been cast as a matter of cosmic significance, a test of a New Humanism, in which the 'enlightened states' (*Foreign Affairs*) open a new era of human history guided by 'a new internationalism where the brutal repression of whole ethnic groups will no longer be tolerated' (*Tony Blair*). The enlightened states are the United States and its British associate, perhaps also others who enlist in their crusades for justice." In this vein, two appendixes appear in this volume to add to Vezina's chapter: speeches by Bill Clinton and Tony Blair on their humanitarian interventionism in the former Yugoslavia (see Appendix C and D). The very sad irony, as described both by Chomsky and Vezina, is that the NATO air war perpetrated a humanitarian catastrophe far greater than that which Milošević has been accused of causing, leading to the first refugees to flee Kosovo, to an escalation in ethnic fighting, and Serb and Albanian casualties that far exceeded anything suffered by Kosovo Albanians before the NATO campaign (Chomsky, 1999, ¶ 7). An even greater irony that gave the lie to NATO intentions was the fact that within NATO itself one of its own members, Turkey, and with millions of dollars in military aid from the U.S., was simultaneously conducting a war against the Kurds in dimensions far greater, and far bloodier, than anything we saw in Kosovo. And yet it largely passed without mention.

The "Responsibility to Protect" (R2P) also comes in for close examination. In his chapter, Thomas Prince is not dismissive of R2P; he instead wants it to live up to the best of its promises, to eschew the politicized selectivity that has been the norm when "humanitarian" principles have been invoked for military interventions, and to re-adopt the broader understanding of human rights enshrined in UN declarations, which include social and economic rights. He gives fair play to both advocates and critics of R2P, while raising numerous critical and important questions of R2P. Prince's approach can best be summed up by looking at one of his concluding statements: "While supporters say that ambiguity is not a reason to do nothing, it should neither be a reason to race in, or ignore the creation of protocols and guidelines. Whatever guidelines and protocols are devised they need to be applied equally, so that allies of the U.S. and other powerful states are subject to the same requirements and obligations as those nations who pursue more independent politics." The chapter by Justin De Genova is very wary of any proclamations of humanitarian intent on the part of interventionist, imperial powers. As he stated at the outset: "This chapter looks at the U.S. as a primary example of how a Western nation can disregard the harm it causes within the international community when it intervenes in another sovereign state's affairs, using the excuse of humanitarian issues to further its worldwide influence."

Perhaps the most painful counterpoint to declared principles of humanitarian protection comes in the chapter on torture by Nageen Siddiqui. She provides us with a condensed review and analysis of the role of torture in U.S. foreign policy in the so-called "war on terror," in a very sobering account to the "other side" of humanitarian interventionism. Those who profess it are often the same as those who defend the need for the "lesser evil."

Occupation

Canada's role in the war in Afghanistan occupies the centre of attention of two chapters, by Kate Roland and Rosalia Stillitano. Haiti is the focus of the chapter by Katelyn Spidle, placed in this section given the extent to which Haiti has become an international protectorate, and was also subject to occupation by the Canadian military as part of the coup against Jean Bertrand Aristide in 2004.

Canada's involvement in the occupation of Afghanistan has been a source of very serious political challenges to the way Canadians prefer to see themselves in an international context. At first, the public rhetoric was that of victorious war: Prime Minister Jean Chretien, in an address to the nation in October of 2001, declared: "I cannot promise that the campaign against terrorism will be painless, but I can promise that it will be won" (Chretien, 2001). In the summer of 2005 the Canadian government decided to transfer its military operations to Kandahar, still one of the most violent regions of Afghanistan, if not the most violent. However, "this was presented to Canadians as a simple re-positioning of the troops in that country" (Coulon & Liégeois, 2010, p. 43), with little indication that the role of Canada would be counterinsurgency, not peacekeeping. As others have also noted, "no official, civilian or military, used the word war to describe what was going on in southern Afghanistan" (Gross & Lang, 2007, p. 185). In their briefing notes, National Defence described the mission "as a more robust peace support role" (Gross & Lang, 2007, p. 186). Then later, in 2007, the Canadian Strategic Counsel advised the government of Prime Minister Stephen Harper "to present the military intervention in Afghanistan in a manner that placed it within the Canadian peacekeeping tradition. It suggested avoiding 'negative' expressions and using more positive words such as 'peacekeeping,' 'reconstruction,' 'stability,' and helping 'women and children.' In short, they advised speaking of peace and not of war" (Coulon & Liégeois, 2010, p. 46).

The Canadian government presented the mission as the realization of its 3D strategy (defence, diplomacy and development—now often called the "whole of government" approach designed to aid "failed states"). The Minister of National Defence, Bill Graham, insisted that "in order to be efficient in robust peacekeeping operations today, it is obvious that our troops must at once be warriors, diplomats and humanitarian workers" (Coulon & Liégeois, 2010, p. 43; see also Phillips, 2008, ¶ 6). As Coulon and Liégeois argue reasonably, "considering Canada's particular history on the international scene and its relationship with the UN, when Canadians listen to the Prime Minister or view the Army's slide presentation, they are led to believe that there are Blue Helmets with the UN in Afghanistan and that they are fighting terrorism" (2010, p. 44). They also note that "even the leaders of the UN and NATO contradict each other. When one of the authors of this study asked some of these leaders if the mission in Afghanistan was a *peacekeeping* operation, he received both positive and negative answers" (Coulon & Liégeois, 2010, p. 44).

We find similar equivocation among Canada's other NATO partners. For example, in France, the day after the death of ten French soldiers near Kabul in August 2008,

> "the Minister of Defence launched into acrobatic semantics trying to explain the French role in Afghanistan. He refused to use words such as 'war' or 'counterinsurgency' and insisted on saying that France is involved in a peace mission in that country. This induced a scathing reply from an eminent deputy in his own party, Pierre Lellouche, who is also a French specialist in military affairs. When asked what he thought of the emotions evoked by the death of ten soldiers, he replied: 'The reproach we can make of the French political and military authorities is that they have not clarified the presence of our country in Afghanistan. Contrary to the claims of the Minister of Defence, Hervé Morin, this is a war and not a policing operation'." (Coulon & Liégeois, 2010, p. 44).

Officially in Germany, until quite recently there was no acknowledgment of what was happening in Afghanistan as being in fact a war (see for an example: Spörl, 2010), and the same has also been true in the case of Italy.

With all of the mixed signals that have been deliberately sent by governments to the public, it is not surprising to see some confusion in public opinion. For example, a poll in March 2006 reported that,

> "there appears to be some confusion about the primary mandate of the mission: most people think it is about peacekeeping which is a traditional role for the Canadian armed forces. Equally important, the Canadian public is almost equally divided about whether the Canadian forces should have an active combat role. Canadians have yet to be conditioned about the new active combat role that Canadian troops are being asked to undertake. This simply underscores the tremendous ambivalence Canadians have about the Afghanistan mission and the potential for this issue to become a major 'hot button' for the Harper government as opinions are clearly in the 'early stages' of being formed, but may shift with time and as events unfold." (Strategic Counsel, 2006, p. 4)

The report found that "about 70% believe that the main purpose of the Canadian troops in Afghanistan is related more to peacekeeping than combat" (Strategic Counsel, 2006, p. 9). Had Canadians understood that the troops' mission was to be active combat, a clear majority, 62 per cent, said they would have opposed sending troops to Afghanistan (Strategic Counsel, 2006, p. 8). Indeed, just as the report repeatedly notes that policy makers should expect volatility in public opinion, as the public would become better informed and more aware of the actual Canadian mission in Afghanistan, almost all polls for several years have shown a consistent majority of Canadians opposed to the war.

Roland focuses considerably on the contradiction between a popularly imagined "Brand Canada," a Canada of peacekeepers and non-aggressors, and the actuality of our war in Afghanistan. She examines what Canadians seem to know about the use of the military in Canadian foreign policy, and specifically how it applies to Afghanistan, by looking at: Canada's power structure and foreign policy with respect to the Canadian military mission in Afghanistan; what Canadians have been told about the Afghanistan mission and what their reactions are in light of what they have been told; and, she examines one example of "off-brand," seemingly "un-Canadian" military behavior to examine these dynamics. In the final analysis, Roland calls for greater attempts to seek consensus in a divided parliament ruled by a minority government (a situation that has persisted for several years and is likely to continue), inviting all stakeholders into crafting an appropriate Canadian military and foreign policy, return to peacekeeping, and better informing the Canadian public.

Stillitano makes some similar points, arguing that the problem with Canadian involvement in Afghanistan is not a problem with the military as such, but rather "the problem lies more in what the Canadian government is using the military for, which is primarily counterinsurgency warfare through the militarization of humanitarian aid. The problem is that the Canadian army is becoming Americanized; we are slowly but surely loosing our identity as neutral peacekeepers." Stillitano also casts an unusually critical glance at nation-building—unusual because it is often equated by critics with a strategy that would sink NATO into a never-ending quagmire. Instead, Stillitano sees it differently, saying that "nation-building is not about the interest of Afghans as it should be: it is an exit strategy." By this we might assume that she means a superficial nation-building that hastily puts in place the semblance of a centralized nation-state, regardless of whether or not that state is actually integrated into the lives of Afghans and, more importantly, whether or not that state is beneficent one that is supported as legitimate by most Afghans. One may doubt, however, whether Stillitano has reason to worry: there is no sign from the U.S. or NATO, at this point, that they are running for the exits.

In Haiti, the only persons running for the exits have been Haitians themselves, while thousands of foreign NGOs have effectively colonized the once independent republic, thanks in part to Canadian military intervention in 2004 that helped to unseat the democratically elected government of Jean Bertrand Aristide. In this volume, Spidle focuses in particular on the NGO-U.S. occupation connection:

> "The U.S. has, in past decades, maintained its stronghold over Haiti by either indirectly occupying the country through its funding of NGOs, or directly occupying the country through military invasion. The NGOs operating in Haiti do not improve the social,

political or economic situation in the country; rather, they create and perpetuate a dependency on foreign aid for its basic services, jobs, and food. In light of the earthquake, military intervention, justified as humanitarianism, has only strengthened that dependency: first, by hindering the activities of NGOs and thus rendering them less effective, and second, by undermining the Haitian government's ability to react or respond to the disaster. The U.S. government has essentially overthrown the Haitian government by installing a military force in the country which has assumed nearly all of its government functions; it dictates the activities of NGOs, controls the airport and ports, and patrols to maintain stability and order."

Far from nation-building, Western intervention in Haiti has been more along the lines of establishing a permanent international protectorate, an aid-dependent basket case whose policies are being dictated and written by foreign "donors." We can see this in more global terms, and as counterintuitive as it may seem, we can critique this situation by using the explanation of someone who advocates in favour of intervention and state-building: Francis Fukuyama. Fukuyama was an official in the administration of President Ronald Reagan, and later became active in the Project for the New American Century, the leading think tank associated with "neoconservatism." He also actively advocated in favour of the invasion of Iraq. This is not an anti-war critic, an anti-imperialist, or someone who rejects American exceptionalism—which makes his commentary even more interesting. In State-Building: Governance and World Order in the 21st Century he remarks that the "humanitarian interventions of the 1990s led to an extension of a de facto imperial power over the 'failed state' part of the world" (p. 97). He writes of the United Nations Office of the High Representative in Bosnia and Herzegovina (OHR) that,

"the OHR used its power to dismiss presidents, prime ministers, judges, mayors, and other elected officials. It could pass legislation and create new institutions without reference to the preferences of the Bosnian people. Much of the administrative capacity of the Bosnian government lay in the hands of international experts rather than indigenous civil servants, to the point that some observers compared it to the British Raj." (Fukuyama, 2004, p. 103)

Writing on the situation in East Timor, he reiterates: "This international imperium may be a well-meaning one based on human rights and democracy, but it was an imperium nonetheless and set a precedent for the surrender of sovereignty to governance by international agencies" (Fukuyama, 2004, p. 98). This imperial effort has been dubbed by the U.S. as "nation-building" (which, more correctly, as Fukuyama himself notes, should be called state-building). In particular, Fukuyama notes that the practice of state-building has largely failed to achieve its aims, anywhere: "Neither the United States nor the international community has made much headway in creating self-sustaining states in any of the countries it has set out to rebuild" (Fukuyama, 2004, p. 103). He notes further that, "the rhetoric of the international community stresses 'capacity-building' while the reality has been rather a kind of 'capacity sucking out'....The international community, including the vast numbers of NGOs that are an intimate part of it, comes so richly endowed and full of capabilities that it tends to crowd out rather than complement the extremely weak state capacities of the targeted countries." (Fukuyama, 2004, p. 103)

In a cold statement of pragmatism, another of the leading "new imperialist" intellectuals, Michael Ignatieff, argues: "humanitarian relief cannot be kept distinct from imperial projects, not least because humanitarian action is only possible, in many instances, if imperial armies have first cleared the ground and made it safe for humanitarians to act" (2003c, pp. 16-17).

From a perspective critical of the new imperialists, Matthew Connelly explains that "the essence of empire, is not military force, but the exercise of untrammeled power" (2006, p. 32). He follows with a very striking statement: "And imperialists have long understood that an entrance exam or a vaccination program are less costly and more compelling instruments of influence, especially when infused with an appealing idea–like *mission civilisatrice* or *médecins sans frontières*" (Connelly, 2006, p. 32). Here Connelly also takes aim at international and nongovernmental organizations whose power is most obvious in so-called "failed states," but whose power is significantly magnified when those organizations work in concert with local governments, producing power that is "as great as any empire" (Connelly, 2006, p. 32).

Soft Power

"Arms have often established empires, but it takes more than arms to maintain them." (Hobsbawm, 2008, p. 53)

The "soft power" concept appeared to have attracted serious attention from a number of the seminar participants, who were critical and yet sympathetic for the most part, similar to what we see in this volume dealing with R2P.

Zoe Dominiak in particular offers a detailed and sympathetic overview of the concept, relying extensively on the writings of Joseph Nye. Dominiak's perspective appears to be optimistic about the efficacy of soft power, while reinforcing the claim that "information is power." Miles Smart, on the other hand, was impressed with neither the concept nor the means associated with soft power:

"The strategic positioning of the U.S. on the international stage has always employed a certain amount of soft power to attract sympathies and alliances. However, the true strength and source of U.S. power globally was and is achieved through military and economic might, both applied and implied."

Miles Smart's treatment of soft power as strategy is particularly critical about the jarring contrast between U.S. self-representation abroad versus its actual conduct. As Smart says, "the attractiveness of U.S. democracy and liberty is severely limited as a resource for soft power when the U.S. operates counter to its own ideals." In anthropological terms, Smart sees the concept of "soft power" as closest to what anthropologists understand as hegemony: "hard power can achieve and even maintain dominance, but legitimacy is the ultimate goal. Legitimacy allows the powerful to maintain their position without force but rather through acceptance and localized support." Soft power thus seeks rule with the consensus of the ruled, premised on the hope that the ruled will internalize the ideas of dominant elites.

Lesley Foster's chapter differs somewhat, in that it is not intended as an explicit treatment of the concept of soft power, as much as it is a critical exploration of the corporate, non-state ways that American power and hegemony have been implanted and enforced internationally. Foster looks at the workings of the military-industrial complex, with a focus on the corporate industrial side, and specifically the workings of Coca-Cola in Colombia. She frames this within an analysis of "security-led investments" where private corporations acquire a military arm in order to better penetrate a market and subjugate workers. Foster raises an exceptional point concerning the other wars currently being fought, not by states but by corporations. As she explains: "Coca-Cola's actions take on a different form of hard and soft power in regards to the normalized, dominant idea of violence and war and, in doing so deflects the regular public attention that the traditional ideas and forms of violence and war might receive. Corporate war does not carry the same urgent implications that other forms of war carry, such as the current 'war on terror'," primarily because it does not represent a stated threat to the "free world" but "actually works in conjunction with it, protecting the neoliberal entitlement to own and conquer." Foster counts the growth and spread of private military contractors, of mercenary groups, as part of the global spread of American militarism, and locates it as a direct by product of neoliberalism. In addition, Foster ties post-9/11 terrorism hysteria to the strengthening of "counter-terrorism" by the Colombian state, and private foreign investors, in quashing workers' rights and social justice activism.

The final product of this first seminar, we think readers will agree, is a large and critical survey of contemporary imperialism, in historical and global context, attentive to local situations and the role of images, ideas, and ideologies. We hope that such efforts, multiple, varied, and cumulative, will help to bring about a radical shift in our awareness and understanding of the world in which we live, and in which we produce knowledge as both anthropologists and sociologists. On the role and duty of scholars in confronting empire Connelly writes:

"As scholars, we must work harder to illuminate the complex interconnections and complicities between them, and bring those findings to the broadest possible public. And it is that very complexity that commands us to speak and write clearly and with all the specificity and evidence we can muster. If we do not, then the American [and Canadian] academy, that most sovereign of institutions, will have to admit that it has become nothing more and nothing less than a finishing school for new imperialists." (2006, p. 33)

References

August, T. G. (1985). *The Selling of the Empire: British and French Imperialist Propaganda, 1890-1940*. Westport, CT: Greenwood Press.

Betts, R. F. (1968). *Europe Overseas: Phases of Imperialism*. New York: Basic Books.

Bongie, C. (1991). *Exotic Memories: Literature, Colonialism, and the Fin de Siècle*. Stanford, CA: Stanford University Press.

Boot, M. (2001). The Case for American Empire: The Most Realistic Response to Terrorism is for America to Embrace its Imperial Role. *The Weekly Standard*, October 15.

http://webcache.googleusercontent.com/search?q=cache:wtOP4eOhz-sJ:anglais.u-paris10.fr/IMG/doc/The_Case_for_American_Empire_The_most_realistic_response_to_terrorism_is_for_America_to_embrace_its_imperial_role-2.doc

——————— . (2003a). American Imperialism? No Need to Run Away from Label. *USA Today*, May 6.

http://www.cfr.org/publication/5934/american_imperialism_no_need_to_run_away_from_label.html

——————— . (2003b). U.S. Imperialism: A Force for Good. *National Post*, May 13.

http://www.cfr.org/publication/5959/us_imperialism.html

——————— . (2003c). Washington Needs a Colonial Office. *Financial Times*, July 3.

http://www.cfr.org/publication/6096/washington_needs_a_colonial_office.html

——————— . (2003d). Enlightened Imperialism Could Save Liberia. *USA Today*, July 28.

http://www.cfr.org/publication/6162/enlightened_imperialism_could_save_liberia.html

Bricmont, J. (2006). *Humanitarian Imperialism: Using Human Rights to Sell War*. New York: Monthly Review Press.

Bush, G.H.W. (1990). Address before a Joint Session of Congress (September 11, 1990).

http://millercenter.org/scripps/archive/speeches/detail/3425

Boron, A. (2005). *Empire and Imperialism: A Critical Reading of Michael Hardt and Antonio Negri*. London: Zed Books.

Carrington, C. (1950). *The British Overseas: Exploits of a Nation of Shopkeepers*. Cambridge, UK: Cambridge University Press.

Chomsky, N. (1999). Kosovo Peace Accord. *Z Magazine*, July. http://www.chomsky.info/articles/199907--.htm

——————— . (2003). *Hegemony or Survival: America's Quest for Global Dominance*. New York: Henry Holt and Company.

Chretien, J. (2001). Chretien: Cdn troops 'will do Canada proud'. *CTV News*, October 7.

http://www.ctv.ca/servlet/ArticleNews/story/CTVNews/1025062429054_20471629

Cohen, B. J. (1973). *The Question of Imperialism: The Political Economy of Dominance and Dependence.* New York: Basic Books.

Connelly, M. (2006). The New Imperialists. In C. Calhoun, F. Cooper, & K. W. Moore (Eds.), *Lessons of Empire: Imperial Histories and American Power* (pp. 19-33). New York: The New Press.

Coulon, J., & Liégeois, M. (2010). *Whatever Happened to Peacekeeping? The Future of a Tradition.* Calgary, AB: Canadian Defence & Foreign Affairs Institute.

http://www.cdfai.org/PDF/Whatever%20Happened%20to%20Peacekeeping%20The%20 Future%20of%20a%20Tradition%20-%20English.pdf

Eakin, E. (2002). "It Takes an Empire" Say Several U.S. Thinkers. *The New York Times*, April 2.

http://www.hartford-hwp.com/archives/27c/498.html

Elkington, J., & Kendall, G. (2009). The Future of Oil. *The Guardian*, November 11.

http://www.guardian.co.uk/environment/2009/nov/11/future-of-oil

Ferguson, N. (2004). *Colossus: The Rise and Fall of the American Empire.* New York: Penguin Books.

Forte, M. (2010). Militainment: U.S. Military Propaganda in the News Media, Hollywood, and Video Games. *Zero Anthropology*, June 13.

http://zeroanthropology.net/2010/06/13/militainment-u-s-military-propaganda-in-the-news-media-hollywood-and-video-games/

Fukuyama, F. (2004). *State-Building: Governance and World Order in the 21st Century.* Ithaca, NY: Cornell University Press.

Gross, J., & Lang, E. (2007). *The Unexpected War: Canada in Kandahar.* Toronto: Viking Canada.

Hardt, M., & Negri, A. (2000). *Empire.* Cambridge, MA: Harvard University Press.

Harvey, D. (2003). *The New Imperialism.* New York: Oxford University Press.

Heller, H. (2006). *The Cold War and the New Imperialism: A Global History, 1945-2005.* New York: Monthly Review Press.

Hobson, J. A. (1905). *Imperialism: A Study.* London, UK: George Allen & Unwin.

Hobsbawm, E. (2008). *On Empire: America, War, and Global Supremacy.* New York: Pantheon Books.

Ignatieff, M. (2002). Nation-Building Lite. *The New York Times Magazine*, July 28.

http://www.nytimes.com/2002/07/28/magazine/nation-building-lite.html?pagewanted=all

————— . (2003a) The American Empire; The Burden. *The New York Times Magazine*, January 5.

http://www.nytimes.com/2003/01/05/magazine/the-american-empire-the-burden.html?pagewanted=all

————— . (2003b). America's Empire Is an Empire Lite. *The New York Times*, January 10.

http://www.globalpolicy.org/component/content/article/154/25603.html

————— . (2003c). *Empire Lite: Nation-Building in Bosnia, Kosovo and Afghanistan.* Toronto, ON: Penguin Canada.

————— . (2004). Lesser Evils. *The New York Times Magazine*, May 2.

http://www.nytimes.com/2004/05/02/magazine/lesser-evils.html?pagewanted=all

International Criminal Court (ICC). (1998). Crimes within the Court's Jurisdiction. New York: Development and Human Rights Section, United Nations Department of Public Information.

http://www.un.org/icc/crimes.htm

Johnson, C. (2000). *Blowback: The Costs and Consequences of American Empire.* New York: Henry Holt and Company.

—————— . (2004). *The Sorrows of Empire: Militarism, Secrecy, and the End of the Republic*. New York: Henry Holt and Company.

Leblanc, D. (2005). JTF2 to Hunt al-Qaeda. *The Globe and Mail*, July 15.

http://www.theglobeandmail.com/servlet/story/LAC.20050715.AFGHAN15/TPStory/?query=%22rob+from+canada%22

Lutz, C. (2009a). Anthropology in an Era of Permanent War. *Anthropologica*, 51(2), 367-379.

—————— . (2009b). Introduction: Bases, Empire, and Global Response. In C. Lutz (Ed.), *The Bases of Empire: The Global Struggle against U.S. Military Posts* (pp. 1-44). New York: New York University Press.

Macalister, T. (2009a). Key Oil Figures Were Distorted by US Pressure, Says Whistleblower. *The Guardian*, November 9.

http://www.guardian.co.uk/environment/2009/nov/09/peak-oil-international-energy-agency

—————— . (2009b). Peak Oil: What Does the Data Say? *The Guardian: DataBlog*, November 13.

http://www.guardian.co.uk/news/datablog/2009/nov/13/peak-oil-iea-uppsala

Magdoff, H. (2003). *Imperialism Without Colonies*. New York: Monthly Review Press.

Mooers, C. (Ed.). (2006). *The New Imperialists: Ideologies of Empire*. Oxford, UK: Oneworld Publications.

Morgan, D. (2003). A Debate over US "Empire" Builds in Unexpected Circles. *Washington Post*, August 10.

http://www.globalpolicy.org/component/content/article/154/25629.html

Phillips, K. (2008). Afghanistan: Canadian Diplomatic Engagement. InfoSeries, PRB 07-38E. Ottawa: Library of Parliament.

http://www2.parl.gc.ca/Content/LOP/ResearchPublications/prb0738-e.htm

Robb, D. L. (2004). *Operation Hollywood: How the Pentagon Shapes and Censors the Movies*. Amherst, NY: Prometheus Books.

Spörl, G. (2010). Facing Reality in Afghanistan: It's Time for Germans to Talk About War. *Der Spiegel Online International*, April 12.

http://www.spiegel.de/international/germany/0,1518,688424,00.html

Stahl, R. (2010). *Militainment, Inc.: War, Media, and Popular Culture*. New York: Routledge.

Strategic Counsel. (2006). A Report to the Globe and Mail and CTV: Perceptions and Views of Canadian Armed Forces Troops in Afghanistan, March. Toronto, ON: The Strategic Counsel.

http://www.thestrategiccounsel.com/our_news/polls/2006-03-13%20GMCTV%20Mar9-12%20(Mar13)%20Afghanistan%20-%20Rev.pdf

Taibbi, M. (2010). Lara Logan, You Suck. *Rolling Stone*, June 28.

http://www.rollingstone.com/politics/matt-taibbi/blogs/TaibbiData_May2010/122137/83512

Turse, N. (2008). *The Complex: How the Military Invades Our Everyday Lives*. New York: Henry Holt and Company.

CHAPTER ONE

Foxtrot Tango Alpha: A Discourse on Supporting the Troops

Cameron Fenton

On February 16, 2003, over 250,000 people marched through downtown Montreal to protest the George W. Bush administration's invasion of Iraq—the largest anti-war demonstration in Canadian history (Christoff 2003, ¶ 1). Around the world, that date was marked with chants, slogans and speeches against war and military intervention. A spokesperson for *Collectif Échec à la Guerre*, expressed the stand as clearly as possible, "No to War" (Richard 2003, ¶ 5). Seven years later, a new paradigm has taken over the mainstream anti-war movement. The relentless militarization of North American society has replaced anti-military critiques within the anti-war movement with the hypocritical claim to "support the troops, but not the war" (Marshall, 2005, ¶ 1). Transfer the logic of this statement to another setting, and the fundamental flaw is clear. Imagine someone explaining that he or she hates the game of hockey, and believes in disbanding the NHL, but is nonetheless an avid supporter of the Montreal Canadiens.

Armies are built up of soldiers, wars are fought between armies. War—though it may be orchestrated by generals and politicians—is fought by "the troops." It is these soldiers who act as the blunt instrument of neo-imperial foreign policy; it is their feet on the ground, their fingers on the triggers, and their bullets in the bodies of civilians. Meanwhile, thanks to ballooning military budgets in Canada and the U.S., and the public relations campaigns they finance, militaries have been branded as humanitarian instruments and a vital tool for global development.

Human welfare by the bomb is an oxymoron by any stretch of the imagination, and yet, this paradox has been used to sell Canadian military action for nearly two decades, the "mythic reality" of war (Hedges, 2003, p. 21). It would be too simple to explain this situation by blaming the genuine ignorance of "the masses," the reality can be directly linked to the rise of militarism in Canadian popular culture. Drawing on historical examples of the conduct, training and use of military forces in humanitarian deployments, this paper will argue that to be pro-troop but anti-war is hypocrisy, and the result of a fundamentally flawed system that sells the political snake oil of a military culture.

Apples and Orders: From Somalia to Torture

In early April 2010, a video emerged on WikiLeaks that shows a U.S. military Apache attack helicopter opening fire on a crowd of civilians in Baghdad. They killed twelve people, including two journalists working with Reuters.

On February 12, 2010, Special Operations forces in Afghanistan killed three innocent women, two of whom were pregnant, mothers of ten and six children respectively. It was later discovered that the soldiers involved dug their bullets out of the bodies in order to sell the murder as an unrelated stabbing (Oppel, 2010).

The misconduct of individual soldiers is typically countered by one of two schools of thought—the Nuremberg defense, or "bad apple" syndrome. The Nuremberg defense, named for the post-World War II trials where it was employed, places the blame for misdeeds on the highest ranks of the military, attempting to absolve the actions of individual soldiers under the guise that they were "just following orders" (D'Amato, Gould and Woods, 1969). In Canada, the most publicized example of this remains the largest black mark in Canadian military history, the Somalia Affair. The controversy stemmed from the now defunct Canadian Airborne Regiment's deployment as part of a 900 soldier humanitarian force in *Operation Deliverance,* part of the U.S.' *Operation Restore Hope,* in Somalia during the early 1990's (Razack, 2004, p. 69). Canadian Peacekeepers were on an assignment referred to by then Minister of Foreign Affairs, Barbara McDougal as "shoot first, ask questions later" (Murphy, 2007, p. 164).

The Somalia Affair involved two major events in March 1993—the shooting of two Somali men, one of whom was killed in what military surgeon and eventual whistleblower, Maj. Barry Armstrong, called an "execution style shooting" (Canadian Broadcasting Corporation [CBC], 1993). The second was the beating death of sixteen year old Shidane Arone—taken into custody under suspicion of theft. Arone was tortured, humiliated and beaten by Canadian soldiers—employing all measure of cigarettes, broomsticks and iron bars—who documented the ordeal with Polaroids for a trophy (Razack 2004, p. 4). Over the next two years, photos, videos and testimony evidenced the Canadian Airborne, considered Canada's most elite unit, as an excessively violent group with strong racist ideologies (CBC, 1995). Hazing rituals for new additions to the unit included a black soldier being tied to a post and having human feces smeared on his face to spell out "KKK" (CBC, 1993). Video from days before the incidents in Somalia showed Canadian soldiers referring to the mission as "operation snatch Nig-Nog" and "operation snatch niggers" (Razack, 2004, p. 4-5). These two events were the most publicized, but many Somalis came forward in the months and years that followed, filing lawsuits and telling their stories of violence, mistreatment and torture at the hands of Canadian soldiers (Razack, 2004, p. 132).

The eventual blame in the official Somalia Inquiry report, *Dishonored Legacy*, fell on the shoulders of high level officers, all the way up to then head of the armed forces General Jean Boyle, the inquiry report said these officers had "failed" the soldiers on the ground (Razack, 2004, p. 6). Colonel Serge Labbe, Canadian Peacekeeping Commander in Somalia, wrote in the official report that the soldiers' actions were "consistent with the actions of well trained soldiers" (Razack, 2004, p. 84). Former commander of the Canadian Airborne, Lt. Carol Mathieu, also defended the soldiers' actions, even applauding the regiment, ending his official testimony with their motto, "I salute you, *ex coelis*," claiming that history would vindicate his men (CBC, 1997). Eventually, only two of the soldiers directly involved in the killings faced legal repercussions, the majority acquitted entirely, and two dismissed from the military. In fact it was uncovered in 2008 that Col. Lambe had been promoted to General in 2000, working as chief of staff of Gen. Hillier throughout the occupation of Afghanistan (CBC, 2008). No action was taken on the report's 162 recommendations for dealing with the "systemic, structural and pervasive" (CBC, 1997) problems within the Canadian Forces , instead the Liberal government of the time opted to slash the military's budget, disband the Airborne, and allow the highest level military commanders to retire by their own accord.

This defense has lost favour over the years, as military officers have developed political agendas and made themselves quintessential parts of a militarized culture. It has been replaced by the Bush era rhetoric of a "few bad apples" ruining the bunch (Lucas, 2004, ¶ 1; see also Gowan, 2004). The most publicized use of this defense has surrounded the use of torture, or "enhanced interrogation" and has tentacles reaching all the way through both the Canadian and U.S. administrations. While the surface of Canada's role in handing over Afghan prisoners to be has only been scratched with the recently stagnated Afghan detainee commission, torture seems to underlie every action of the U.S.' occupations of Afghanistan and Iraq.

From Abu Ghraib to Guantánamo Bay, the world has been shown the result of what Noam Chomsky refers to as a sixty year old CIA "'torture paradigm', developed at a cost that reached $1 billion annually" (Chomsky, 2009, section 3 ¶1). Photos, though now digital and in higher resolution, that looked strikingly like those that surfaced from Somalia, depict American soldiers inflicting grossly inhumane treatment on prisoners, with smiling faces and thumbs up.

The soldiers responsible have been prosecuted, and many are serving jail time, yet those responsible for the training of these people remain free, training new recruits to make the same mistakes (CBC, 2005).

Torture is also simply the tip of the iceberg when it comes to war crimes, and crimes against humanity in Iraq and Afghanistan. Iraq Veterans against the War (IVAW) resurrected the Winter Soldier tribunals of the Vietnam War in order to tell the true stories of the occupations. Participants were asked questions such as "Did you witness or participate in any of the following: Civilians hurt or killed at checkpoints? Purposeful killing of civilians or unarmed combatants? Killing or wounding of prisoners? If yes, was this unit SOP [standard operating procedure] or common practice?" (Leve, 2008). Referring to the 2005 massacre in Haditha, where 24 unarmed Iraqi civilians were killed, one of the soldiers explained the repercussions: "The people on the ground are looking at serious prison time. Like life. The people who were giving orders were only relieved of command. And I don't think that's right" (Leve, 2008). This is the effect of the bad apple doctrine, targeting those that pull the trigger, yet leaving those who create the policies and issue the orders free and clear. The truth is that the same systemic problems with the military that led to the Somalia Affair for Canada are at the heart of Canadian and American misconduct in Iraq and Afghanistan.

Soldierly Bravado, Such an Unspeakable Gift

In 2007, U.S. soldiers deployed with Bravo Company 2-16 in Baghdad opened fire on a crowd of Iraqi civilians from an Apache helicopter. Twelve people were killed, including two Reuters journalists, while soldiers in the helicopter said:

> U.S. SOLDIER 3: I've got eleven Iraqi KIAs . One small child wounded. Over.
> U.S. SOLDIER 1: Roger. Ah, damn. Oh, well.
> U.S. SOLDIER 3: Roger, we need—we need a—to evac this child. She's got a wound to the belly. I can't do anything here. She needs to get evac'ed. Over.
> U.S. SOLDIER 1: Well, it's their fault for bringing their kids into a battle.
> U.S. SOLDIER 2: That's right. (González and Goodman, 2010)

According to Josh Stieber, a former member of Bravo 2-16 and now organizer with IVAW the soldiers "did exactly what they were trained to do" (González and Goodman, 2010).

The gap between the politically acceptable depiction of the soldier and the reality of the man or woman on the ground is a chasm that can only be crossed by immense feats of logical long-jump. Both pro- and anti-military groups often make the same mistake, presenting soldiers as either GI-Joe defenders of the homeland or blood thirsty maniacs, hell-bent on consuming the hearts of their enemies. While both of these may describe individual members of any military, the fact is that most of these people are simply that, people. What makes them different from civilians is the job training that militaries provide—training someone to kill people. Like any other job, when the boss invests the time and energy to train you to do something—whether that be cooking a medium rare steak, selling long distance phone plans, or dropping a few hundred pounds of ordnance on an Afghan village—your job is to get it done.

According to Retired General Rick Hillier, former chief of staff for the Canadian Forces, "we're not the public service of Canada, we're not just another department. We are the Canadian Forces, and our job is to be able to kill people" (Leblanc, 2005).

The Canadian Forces Leadership and Recruit School (CFLRS) is the primary training institution for Canadian soldiers. It was originally created in 1968 following the passage of the Canadian Forces Reorganization Act, and has existed in various locations as the primary training body for Canadian soldiers. Located in Saint-Jean-sur-Richelieu, southwest of Montreal, Quebec, an estimated 5,000 new recruits pass through its doors each year. According to the Canadian Forces, during their 10-week stint with CFLRS:

> "You'll be up early…very early. You'll do lots of push-ups, sit-ups and chin-ups. You'll run. You'll practice drill. You'll learn about weapons…how to handle them, take care of them and how to use them. You'll be taught orienteering and how to live in the field under tough conditions. You'll learn First Aid and CPR. In short, you'll become a soldier." (Canadian Army, 2010)

The program is broken up into ten basic categories: Military Bearing, General Safety, First Aid, Nuclear, Biological and Chemical Defense, Drill, Weapons Training, Military Knowledge, Physical Fitness, Topography, and Survival. There is no mention of human rights, humanitarianism, or even the word peace in the publically available outlines of the Canadian soldier. The closest is a promise that each recruit will "learn to recognize and comply with Canadian Forces policies including military law, regulations, the Geneva Convention, and routine administration" (Canadian Army, 2010).

Looking at the basic training programme presented in the publicly available, recruitment oriented, material of the Canadian Forces, one might forget one of the most important facets of military training—social and mental conditioning. The Canadian Forces refer to this as "Military Bearing," meant to teach "teamwork, loyalty, integrity, honesty and responsibility" (Canadian Army, 2010). Critics on the opposite end of the spectrum prefer the term "brainwashing." In his book *War*, Gwynne Dyer states "the way armies produce [a] sense of brotherhood in peace-time is basic training, a feat of psychological manipulation on the grand scale" (2004, p. 34). Dyer, a former naval officer, argues that a functional soldier cannot be of the same mind as a civilian, and her training is specifically designed to break a person down, and rebuild them in order to create someone who will follow orders, regardless of if those orders contradict their basic instincts, or personal ideologies (Dyer, 2004).

For a person "from a civilian environment that does not share the military values, basic training provides a brief but intense indoctrination whose purpose is not really to teach the recruits basic military skills but rather to change their values and loyalties" (Dyer, 1004, pp. 34-35). The result of this process is to transform the recruit into a functioning member of the military machine, through a process of intensive socialization. Militaries work in a state of exceptionalism where what is militarily justifiable is often not morally justifiable. Josh Stieber, mentioned above, explained how training blurs the definition of morality:

> "[In training] leaders would ask the younger soldiers what they would do if somebody were to pull a weapon in a marketplace full of unarmed civilians. And not only did your response have to be that you would return fire, even if you knew it was going to hurt innocent civilians...the answer had to be yes...these things are just hammered into you through military training." (González and Goodman, 2010)

If the military is simply a machine to transform civilians into ravenous bloodthirsty killers, what is the next the course of action?

Blame the Troops? Deconstructing the Military Normal

> "Rather than a few bad apples...the contents of the entire wretched barrel are, in fact, rotten. If the military is capable of producing 'personalities' that kill babies, rape women, and torture the innocent, then what is responsible for the degradation and dissolution of these military personnel? How and why do U.S. soldiers lose their humanity?" (Smith, 2006)

Armies are the physical force extension of state power, and in a nation such as Canada, where the values of democracy are trumpeted, that should make the military a tool of the people. This also means that as long as these soldiers march with the flags of our nations stitched to their sleeves, we are culpable for their actions. As the civilian causality numbers continue to rise year after year in Afghanistan so increases the fuel for blowbacks such as the 11 September 2001 terrorist attacks. As Jeremy Scahill argued on a 2009 episode of Al Jazeera's *Faultlines*, "what we're doing in Afghanistan right now is making us less safe...we are giving a motive to those people who want to attack us" (Lewis, 2009). In order to end this seemingly relentless cycle we must first understand and confront the systemic militarization of our culture that Nick Turse refers to as "the Complex" (2009).

According to a report from the Canadian Center for Policy Alternatives, military spending is the highest it has been since the Second World War (Robinson and Staples, 2007) and has increased, reaching $18.2 billion in 2008, up over 35 per cent from 2001 levels. This upsurge in funding has not only increased equipment and technology purchasing, but has funded a public relations campaign aimed to build the heroic narrative of the Canadian soldier deployed in Afghanistan. The new Canadian immigration guide *Discover Canada* (Citizenship and Immigration Canada [CIC], 2010) dedicates a sizable proportion to vaunting the military narrative of Canadian history, using the word "war" 55 times in a 62 page document, and selling the Canadian Forces as one of the foremost career options for new Canadians. From updated, slick looking web pages, recruitment commercials, yellow "support our troops" ribbons, to Hockey Night in Canada special salutes that hark back to the public indoctrination schemes of totalitarian regimes, the government program has all been geared at creating the new military normal. This system of cultural indoctrination makes each and every citizen complicit in the actions of Canada's soldiers, making a reality of General Hillier's dream that "when a soldier steps on foreign soil...every single Canadian should be walking with him or her" (quoted in Petersen, 2008).

During the Vietnam War one of the strongest forces in the anti-war movement was the resistance of American soldiers to follow orders. An entire movement of enlisted men refused to fall in line and commit what they knew were atrocities. The difference was that at that time the war resisters were supported by a powerful movement of anti-war activists that knew the only way to support the troops in the short term was to bring them home, and to end neo-imperial wars of expansion in the long term. In order for any modern anti-war movement to be successful in ending the occupations of Afghanistan and Iraq, and the expansion of North American militarism around the globe, the military system must first be examined, critiqued and disassembled. Soldiers of all levels need to be held accountable for their actions, regardless of the number of stripes on their arms, or if their uniform is a Tory blue suit, because from order givers to order takers, to the tax payers who fund the destruction, we are all responsible for what our governments and militaries do in our name.

References

Canadian Army. (2010). Basic Training. *National Defence Canada*.
　　http://www.army.forces.gc.ca/land-terre/joining-enroler/training-entrainement-eng.asp
Canadian Broadcasting Corporation (CBC). (1993). The Whistle Blower (television program). *The CBC Digital Archives Website*.
　　http://archives.cbc.ca/war_conflict/peacekeeping/topics/723/
————— . (1995). Rampant racism in the Airborne Regiment (television program). *The CBC Digital Archives Website*. http://archives.cbc.ca/war_conflict/peacekeeping/topics/723/
————— . (1997). Somalia debacle a high level coverup (television program). *The CBC Digital Archives Website*. http://archives.cbc.ca/war_conflict/peacekeeping/topics/723/

———————. (2005). *A Few Bad Apples* (documentary). Canadian Broadcasting Corporation.

———————. (2008). Canadian colonel criticized over Somalia affair promoted to general. *CBC News Online*.

http://www.cbc.ca/canada/story/2008/07/25/promotion-labbe.html#ixzz0mJU5NAtn

Chomsky, N. (2009). The Torture Memos and Historical Amnesia. *The Nation*, May 19.

http://www.thenation.com/doc/20090601/chomsky

Christoff, S. (2003). Riot Police Brutalize Anti-War Protestors Outside of American Consulate. Press Release. http://archives.lists.indymedia.org/imc-montreal/2003-March/001383.html

Citizenship and Immigration Canada (CIC). (2010). *Discover Canada: The Rights and Responsibilities of Citizenship*. Ottawa: Minister of Public Works and Government Services.

http://www.cic.gc.ca/english/pdf/pub/discover.pdf

D'Amato, A., Gould, H., & Woods, L. (1969). War Crimes and Vietnam: The "Nuremberg Defense" and the Military Service Roster. *California Law Review*, 57(5), 1055-1110. http://anthonydamato.law.northwestern.edu/Adobefiles/A69d-nurembergdef.pdf

Dyer, G. (2004). War. Toronto: Random House.

González, J., & Goodman, A. (2010). "This Is How These Soldiers Were Trained to Act"– Veteran of Military Unit Involved in 2007 Baghdad Helicopter Shooting Says Incident Is Part of Much Larger Problem (television broadcast). *Democracy Now!*, April 12. http://www.democracynow.org/2010/4/12/this_is_how_these_soldiers_were

Gowan, S. (2004). Bad Apples in a Bad Barrel. *Counterpunch*. http://www.counterpunch.org/gowans05292004.html

Hedges, C. (2003). *War is a Force that Gives Us Meaning*. New York: Anchor Books.

Leblanc, D. (2005). JTF2 to hunt al-Qaeda. *The Globe and Mail*, July 15.

http://www.theglobeandmail.com/servlet/story/LAC.20050715.AFGHAN15/TPStory/ ?query=%22rob+from+canada%22

Leve, A. (2008). Patriot missiles: Iraq Veterans Against the War. *Times Online*, March 2.

http://www.timesonline.co.uk/tol/news/world/us_and_americas/article3444835.ece

Lewis, A. (2009). *Fault Lines: Afghanistan* (television program). Al Jazeera: Qatar.

Lucas, J. A. (2004). Torture Gets The Silent Treatment. *CounterCurrents.org*. http://www.countercurrents.org/us-lucas260704.htm

Marshall, L. (2005). Why I Don't Support the Troops. *CounterCurrents.org*. http://www.countercurrents.org/us-marshall020905.htm

Murphy, R. (2007). *UN Peacekeeping in Lebanon, Kosovo & Somalia: Operation & Legal Issues in Practice*. Cambridge, UK: Cambridge University Press.

Oppel, R. A. (2010). U.S. Admits Role in February Killing of Afghan Women. *The New York Times*, April 4.

http://www.nytimes.com/2010/04/05/world/asia/05afghan.html?src=un&feedurl=http% 3A%2F%2Fjson8.nytimes.com%2Fpages%2Fworld%2Fasia%2Findex.jsonp

Petersen, K. (2008). Peace of Walking with Warriors. *Dissident Voice*, March 20.

http://dissidentvoice.org/2008/03/peace-or-walking-with-warriors/

Razack, S. (2004). *Dark Threats and White Knights: The Somalia Affair, Peacekeeping and the New Imperialism*. Toronto: University of Toronto Press.

Richard, J. (2003). Montreal antiwar demonstration the largest in Canadian history. *World Socialist Website*, February 17.

http://www.wsws.org/articles/2003/feb2003/mont-f17.shtml

Robinson, B., & Staples, S. (2007). More Than The Cold War: Canada's military spending 2007–08. *Canadian Center for Policy Alternatives: Foreign Policy Series*, 2(3), 1-10.

http://www.policyalternatives.ca/sites/default/files/uploads/publications/National_Office_Pubs/2007/More_Than_the_Cold_War.pdf

Smith, Sgt. M. (2006). Bad Apples from a Rotten Tree: Military Training and Atrocities. *Counterpunch*, August 5-6.

Turse, N. (2009). *The Complex: How the Military Invades Our Everyday Lives*. New York: Holt Paperbacks.

CHAPTER TWO

The Militarized Society

Corey Anhorn

As a child growing up in the prairies, the military was a ubiquitous part of my life—even if I never realized it at the time. From early on, my days did not consist of "Cops and Robbers" or "Cowboys and Indians." Rather, my friends and I bought cheap plastic M16 and 9mm replicas and donned opposing headband colours. We played "War." Growing older, I became interested in the field craft of Boy Scouts and the sharp drill of Cadets. During my visits to California, I was always secretly envious of the Marines in their blue dress uniforms, an envy that grew every time I passed by the local recruitment offices or heard of someone else signing up for service.

I now find myself, years later, a member of the Canadian Forces. While my choice to join the service was not one taken lightly, I have nonetheless come to realize just how easy it can be to become entranced by the perceived glamour and glory that military service offers. As the militarization of culture and society becomes increasingly more apparent both in Canada and the U.S., the need for an honest discussion of the potential ramifications of such a militarization is needed more than ever. By focusing my research on how the entertainment industry and corporate media are becoming increasingly linked to the military and military culture, I hope to illuminate some of the potential outcomes this partnership.

I begin with the exploration of how the military and war are represented in North American societies through a number of topic questions:

- What role do youth programs such as Boy Scouts or the Junior Reserve Officer's Training Corps (JROTC) play in the militarization of society, if any?

- Does the military co-opt or appropriate the media for its own use, or do the media willingly acquiesce for their own reasons? How are service members portrayed and viewed by the society at large?
- In what other ways has the military, or militarization, worked its way into civil society?

I feel as though it is increasingly important to study the militarization of society and culture to better understand how it has begun to permeate all aspects of our life and what can be done to keep this continued militarization at bay. As a member of the military on the one hand, yet a hopeful anthropologist on the other, the opportunity to study this burgeoning entanglement of society and war is one that I simply cannot avoid.

Youth Programs

Perhaps one of the most startling aspects of the militarization of society is the way in which the educational system and youth programs such as the Boy Scouts of America have shifted over the past decade. The Boy Scouts of America, part of the global "Scout Movement" beginning in 1910, is an institution that has long been a staple in the American way of life. Through participation in outdoor activities, educational programs and character development, the Scouts are looked upon fondly as an organization which guides American youth towards self-reliance and a keen sense of civic duty. These guiding values were further expanded through the creation of the "Explorers" program in 1959, which worked to give on-the-job training to youth in fields such as law enforcement, fire and rescue work or aviation. Yet, as recently as 2009, the same youth who had been previously known for their crisp brown khakis and sashes brimming with badges were now wearing full suits of Kevlar and breaking down doors.

With approximately 145,000 members aged 14-21 currently enrolled in one of the 12 career-related programs organized into "posts," 24 per cent of these members—numbering a staggering 35,000 by recent estimates—have chosen to follow the "law enforcement" path. As Jennifer Steinhauer writes, "since the attacks of Sept. 11, 2001, and the wars in Iraq and Afghanistan, many posts have taken on an emphasis of fighting terrorism and other less conventional threats" (Steinhauer, 2009). Indeed, these Scouts are led and taught by active police officers and border agents who place their charges into intricate scenarios that are surprisingly realistic. From conducting armed patrols through imagined fields of marijuana to encounters with role-players wearing traditional Arab dress, the program does claim to be neutral. "This is about being a true-blooded American guy and girl," Sheriff's Deputy A.J. Lowenthal comments, "If we're looking at 9/11 and what a Middle Eastern terrorist would be like...then maybe your role-player would look like that" (Steinhauer, 2009). Armed with plastic airsoft replica rifles, decked in paramilitary clothing and trained in up-to-date counter-terrorism drills, these Scouts—mainly children—resemble more a group of military recruits than a team of campers. Yet, the creep of militarism into civil society has not ended there.

Figure 2.1: Boy Scout Meets Marine Machine Gunner in Hawaii

Original caption: Gunnery Sgt. Pel Jaerith, company maintenance chief, Combat Assault Company, 3rd Marine Regiment, introduces the M2 .50 caliber machine gun to seven-year-old Thomas Yamada during "Scouting in Hawaii's" 100th anniversary Makahiki Show at Ala Moana Regional Park, April 24, 2010. Photography by the U.S. Marine Corps, cleared for release, placed in the public domain by the USMC.

Figure 2.2: Boy Scouts at the Pentagon, meeting with Army Chief of Staff

Original caption: Chief of Staff of the Army Gen. George W. Casey Jr., left, hands out Army hats to members of the Boy Scouts of America during a visit to his office at the Pentagon, March 1, 2010. They Boy Scouts are in Washington, D.C., to give their annual "Report to the Nation." Department of Defense photo by Cherie Cullen. (Creative Commons License: Share, Remix, Attribution.)

The Junior Reserve Officer's Training Corps, or JROTC, has undoubtedly been a staple of the secondary school system in the United States since its creation in 1916. However, only recently has there been such an expansive growth in an organization which outwardly claims to "help motivate young Americans toward military service [while their programmes] educate America's youth about the military" (U.S. Army, 2001). Until 1967, the number of JROTC units attached to secondary schools was limited to 1,200 at which point it was raised to 1,600. Subsequently, this cap was lifted to 3,500 units in 1992. However, these congressional limits were removed completely in 2001—allowing for an unprecedented growth of JROTC units across the United States (U.S. Code, 2009). This growth, it must be noted, has since been focused on particularly impoverished areas of the country. One only has to look to the city of Chicago, Illinois, to see the outcome of this expansion. With the highest amount of public military academies in the country (six in the city, amounting to one-third of the country's total) (McDuffee, 2008), one in 10 public high school students in Chicago is a cadet in JROTC (AFP, 2007). During their time at these academies, students are required to take courses on subjects such as military history or military protocol and dress and act in a military manner. Yet, while the U.S. Armed

Forces state that the JROTC program is not used as a recruiting tool—the opposite seems true. The military chiefs of staff themselves, in 2000, stated that somewhere between 30 and 50 per cent of JROTC cadets went on to sign up for military service, depending on the branch (House Armed Services Committee, 2001).

Figure 2.3: Training Children of Soldiers to be Like Soldiers

Original caption: A girl crawls low while maintaining control of her "weapon" as part of the 1st Cavalry Division's 6th Squadron, 9th Cavalry Regiment Saber Spur Ride to allow the children of soldiers to train as soldiers for a day on Fort Hood, Texas, June 20, 2008. The child is performing the last leg of a rigorous obstacle course that included a rope climbing exercise and a zip line. Photograph by U.S. Army Pvt. Sharla Perrin. (Creative Commons License: Share, Remix, Attribution.)

Mainstream Media

The media are perhaps one of the most obvious, yet subtly insidious, ways through which the military has crept into our daily lives. Through consistent and generally glowing depictions of service members fighting gallantly against those who work to harm us or others, we have come to simply acquiesce that our militaries (here I mean "Western militaries") are the good guys in nearly all cases. Films are perhaps the most prolific example of the blurring of lines between the civilian and military world, with the Pentagon maintaining a movie liaison office as part of the Office of the Assistant Secretary of Defense for

Public Affairs. The impact of this partnership has not been slight—nearly every major military film recorded in the United States over the past 40 years has either been asked to change portions of their content to show the U.S. military in a better light or has agreed to in exchange for the benefits it entails in production.

Filmmakers hoping to have access to military equipment, personnel, or land with which to film have had to alter their films in order to fall in line with what the Pentagon wants to depict. As producer Peter Almond explains in David L. Robb's book *Operation Hollywood: How the Pentagon shapes and censors the movies*, "the problem...with these big-scale projects that involve military assets is that we're kind of dependent on them for comparatively inexpensive use of the assets in making our stories. So they have us kind of over a barrel" (Robb, 2004, p. 56). *Operation Hollywood* goes on to name the staggering list of films that willingly gave into (or fit into) Pentagon demands, with blockbusters such as *Golden Eye, Top Gun, The Hunt for Red October* and *Armageddon* among the most prominent mentioned. Indeed, as recently 2009, the military has been intertwined with the film industry to promote its agenda. According to the U.S. Air Force's official website, four branches of the U.S. military worked with the staff of *Transformers: Revenge of the Fallen*, a film that has grossed $836,297,228 worldwide since June 24, 2009. Beyond simply receiving technical expertise or loads of equipment however, it seems as though those primarily involved in the film have had no qualms in praising their military partners. The film's producer, Lorenzo di Bonaventura, was quoted as saying "for us what is most interesting about it is our interaction with them, because you actually get to see these people who have made a life choice and the honesty of that choice comes through each and every time you meet these guys" (Davidson, 2009, ¶ 10). If this is not enough, the film's female lead actor, Megan Fox openly espoused her support for the partnership; "I enjoyed being able to walk on the set and there are a hundred real soldiers...It was just an overall pleasant experience, and I have an immense amount of respect for the Soldiers and for our troops" (Davidson, 2009, ¶ 8). Coming from one of the nation's pre-eminent sex symbols, and someone who young males within the recruitment age follow intensely, these comments may carry a lot of weight.

The link between media and the military does not end with the film industry, however. Nick Turse, author of *The Complex: How the Military Invades Our Everyday Lives* talks about the Xbox game "Close Combat: First to Fight" and how it was not only originally used as a training tool for the U.S. Marine Corps, but was also created under the direction of more than 40 active-duty Marines, just returned from Iraq, and who worked with the development team to put into "First to Fight" the exact tactics that they themselves used in combat (Turse, 2008). Moreover, the military has begun targeting social media sites and blogs as a means of tracking public opinion and to raise recruitment levels.

They have even gone as far as to produce a "blog assessment flowchart" in the U.S. Air Force in order to engage in "counter-blogging" against in order to, as Capt. David Faggard, Chief of Emerging Technology at the Air Force Public Affairs Agency in the Pentagon said in 2008, "counter the people out there in the blogosphere who have negative opinions about the US government and the air force" (Scott, 2008, ¶ 5). Beyond this, the U.S. military now has a presence on nearly every social media site popular today, from Facebook to Twitter. Lt. Gen Benjamin Freakley, the officer in charge of Army recruiting notes that Facebook has been essential in finding new avenues for recruitment: "They live in the virtual world," he says. "[On Facebook] you could friend your recruiter, and then he could talk to your friends" (Meghani, 2009, ¶ 4).

Conclusion

The problems associated with the ever-expanding militarization of society are obvious: children are brought up in organizations such as the Scouts that may eventually lead to their emulation of counter-terrorist operations. Films work, overwhelmingly, to glorify the military and to whitewash over much of the hardship that service members, their families and veterans face. Indeed, the militarization of American culture has become increasingly normalized, to the point where the government allows live-fire military exercises to continue unabated despite local protest (San Diego Union-Tribune, 2009) and where heavily-armed SWAT teams have seen an increase of 1,500 per cent since the early 1980s. This expansion has not occurred solely in the U.S., however. Since beginning its role in the conflict in Afghanistan, Canada too has seen a shift towards militarization with such initiatives as "Project Hero"—a program that pays for the undergraduate education of children of Canadian Forces personnel who have lost their lives while serving in an active mission (Project Hero, 2010). With the increasingly intertwined nature of civil society and the military, it may be argued that our faculty for critical thought of military ventures is being severely reduced, if not eliminated completely. When a filmmaker is unable to complete his work without the support of the military, what are they to do? Likewise, impoverished youth often see JROTC programs as the only way "out." Society then is locked in a Catch-22.

Undoubtedly, the points discussed here do not by any means cover the breadth of the militarization of society. Surely, it is nigh impossible to cover all of the facets central to cultural and social militarization in such a short space. Yet, by illuminating some of the pitfalls and danger areas that are the crux of the social ramifications of this militarization, I hope that it will work to open a larger discourse on the topic itself. For, as Eisenhower most poignantly stated in his farewell address of 1961, "only an alert and knowledgeable citizenry can compel the proper meshing of the huge industrial and military machinery of defense with our peaceful methods and goals, so that security and liberty may prosper together" (Eisenhower, 1961, Section 4, ¶ 6).

References

AFP. (2007). Military Training Program for Teens Expands in US. *American Free Press*, November 25.

http://afp.google.com/article/ALeqM5gpoWMq8VcFOJBYp3U8yigxhLkuJg

Davidson, J. (2009). Military unites with Hollywood on "Transformers." *American Forces Press Service*, June 23. http://www.af.mil/news/story.asp?id=123155579

Eisenhower, D. D. (1961). Farewell Address.

http://www.ourdocuments.gov/doc.php?flash=true&doc=90&page=transcript

House Armed Services Committee. (2001). Hearings on National Defense Authorization Act

For Fiscal Year 2001—H.R. 4205 and Oversight of Previously Authorized Programs before the Committee on Armed Services, House of Representatives, 106th Congress, Second Session, Full Committee Hearings. Washington, DC: U.S. House of Representatives.

http://commdocs.house.gov/committees/security/has041000.000/has041000_0f.htm

Meghani, S. (2009). Pentagon reaches out on Facebook, Twitter: Social Networking Sites Offer Another Way to Reach Tomorrow's Soldiers. *MSNBC*, May 1.

http://www.msnbc.msn.com/id/30519203/ns/technology_and_science-tech_and_gadgets/

McDuffee, A. (2008). No JROTC Left Behind: Are military schools recruitment pools? *In These Times*, August 20. http://www.inthesetimes.com/article/3855/no_jrotc_left_behind/

Project Hero. (2010). Project Hero Program.

http://www.projecthero.ca/program.html

Robb, D. L. (2004). *Operation Hollywood: How the Pentagon Shapes and Censors the Movies*. New York: Prometheus Books.

Scott, D. M. (2008) The US Air Force: Armed with Social Media. *WebInkNow*, December 15.

http://www.webinknow.com/2008/12/the-us-air-force-armed-with-social-media.html

Steinhauer, J. (2009). Scouts Train to Fight Terrorists, and More. *The New York Times*, May 13.

http://www.nytimes.com/2009/05/14/us/14explorers.html

Turse, N. (2008). *The Complex: How the Military Invades Our Everyday Lives*. New York: Henry Holt and Company.

San Diego Union Tribune. (2009). County Says War Games Can Continue Without Loudspeakers. *The San Diego Union-Tribune*, July 22.

http://www.signonsandiego.com/news/2009/jul/22/county-says-war-games-can-continue-without-loudspe/?northcounty&zIndex=136126

U.S. Army. (2001). United States Army Posture Statement FY01: Chapter 5, Meeting the Recruiting Challenge. Washington, DC: Office of the Chief of Staff, U.S. Army, Congressional   Activities   Division   (DACS-CAD). http://www.army.mil/APS/aps_ch5_2.htm

U.S. Code. (2009). USC Chapter 102—Junior Reserve Officers' Training Corps. Washington, DC: Office of the Law Revision Counsel.

http://uscode.house.gov/download/pls/10C102.txt

CHAPTER THREE

The African Response to AFRICOM

Ricky Curotte

The desire of the U.S. to establish a permanent U.S. Army Africa Command (AFRICOM) signals the growing strategic, political and economic importance of Africa in the post-Cold War world-view of the U.S. At the Cold War's end, American interests in Africa were handled by a single command centre in Europe, the Pacific and the Atlantic. According to official statements, AFRICOM is dedicated to enhancing "efforts to bring peace and security to the people of Africa" and to promoting the "goals of development, health, education, democracy and economic growth" (Office of the Press Secretary, 2007). Nevertheless, AFRICOM's actions in Africa are being conducted according to George W. Bush's "War on Terror" and his successor Barack Obama's "fight against violent extremism."

The announcement of AFRICOM has caused considerable protest from all levels of African society. Given the history of neglect demonstrated towards Africa, sceptics of AFRICOM argue that the U.S. is more concerned with curbing the growing influence of China on the continent and securing African sources of oil, as they are deemed more reliable than Middle Eastern sources. Furthermore, the American-led invasion of Iraq, the occupation of Afghanistan, and more recently, the American-backed invasion of Somalia—all missions claiming humanitarian goals—have served to fuel African protests, and have destabilized those areas.

Collectively, every state in Africa, with the exception of Liberia, has refused to allow the establishment of AFRICOM's headquarters on African soil. Many African states cite the implications that the establishment of such a large command could present with regard to sovereignty. They point to the degree of influence the U.S. has exerted in Algeria as a major African partner in their War on Terror as proof that aid will be dispensed to African countries that will serve U.S. interests. Therefore, African protests against AFRICOM arise out of the widespread scepticism shared regarding the true motive of AFRICOM, as it appears to be dedicated to protecting American interests instead of addressing African needs.

Figure 3.1: An AFRICOM Graphic Used for Publications

Africa covered by the U.S. military, emphasizing the supposed "humanitarian" nature of a military command. Photograph by U.S. Army Africa. (Creative Commons License: Share, Remix, Attribution.)

Throughout the twentieth century, Africa was regarded by the U.S. military and diplomatic community as unimportant to their strategic interests. According to Peter Pham, Africa during the twentieth century was the "step child of U.S. foreign policy, with official attitudes and policies in Washington ranging from benign neglect at best to callous indifference at worst" (Pham, 2007, p. 40). During the Cold War, the Americans and their allies propped up friendly African governments as a bulwark against Soviet expansion on the continent. Nevertheless, as the Iron Curtain fell, so did Africa's strategic significance. Following the Cold War, the U.S. divided its global interests along the lines of military commands, dividing Africa among three separate commands in Europe, and the Pacific, whereas more important regions such as Europe had a single command. According to Sean McFate, the justification for placing interest in Africa among three commands was that "each viewed its strategic imperative as being elsewhere, leaving Africa as a secondary or even tertiary concern" (McFate, 2008, p. 11). Therefore, the desire of the U.S. to establish a permanent AFRICOM signals the growing strategic, political and economic importance of Africa in the post-Cold War world.

Figure 3.2: The U.S. Military Building a New Interest in Africa

U.S. Army Gen. William E. Ward, centre, U.S. European Command deputy, and U.S. Ambassador to Ghana Pamela Bridgewater, rear, inspect Ghanaian military members at Burma Camp in Accra, Ghana, 06 August 2007. Ward visited the nation in an effort to bolster relations with African nations. DoD photo by Capt. Darrick Lee, U.S. Air Force. (Creative Commons License: Share, Remix, Attribution.)

This chapter first explores how the American government justifies the establishment of a permanent military command for Africa. In addition, it will be demonstrated that behind the desire to aid Africa with humanitarian development and security are American concerns with the War on Terror, the need for African sources of oil, and a desire to reverse declining U.S. influence on the continent. The section after that explores the sources of African protests, which have grown out of the widespread scepticism across Africa and have succeeded in preventing the establishment of AFRICOM on African soil. Therefore, AFRICOM must conduct its mission from Stuttgart, Germany. Nevertheless, AFRICOM has produced more destabilization in Africa then it has prevented. Therefore, I contend that an alternative to AFRICOM's military emphasis would be African involvement in diplomatic and humanitarian efforts to foster development in Africa in areas where AFRICOM has failed. It will be argued that African solutions to African problems do exist, and that they require only secondary support from the U.S. It will be found, though, that an African-led diplomatic and humanitarian approach is being hindered by AFRICOM, as such an initiative thwarts American interests in Africa.

American Justifications

Efforts to establish a permanent African command centre accelerated during the administration of President George W. Bush. Following Bush's departure, his successor, current President Barack Obama continued with the creation of a command centre as an important tool in his war against "violent extremism." For Obama, an African command is necessary because, "there will be situations that require the United States to work with its partners in Africa to fight terrorism with lethal force;" he went on to assert that "having a unified command operating in Africa will facilitate this action." (Volman, 2009, p. 15). Even though the plans for establishing an African command has been pursued by two different administrations, it is clear that both are dedicated to encouraging the formation of like-minded government suited to American national interests.

Enhance Security

According to proponents of AFRICOM, the formation of a new strategic command is concerned with the belief that Africa's destabilization has repercussions for global, and more importantly, American interests. This is a point expressed by former President George W. Bush: "Africa is increasingly vital to our strategic interests. We have seen that conditions on the other side of the world can have a direct impact on our own security" (Office of the Press Secretary, 2008). Arguably, these statements originate within the context of the War on Terror, as Africa was one of the earliest sites of Al Qaeda terrorist attacks. As pointed out by Carmel Davis, "Al Qaeda's first major terrorist operation was the bombing of the U.S. embassies in Nairobi and Dar es Salaam in 1998. Al Qaeda struck again in Kenya in 2002, bombing a discotheque and attempting to shoot down an Israeli airliner" (2009, p. 125). Adding to American concerns is the importance expressed by Al Qaeda agents of Africa. As pointed out by Abu Azzam al-Ansari of the Global Islamic Media Front:

> "There is no doubt that al-Qaeda and the holy warriors appreciate the significance of the African regions for the military campaigns against the Crusaders. Many people sense that this continent has not yet found its proper and expected role and the next stages of the conflict will see Africa as the battlefield....This is a continent with many potential advantages and exploiting this potential will greatly advance the jihad. It will

promote achieving the expected targets of jihad. Africa is a fertile soil for the advance of jihad and the jihadi cause." (Kfir, 2008, p. 111)

Consequently, regions with significant Muslim populations, such the Maghreb, the Nigerian Delta and East Africa, are of concern as potential hotbeds of Islamic extremism, which is the biggest security concern in Africa. As noted by Jeremy Keenan, "US military intelligence sees this zone as a conduit for potential terrorists moving between what it sees as the traditional terrorist havens of Afghanistan, Pakistan, Yemen, Somalia and the Sudan, and the Western Saharan-Sahel regions of Niger, Mali, Southern Algeria, Mauritania and the Senegal Valley" (Keenan, 2004a, p. 480). Furthermore, the American intelligence community holds that these pockets of Islamic terrorist groups emerge out of the destabilization of many African governments, who also lack the military capacity to meet the challenge these groups pose. Consequently, according to Catherine Besteman, "arguing that security is a necessary precondition for development, officials say AFRICOM will be heavily involved in military-to-military [relations] to improve African military capabilities" (Besteman, 2009, p. 123).

Humanitarian Aims

In the face of mounting criticism concerning AFRICOM as part of the militarization of Africa, officials have fervently presented AFRICOM as dedicated to the humanitarian needs of Africa. One such official, Navy Rear Admiral Robert Moeller, who led the AFRICOM transition team, stated that "by creating AFRICOM, the Defence Department will be able to coordinate better its own activities in Africa as well as help coordinate the work of other U.S. government agencies, particularly the State Department and the U.S. Agency for International Development" (Pajibo et al., 2007). Thus, in conjunction with military support, the humanitarian arm of AFRICOM can succeed in bringing stability to regions of Africa where aid is needed. This is a point shared by Christopher Isike et al., who note that "in Africa, where state corruption, weak social and security infrastructure and their multiplier effects of pervasive poverty and armed insurgency are very much in evidence, AFRICOM could serve as an instrument to create a truly secure African environment where development can thrive" (2008, p. 32).

Figure 3.3: Promoting AFRICOM

U.S. Army Africa's interactive exhibit at the Annual Meeting and Expo of the Association of the U.S. Army (AUSA), held in Washington, DC, 5-7 October 2009. Photograph by U.S. Army Africa. (Creative Commons License: Share, Remix, Attribution.)

Figure 3.4: Promoting AFRICOM as "Security, Stability and Peace" for Africa

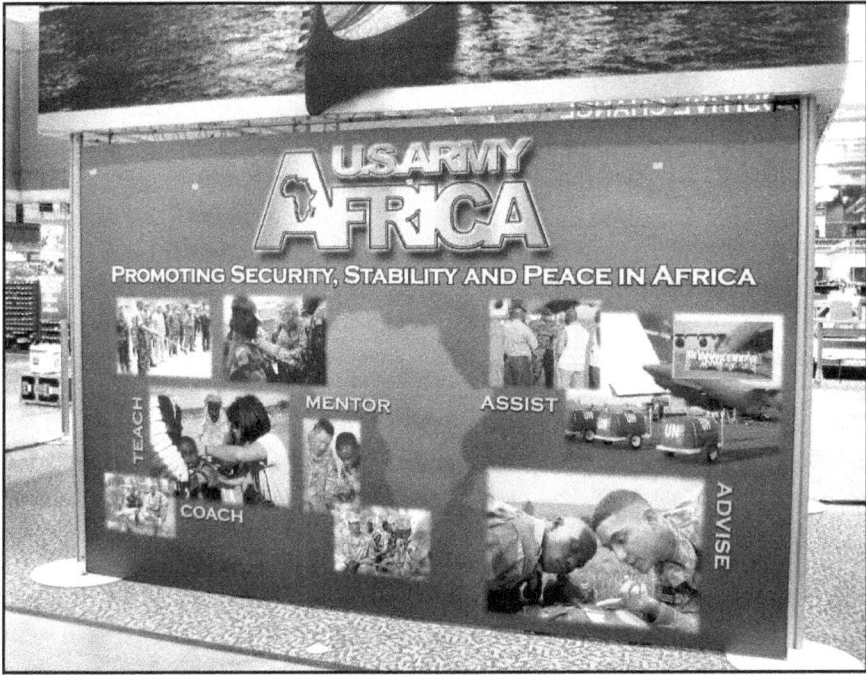

Another side of the U.S. Army Africa's interactive exhibit at the Annual Meeting and Expo of the Association of the U.S. Army (AUSA), held in Washington, DC, 5-7 October 2009. Photograph by U.S. Army Africa. (Creative Commons License: Share, Remix, Attribution.)

President Ellen Johnson Sirleaf of Liberia hailed the establishment of USAFRICOM as "a model for the future in helping governments that are willing to help themselves" (Gordon, 2007). Nevertheless, she is one of the very few high ranking African officials to embrace AFRICOM in such a positive light. Additionally, numerous scholars, considering the U.S.' history of neglect, and of intervening when it suits their strategic interests, suggest that heads of states, such as Johnston Sirleaf, are mistaken if they believe that AFRICOM motives in Africa are altruistic.

Hidden Motives

Dependence on Foreign Oil

The U.S. is becoming alarmingly dependent on foreign sources for oil to satisfy its industrial and personal consumption. According to the Cheney Report published in 2001: "Without a change in current policy, the share of U.S. oil demand met by net imports is projected to increase from 52 percent in 2000 to 64 percent in 2020" (National Energy Policy Group, 2001). Therefore, secure reliable sources of foreign oil have become a major security concern for the U.S. This concern was echoed five years later, during former president Bush's State of the Union Address, which called for the U.S. to "replace more than 75% of our oil imports from the Middle East by 2025" and to "make our dependence on Middle Eastern oil a thing of the past" (Bush, 2006). In 2007, Africa surpassed the Middle East in oil exports to the U.S. (for more data, see Energy Information Administration [EIA], 2010). Arguably, the destabilization in the Middle East contributes to the appeal of African oil. As noted by Davis, "African oil would increase in importance if supply from the Middle East were to be disrupted by political shocks, such as a regional war in the wake of a possible U.S. withdrawal from Iraq or a U.S. attack on Iran" (2009, p. 124). Equally alarming, emerging industrial powers will be as dependent in the future on foreign oil as the U.S. is presently. Competition is inevitable. This looming battle for foreign oil becomes all the more likely when we consider that even "former major oil exporters such as China and Indonesia are now net importers of oil while countries such as Mexico, Algeria, Iran and Malaysia may join them by the end of the second decade of the 21st century" (Isike et al., 2008, p. 23).

For Besteman, it is no coincidence that the creation of an African command is being discussed at a time when the U.S. has it sights on African sources of oil. For Besteman, "Africa's increasing importance as a source of oil (to say nothing of the continent's other precious resources) is undoubtedly what provoked the creation of AFRICOM. The same logic led to the creation of CENTCOM in 1980, a dire harbinger of AFRICOM's likely future" (2008, p. 21). In this context, it can be predicted that AFRICOM will be predominantly concerned with oil producing regions, such as the Nigerian Delta. The importance Nigeria to American security interests was noted by Isike et al.: "any attempt at destabilizing oil production activities in oil-rich states like Nigeria is viewed as a threat to America's energy security that must be contained" (2008, p. 23). Another new source of oil in Africa is Algeria. The growing interest in Algerian oil was noted by Keenan: "Algeria increased its export of 'Saharan Blend' to the U.S. during the first five months of 2004 by some 400 per cent over the same period of 2003, from 48,000 bpd (barrels per day) to 193,000 bpd." (2004a, p. 492). Thus, just as Besteman observed that the creation of AFRICOM at a time when African oil is in high demand was no coincidence, neither is the focus on Algeria as the center of the War on Terror in Africa.

War on Terror

Critics of AFRICOM point to the expansion of the War on Terror in the Sahel as an example of America protecting its interest in oil under the guise of protecting its security. According to Keenan, "through AFRICOM the U.S. has used the pretext of the 'War on Terror' in the Sahel to firm up its basing rights and militarization (aid!) programmes in sub-Saharan Africa, especially where US strategic interests are at stake" (2004a, 492). Nowhere does Keenan's contention resonate more loudly than in the case of Algeria. Initially, when the U.S. announced its expansion of the War on Terror into the Sahel, regional powerhouse Algeria was at the forefront of protest of such actions. As noted by Keenan, "in 2003, Algeria's Foreign Affairs Minister at that time, Abdelaziz Belkhadem (currently Prime Minister), fearful that reports of a US military presence would cause domestic problems, was quick to point out that his country's policy had always been to deny a foreign military presence on its territory" (Keenan, 2006a, p. 602). Shortly thereafter, with the emerging threat of *Groupe Salafiste pour la Predication et le Combat* (GSPC), led by former Algerian counterterrorist agent, El Para, the U.S. was able to convince Algeria to accept American aid. According to Keenan, El Para was used to justify the American military presence in the Sahel and the suppression of Tuareg tribes. Some critics argue that the threat that GSPC posed is over-hyped. Jeremy Keenan argues that "the lack of effort by either the Americans or Algerians to 'take [El Para] out of Chad' strongly supports the conclusion of terror in the Sahara...that he was the key instrument in the U.S.-Algerian attempt to launch their 'War on Terror' into the Sahel" (Keenan, 2004b, p. 696). Furthermore, Keenan attacks Algerian claims of an impending Tuareg uprising as unlikely, given that "Algerian Tuareg know that any rebellion would be crushed easily with heavy loss of life" (Keenan, 2006b, p. 765).

The Horn of Africa remains an important region of American security interest. Critics of AFRICOM point out that American intervention in the Ethiopian invasion of Somalia has served to further destabilize the country. As noted by Bah and Aning, "the role of the U.S. in the continuing crisis in Somalia has also deepened reservations about its policies on the continent. U.S. support for the Ethiopian government's unilateral invasion of Somalia to oust the Union of Islamic Courts (UIC)—credited for restoring a degree of order to Mogadishu—created unease in Africa" (2008, p. 128).

Chinese Gains in Africa

The expansion of Chinese influence in Africa, and the potential threat this reality presents to American interests in Africa, has been seized upon by proponents of AFRICOM. According to Daniel Volman, the U.S. government has become increasingly concerned by the "growing efforts of China to expand its access to energy supplies and other resources from Africa and to enhance its political and economic influence throughout the continent" (Volman, 2009, pp. 4-5). This contention is one that has become a major source of skepticism by the African media. According to Stephen Burgess, it is widely held in Africa that, "the U.S. action in establishing AFRICOM had little to do with altruistic reasons and more to do with selfish motives of establishing access to oil and natural resources, enabling the U.S. to fight terrorism, and countering China's growing influence on the African continent" (Burgess, 2009, pp. 4-5).

Without a doubt, Chinese economic and political interests in Africa pose a major threat to American interests in Africa. As noted by Sean McFate, "over 700 Chinese state companies conduct business in Africa, making China the continent's third largest trading partner, behind the U.S. and France, but ahead of Britain" (McFate, 2008, p. 14). Furthermore, as China's influence on the world stage has increased significantly over the last 30 years, China has demonstrated consistent interest in trade relations with the continent. The strong commercial links between China and the African continent have been observed by Paul Tiyembe Zezela, who notes that "trade between Africa and China increased from $817 million in 1977 to $1.7 billion in 1990 and $3 billion in 1995, jumping to $10 billion in 2000 and $39.7 billion in 2005, and reached $55.5 billion in 2006 and is projected to rise to $100 billion in 2010" (2008, p. 173). Equally impressive has been China's role in providing loans dedicated to African infrastructure. "According to World Bank estimates, China's Export-Import Bank infrastructure loans to Africa were estimated at $12.5 billion in mid-2006, more than the total western infrastructural aid to the continent," notes Zezela (2008, p. 176). Consequently, in exchange for generous aid donations, one source of compensation has been rights to African oil sources. As noted by Davis, "China received almost one-third of its oil imports from Africa in the first five months of 2006, and Angola surpassed Saudi Arabia as the largest source of China's oil imports in early 2006" (2009, p. 127).

One appealing element of granting trade concessions to China in exchange for economic aid and relief is the West's history of exploitation and domination in Africa. According to Zezela, in Africa, "China is depicted as a developing country with no history of external imperialism and incapable of being an imperialist power like the nations of the West, a country, moreover, that has unlocked the secrets of rapid development that other developing countries in Africa can productively follow" (2008, p. 174).

The growing influence of China in Africa and its role as an alternative source to American aid and military support holds several implications that highlight significant differences in the Chinese and American approaches to Africa. The Chinese approach is subtle in contrast to the U.S. interventionist approach to African politics. Four important differences in the American and African approaches where identified by Davis (2009, pp. 132-133):

1. Where the U.S. approach is to trade, encourage economic development, and mold African states in ways that extend the frontier of gov-

ernment authority and promote stability, China's approach is to truck and barter and its official policy is not to "interfere in the internal affairs of other countries."

2. Where the U.S. seeks to support political transformation into putatively more stable democratic forms of government and extend the state's authority to the territorial frontiers of countries, China seeks to maintain the political status quo and is not seeking to extend the state's authority.

3. Where the U.S. wants countries in Africa to become like those in the developed world, China is content to support weak and authoritarian states.

4. Where the U.S. wants pervasive governance, China supports states that do not effectively govern the entirety of the territory of their country.

Figure 3.5: AFRICOM's "Information Operations" Network

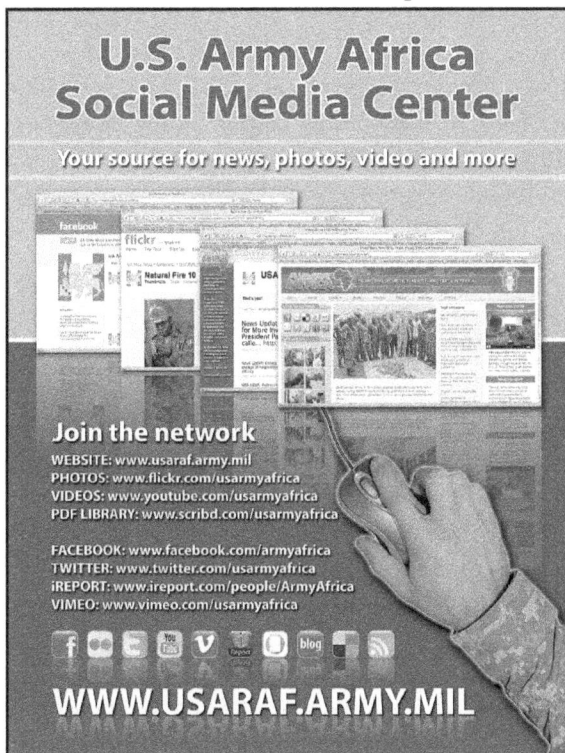

A poster advertising the extent of AFRICOM's employment of social media to sell its preferred representations of its image, mission, and message. This image itself comes from U.S. Army Africa's Flickr photostream. (Creative Commons License: Share, Remix, Attribution.)

African Opposition

Interfering With African Sovereignty

Five decades have passed since Africa went through an extensive process of decolonization. The unrest that still plagues Africa is arguably a consequence of the disinterest demonstrated by their former colonial masters in preparing indigenous Africans for the political and social challenges that awaited them. As Africa struggled to develop, several Western powers have used African political instability as a pretext for intervening in African domestic affairs. A major concern of African states is the consequence that the establishment of AFRICOM will have with respect to sovereignty. As highlighted by Burgess, "coming four years after a combatant command (CENTCOM) had carried out the invasion of Iraq and overthrown Saddam Hussein and weeks after the U.S.-backed Ethiopian invasion of Somalia in December 2006, many African leaders appeared to be concerned that the insertion of the new command on the continent might lead to U.S. offensive military operations" (2009, pp. 3-4). This being considered, the most explicit demonstration of protest that stems from concerns of sovereignty with respect to AFRICOM is the command must operate from outside of Africa, in Stuttgart, Germany. As a consequence, every African country, with the exception of Liberia, is unwilling to allow the military command to set up its headquarters on their territory.

Lack of Consultation

Ample evidence suggests that planners of AFRICOM are going ahead with their plans to expand into Africa with little input from African states. This lack of consultation has raised concerns about what the U.S.' motives are in Africa. This concern was echoed by the Algerian Foreign Affairs Minster who, upon hearing American announcements of AFRICOM, questioned why "did no one ever propose any anti-terror cooperation with Algeria in the 1990's when terrorist violence was rampant and wrought havoc in that country?" (Isike et al., 2008, p. 22).

Nevertheless, there is equal evidence that the U.S. will, when consulted for help, intervene if doing so serves its interests. Jeremy Keenan points to American intervention on behalf of the Algerian government during the 1991 national election. Keenan notes that the ruling government at the time was concerned with the early success of the Islamic Salvation Front or *Front Islamique du Salut* (FIS), also known as *al-Jabhah al-Islāmiyah lil-Inqādh*. If elected, Keenan suggests, they would have ushered in "the world's first democratically elected Islamist government, something that neither the leadership of Algeria's army nor western powers was prepared to allow" (Keenan, 2004a, p. 480). Thus, the Algerian government succeeded in soliciting the help of the U.S. and their former colonial masters, France, in annulling the elections. Keenan, among others, argues that these actions were parallel to a coup in which "the country succumbed to an increasingly dirty 'civil war' in which army elements and their various militias were probably responsible for as many atrocities as Islamic militants" (Keenan, 2004a, p. 481).

More recently, the ire of many African states was provoked by the U.S. and the support lent to Ethiopia in its invasion of Somalia. As noted by Ed Blanche, American intervention on behalf of its Ethiopian allies enabled "the overthrow of Somalia's first stable government in 16 years, dominated by the Islamist Courts Union, which was viewed by the Americans as threat" (Blanche, 2009, p. 47). Another similarity between the American intervention in Algeria and the Ethiopian-backed invasion in 2006 was the destabilization that ensued after both incidents. What followed the overthrow of the ICU, according to Catherine Besteman, was "a humanitarian disaster identified by Refugees International as the worst in the World" (Besteman, 2009, p. 125).

Opposition Raised by Regional African Powers to AFRICOM

A considerable amount of opposition to AFRICOM has been voiced collectively by major African political organizations and individual regional African powers. The African Union, through the Pan-African parliament, notes Pham, symbolically "passed a non-binding motion asking member governments not to accede to the United States of America's government's request to host AFRICOM" (2008, p. 267). South Africa, as a major African power, perceives the establishment of AFRICOM as a challenge to its influence on the continent. This concern has been reiterated by South African Defense Minister, Mosiuoa Lekota, to the South African Development Community, that "Africa has to avoid the presence of foreign forces on its soil, particularly if any influx of soldiers might affect relations between sister African countries" (Kifar, 2008, p. 112). Quite clearly, the political opposition emerges from the recognized potential that AFRICOM can hold for the existing power structure in Africa.

Opposition to AFRICOM is also present throughout the African media, thus demonstrating opposition at the local level. The American-backed invasion of Somalia was heavily criticized in the media by neighbouring Kenya, stating that the "U.S. is using Somalia and neighboring countries to conduct experimental tests on the effectiveness of its new military outfit, AFRICOM" (Burgess, 2009, p. 7). Additionally, one Nigerian editorial referring to the American intervention in the civil war in Liberia—the only African state that has explicitly considered the establishment of AFRICOM on its territory—noted that "the U.S. failure to provide meaningful assistance to Liberia during its violent civil war belied any notion of a genuine altruistic intent" (Burgess, 2009, p. 5).

Therefore, it can be concluded that opposition expressed in the African media is indicative of the profound skepticism of American motives in regards to AFRICOM that is present at all levels of society in many African states.

Precursors of AFRICOM, such as the Pan-Sahel Initiative (PSI), have been criticized for their role in facilitating the suppression of indigenous groups deemed a threat by the states ruling their territory. Given that fighting the War on Terror is a major element of AFRICOM's mission, as the successor of the PSI, it has raised concerns from African states and critical scholars. Under the PSI, the American Government supplied countries, such as Niger, Mali, and Chad, to support counter terror measures with military training and weaponry (Bah & Aning, 2008, p. 126). Keenan observed that the PSI not only failed to bring stability to the Sahel, but has rather prevented it. He points to the fact that "six years of fabricated terrorism and provoked unrest have transformed large, hitherto relatively tranquil, tracts of Africa into zones of more-or-less permanent instability, rebellion, war and terror" (Keenan, 2008, p. 19). Moreover, many friendly African nations have been using military aid to wage offensive conflicts against their neighbors as opposed to defense. Therefore, it can be argued, military aid aimed to bolster the security capabilities of African states may be focused on states open to American interests. As noted by Besteman, "Ethiopia receives support, even though it used U.S. tanks against its own population; Rwanda receives help even though its intervention in the D.R.C. [Democratic Republic of Congo] conflict zone exacerbates violence; Uganda receives support even though northerners continue to suffer human rights abuse by government soldiers" (Besteman, 2009, p. 126).

One specific case of the war on terror as justification for a country taking action against its own citizens can be found in Algeria, with the state's campaign of oppression against the Tuareg. Nevertheless, as noted by Keenan, even though "the region has remained relatively calm both during and since the Kidal rebellion of May 2006, in spite of considerable provocation of the local Tuareg by the U.S.-supported governments of the region" (Keenan, 2006b, p. 761), the Algerian authorities framed the alleged existence of a Tuareg uprising in the context of the War on Terror. It has been argued that the Algerian government's provocation of the Tuareg is common practice of many Sahel governments: they provoke indigenous populations into conflict to justify the need for American aid. Keenan notes that "the more the local governments of the Sahel can provoke and hence portray these minority and marginalized populations as 'rebels/bandits' or as arms, cigarettes, drugs or people traffickers, the more money and arms they are likely to receive from the U.S." (Keenan, 2004b, p. 695). Additionally, the provocation of certain indigenous groups is aided by other groups who share close ties with the government or share a history of conflict with those groups. As noted by Keenan, government informants are "often the worst possible intelligence sources, as the vast majority of them come from ethnic groups that are alien to the region (i.e. non-Tuareg, Tubu, etc) and whose knowledge of the indigenous Sahel populations is usually prejudiced by their experience of the region's several recent rebellions and other, often long-standing inter-ethnic conflicts" (Keenan, 2004a, p. 484). Furthermore, although at the national level these tribal bonds should be blurred, it is often not the case; many African leaders with strong bonds to their tribal groups may be inclined to carry tribal hostilities with them to the highest rungs of government. Fortunately, as noted by Keenan, "people in the Sahel know their governments are benefiting from the U.S. in the form of financial and military support and therefore have a vested interest in both generating and maintaining this climate of terror" (Keenan, 2004a, p. 490).

The Sensitivity of the ΔFRICOM Mission

Security Concerns

Many critics of AFRICOM question the U.S.' militaristic rather than diplomatic approach to fostering security in Africa. This question has been put forward by Catherine Besteman: "If military security is the objective, why is the U.S. enhancing militarism in Africa rather than providing vastly expanded assistance to the beleaguered African Union and other regional peace-keeping and diplomatic organizations?" (Besteman, 2009, p. 117). One answer to this question could be that a stronger military presence, and encouragement of local military dependence on American aid, will facilitate American interests in the continent. Danny Glover and Nicole C. Lee, both leading activists against AFRICOM, predict that "an increased US military presence in Africa will likely follow this pattern of extracting resources while aiding factions in some misguided unilateral US military policy to "bring peace and security to the people of Africa" (Glover& Lee, 2007, p. 6). Furthermore, scholars have pointed to history as an indicator the ineffectiveness of a military-heavy solution in stabilizing war-torn countries. As noted by Isike et al., "there is incontrovertible historical evidence (Algeria, Angola, Chad, Ethiopia, the D.R.C., South Africa, Sudan and Uganda) that militarism is ineffective in curbing conflict in Africa unless the environment that gave birth to the violence is fundamentally altered" (2008, p. 27).

Internal Stability

The military orientated approach followed by AFRICOM will ensure further internal destabilization in many African states instead of preventing it. Rather than encourage democratic governments, AFRICOM emphasis on military support will only serve to strengthen repressive regimes, which may provide the environment for radical political ideologies and encourage violent extremism. This is a contention shared by Pham, who argues that "there is no denying that the environment created by Africa's endemic poverty, social injustice, and political alienation nonetheless enhances the ability of religious and other extremists to propagate their radical ideologies and of terrorists to find local collaborators and other support for their violence" (Pham 2007, p. 43). In response to the exacerbation of political and social instability, some critics of AFRICOM have argued for support being increased to African-led initiatives. One such initiative was the Monitoring Group of the Economic Community of West African States, which saw success in quelling the civil war in Liberia. As noted by Glover and Lee, the "ECOMOG forces in Liberia numbered 12,000, and it was these forces—not U.S. or U.N. troops—that kept Liberia from disintegrating" (Glover & Lee, 2007, p. 6). Therefore, it can be argued that an overwhelming American presence may not be necessary to meet African security needs.

Humanitarian Concerns

The 2006 American-backed Ethiopian invasion of Somalia has been widely criticized for exacerbating the humanitarian crisis in the East African state. As noted by Volman and Minter, two years following the invasion, "over 3.2 million or (43 per cent of Somalia's population), including 1.3 million internally displaced by conflict, were estimated to be in need of food assistance" (2009, p. 5). Moreover, destabilization provides the right environment for radical extremist groups to gain a more profound foothold in the country at the expense of the more moderate groups overthrown in the invasion.

Some Possible Solutions

Diplomacy

Even though AFRICOM praises itself on its diplomatic merits, it can be argued that its manner of conducting diplomacy through military concessions is more suited towards American concerns as opposed to African ones. As highlighted by Isike et al.:

> "Western security needs in Africa would be best assured not by using military means to check China or terrorism in Africa but rather by looking to meaningfully address the region's human security needs that are amplified both by unfair trade relations between the continent and the West and by the benign neglect and scrounging relationship that historically enabled, cuddled and protected corrupt and self-centred leaders to do their bidding throughout the continent." (2008, p. 36)

The Niger Delta, an important source of oil, which the U.S. covets as a solution to its energy needs, is one region where African and American interests contradict. Whereas the U.S. views the insurgencies in the region as the greatest security threat, Volman and Minter suggest that the African "priority is rather to resolve the problems of poverty, environmental destruction, and to promote responsible use of the country's oil wealth, particularly for the people of the oil producing regions" (Volman & Minter, 2009, p. 7).Therefore, if AFRICOM does intend to promote stability in these regions, then it must do so with the input of the African states whom the Command intends to aid. The most effective way to do so is through decision-making that prioritizes African needs over American concerns, which is achievable only through diplomacy.

Decrease the Influence of the Pentagon in Humanitarian Initiatives

On the U.S. side, the most effective means of encouraging a more diplomatic approach to the problems that AFRICOM intends to address would be to allow more input from the State Department and other government departments dedicated to non-military objectives. This shift away from the Pentagon is espoused by Burgess, who argues that "foreign policy decision making power should be shifted back towards the State Department and development policy back towards USAID, which would make AFRICOM a supporting command" (2009, p. 27). Moreover, this approach will allow African humanitarian organizations governments, which are in a better position to recognize African problems, to work along with the U.S. in addressing more serious African security challenges, such as HIV/AIDS, deforestation, corruption, debt relief and poverty—the realities AFRICOM should confront it were serious about its stated humanitarian goals.

Conclusion

It is clear that after four years in operation, AFRICOM has failed in its mission to bring stability to Africa. Instead, it has been met with endless amounts of protest reflecting the widespread distrust of American motives in Africa. It has been shown that this distrust has emerged out of a long history of neglect and indifference from the U.S. towards Africa. Therefore, American claims of a humanitarian purpose while enlarging its military presence in Africa is resented because many of the security and humanitarian crises facing Africa have been caused by American neglect and manipulation in the past. Evidence indicates that America's new found interests are rooted in its own concerns with the War on Terror, its declining political influence in Africa, and its growing demand for reliable sources of oil. It is through AFRICOM that the U.S. hopes to assert itself, politically and military, so that it may protect its own security interests even if that is done at the expense of African interests. This has been demonstrated by its actions in Ethiopia and Algeria and the ensuing havoc, which many Africans perceive to be a foreshadowing of what AFRICOM really about.

Nevertheless, it has been suggested that it is not too late. Arguably, if African states collectively have the ability to forestall the building of AFRICOM's headquarters on African soil, then they can collectively address the real problems they are facing, such as AIDS, poverty, and corruption, which create the conditions that encourage violent extremism and susceptibility to radical fundamentalist ideologies. If AFRICOM wishes to bring stability to Africa, it must deal with these tragic realities. The only solution is to de-emphasize its military role by adopting an approach that prioritizes diplomacy. More importantly, future missions must be limited to supporting African states in addressing the problems they recognize as important. It has been shown that Africa is capable of taking care of its problems. Even though AFRICOM has the resources to help Africa to fight African problems, it will not help because African needs and American desires do not coincide.

References

Bah, A. S. & Aning, K. (2008). U.S. Peace Operations Policy in Africa: From ACRI to AFRICOM. *International Peacekeeping*, 15(1), 118-132.

Besteman, C. (2008). "Beware of Those Bearing Gifts." An Anthropologist's View of AFRICOM. *Anthropology Today*, 24(5), 20-21.

——————— . (2009). Counter AFRICOM. In Network of Concerned Anthropologists (Eds.), The Counter-Counterinsurgency Manual: Or, Notes on Demilitarizing American Society (pp.115-132). Chicago: Prickly Paradigm Press.

Blanche, E. (2009). Africom's Agenda Still Baffles Africa. *New African*, (481), 46-47.

Bush, G. W. (2006). Address before a Joint Session of the Congress on the State of the Union [transcript]. 31 January.

http://georgewbush-whitehouse.archives.gov/news/releases/2002/01/20020129-11.html

Burgess, S. F. (2009). African Responses to US Africa Command. Conference Papers— International Studies Association, 2009 Annual Meeting, January 28.

Davis, C. (2009). AFRICOM's Relationship to Oil, Terrorism and China. *Orbis*, 53(1), 122-136.

Energy Information Administration. (2010). *U.S. Imports by Country of Origin*. Washington, DC: U.S. Department of Energy.

http://tonto.eia.doe.gov/dnav/pet/pet_move_impcus_a2_nus_ep00_im0_mbbl_m.htm

Glover, D. & Lee, N. C. (2007). Say No to Africom. *The Nation*, 285 (16), 4-6.

Gordon, D. (2007). The Controversy over AFRICOM. *BBC News*, October, 03.

http://news.bbc.co.uk/2/hi/africa/7026197.stm

Isike, C., Okeke-Uzodike, U. & Gilbert, L. (2008). The U.S. Africa Command: Enhancing American Security or Fostering African development? *African Security Review*, 17(1), 20-38.

Keenan, J. (2004a). Political Destablisation and "Blowback" in the Sahel. *Review of African Political*

Economy, 31(102), 691–703.

——————— . (2004b). Terror in the Sahara: The Implications of US Imperialism for North & West Africa. *Review of African Political Economy*, 31(101), 475-496.

——————— . (2006a). Military Bases, Construction Contracts & Hydrocarbons in North Africa. *Review of African Political Economy*, 33(109), 601-608.

——————— . (2006b). Turning the Sahel on Its Head: The "Truth" Behind the Headlines. *Review of African Political Economy*, 33(110), 761-769.

——————— . (2008). U.S. militarization in Africa: What Anthropologists should know about AFRICOM. *Anthropology Today*, 24(5), 16-20.

Kifar, I. (2008). The Challenge that is US AFRICOM. *JFQ: Joint Force Quarterly*, (49), 110-113.

McFate, S. (2008). U.S. AFRICAN COMMAND: A New Strategic Paradigm? *Military Review*, 88(1), 10-21.

National Energy Policy Development Group. (2001). *National Energy Policy*. Washington, DC: Government Printing Office.

http://www.pppl.gov/common_pics/national_energy_policy/national_energy_policy.pdf

U.S. Office of the Press Secretary. (2007). President Bush Creates a Department of Defence Unified Combatant Command for Africa, February 6.

http://georgewbush-whitehouse.archives.gov/news/releases/2007/02/20070206-3.html

——————— . (2008). Remarks by President Bush, First Lady, on U.S. Policy in Africa, February 14.

http://www.america.gov/st/texttrans-english/2008/February/20080214133927eaifas0.3938257.html

Pajibo, E. & Woods, E. (2007). AFRICOM: Wrong for Liberia, Disastrous for Africa. *Foreign Policy in Focus*, July 26.

http://www.fpif.org/articles/africom_wrong_for_liberia_disastrous_for_africa

Pham, P. J. (2007). Next Front? Evolving U.S.-African Strategic Relations in the "War on Terrorism" and Beyond. *Comparative Strategy*, 26(1), 39-54.

——————— . (2008). America's New Africa Command: Paradigm Shift or Step Backwards? *Brown Journal of World Affairs*, 15(1), 257-272.

Volman, D. (2009). AFRICOM and the Obama Administration. Association of Concerned Africa Scholars.

http://concernedafricascholars.org/african-security-research-project/?p=43

Volman, D. & Minter, W. (2009). Making Peace or Fuelling War in Africa. *Foreign Policy in Focus*, March 13.

http://www.fpif.org/reports/making_peace_or_fueling_war_in_africa

Zezela, P. T. (2008). Dancing with the Dragon: Africa's Courtship with China. *The Global South*, 2(2), 171-187.

CHAPTER FOUR

The Human Terrain System: A Question of Ethics and Integrity

Mark Shapiro

With the creation of the Human Terrain System (HTS), the U.S. military sang the praises of social scientists working with the military. Embedded with troops, Human Terrain Team (HTT) members conduct social science research in the name of the U.S. military under the guise of anthropology. Arguments against the Human Terrain System call its application of anthropology unethical and detrimental to the profile of the discipline. Ethical concerns exist as to whether informant participation is voluntary, and whether findings are being used for targeting. This essay addresses two fundamental ethical questions pertaining to Human Terrain Teams: whether team members practice anthropology in accordance with the Code of Ethics of the American Anthropological Association and whether the Human Terrain System contributes to a devaluation of the professional integrity of all anthropologists.

As alleged in the media, the germ of the Human Terrain System is to be found in 2002 when femme fatale and current Senior Social Scientist of HTS, Montgomery McFate (PhD Yale, J.D. Harvard Law School) posed the question to her husband, of how she could make anthropology relevant to the military (Stannard, 2007). In 2003 McFate was contacted by the Pentagon, and in 2005 was asked to create a database to map the "human terrain," "the cultural, sociological, political and economic factors of the local population," of Iraq (Rhode, 2007; Human Terrain System [HTS], 2008, p. 3). In 2005 she and Andrea Jackson, Director of Research and Training at the Lincoln Group, addressed the need for social science research within the Department of Defense (DOD) in a paper titled, "An Organizational Solution of DOD's Cultural Knowledge Needs" (McFate and Jackson, 2005). An argument put forth by McFate was that "the national security structure needs to be infused with anthropology, a discipline invented to support war fighting in the tribal zone" (McFate, 2005, p. 43). Under the direction of Steve Fondacaro, a retired Special Operations Colonel, the U.S. Army Training and Command (TRADOC) implemented the Human Terrain System, a proof-of-concept program, embedding social scientists with combat troops in order to better understand the "human terrain' and to make information relevant to commanders in Iraq (Rhode, 2007; HTS, 2008, p. 2). The Human Terrain System worked to embed attachments of military and civilian social scientists and analysts in order to study the "human terrain" and perform anthropological, sociological and ethnographic research (Kipp et al., 2006, p. 9). Human Terrain Teams are made up of "a Team Leader, a Social Scientist, a Research Manager and two Human Terrain Analysts" (HTS, 2008, p. 11).

The military is collecting cultural data on "tribal affiliations, ethnicity, religion and language" in order to map the "human terrain." Information and analysis is being stored in central databases and can be accessed for intelligence purposes by a number of US government agencies (Gonzalez, 2008; Jean, 2010). This information is then layered to create human terrain maps, according to Swen Johnson (CEO of SCIA Socio-Cultural Intelligence Analysis). According to Johnson:

> "One map might show the location of all the tribes in a region. A second map might depict the known locations of all suspected insurgents. By imposing one over the other, an analyst might discover that the bad guys are in a single tribe." (Jean, 2010)

Detailed knowledge of the human terrain may also enable the identification of key players whose alignments might be crucial to military success in the region (Batson, 2008). Information collected by Human Terrain Teams might then be used for targeting insurgents, in clear violation of the American Anthropological Association's Code of Ethics, which maintains that anthropologists must "do no harm" vis-à-vis their research subjects (Commission on the Engagement of Anthropology with the U.S. Security and Intelligence Communities [CEAUSSIC], 2009).

Human Terrain Teams (HTTs) claim that their research subjects are offering their voluntary informed consent in interactions with team members, although the fact that some Human Terrain Team (HTT) members carry arms and travel with armed security attachments paints a different picture (CEAUSSIC, 2009). According to the HTS website, "from the perspective of many local nationals, the consequences of not engaging outweigh the risks of engaging [with the Human Terrain Teams]" (HTS, n.d.). The website states that HTT "members are legally prohibited from performing active intelligence collection" (HTS, n.d.); intelligence is defined according to Mark Crisci (Director of HTS Project Development), however, as information about the *enemy* (Jean, 2010). Crisci makes sure HTTs differentiate between gathering information and gathering intelligence: "Whenever his team encountered someone willing to impart intelligence about an alleged bad guy, its members would bring in a commander to take the information [instead]" (Jean, 2010). It remains that the work of HTTs involves gathering actionable intelligence about insurgents, except that the information gathered is only spoken to an attending soldier and not to the HTT "scout" nearby. HTS was implemented as a tool to not only better understand the people and cultural terrain of the host nations but as well to analyze the dispositions and cultures of insurgents, according to Kipp et al. (2006). In line with the Civil Operations and Revolutionary Development Support (CORDS) program first implemented by the U.S. military in the Vietnam war, Kipp asserts that HTS will be a cultural system analogous to "traditional military intelligence systems" (Kipp et al., 2006, p. 12).

Figure 4.1: Human Terrain Team Member Taking Notes on Afghan Villagers

Original caption: Task Force Gladius Soldier, 1st Lt. Sam Drzewianowski (left), a platoon leader with 1st Platoon, Company B, Special Troops Battalion, 82nd Airborne Division, and Ed Campbell (center left), Human Terrain Team member, both assigned to Task Force Cyclone, speak with village members in Surkh-e Parsa district, Parwan province, Afghanistan, 16 November 2009. Task Force Cyclone checked on current building projects, met with Afghan police officials and talked with civilians about concerns in the area. Combined Joint Task Force - 82 PAO Photo by Spc. William Henry. (Creative Commons License: Share, Remix, Attribution.)

Informed consent is a cornerstone of ethical research principles concerning ethnographic fieldwork and includes divulging any possible risks that participation could entail, according to Roberto González at San Jose State University (Stannard, 2007; Lucas, 2009). Ethical disclosure practices would entail disclosing the uses and possible consequences of information gathered. It is highly questionable whether the HTS can claim to "do no harm" to its informants, and to adhere to the ethical guidelines of anthropology as laid out by the AAA's Code of Ethics. For anthropologists who base their research on information gained from establishing trusting relationships, using that information to subsequently persecute your informants is neither a sustainable method, nor is it ethical according to Hugh Gusterson of George Mason University (Stannard, 2007). In 2007 the American Anthropological Association established an ad hoc Commission on the Engagement of Anthropology with the U.S. Security and Intelligence Communities (AAA, 2007; Lucas, 2009). David Price of St. Martin's University and Roberto González of San Jose State University joined other anthropologists in creating the Network of Concerned Anthropologists and subsequently drafted a "Pledge of Non-participation in Counterinsurgency" with over a thousand signatories (Vergano & Weise, 2008; Lucas, 2009). Other professional organizations, including the American Psychiatric Association, the American Medical Association and the American Psychological Association, also opposed their members' involvements in U.S. counterinsurgency operations "citing fears that scientists are violating professional standards" (Vergano & Weise, 2008).

Figure 4.2: A Human Terrain Team Member at Work in Afghanistan

Original caption: Task Force Cyclone Human Terrain Team's, 1st Lt. Raphael Howard, research manager, speaks with village members of Shaykh Ali, Parwan province, Afghanistan, 19 December 2009. Information gathered will help assess what is needed to better serve and contribute to the local people in the area. Photo by U.S. Army Spc. William E. Henry, Task Force Cyclone, 38th Infantry Division. (Creative Commons License: Share, Remix, Attribution.)

In October 2009 CEAUSSIC submitted its final report on the Army's Human Terrain Proof of Concept Program to the Executive Board of the American Anthropological Association (AAA). Commission members included David Price among others (CEAUSSIC, 2009, p. 1). The AAA's Executive Board Statement on the Human Terrain Project dating from October 2007 (AAA, 2007) raised five main ethical concerns that contravene the Association's Code of Ethics, namely that:

- Human Terrain Team members will not always be able to identify themselves as anthropologists apart from military personnel and thus will create problems regarding full ethical disclosure of their intents and purposes.
- Members' interests may be at conflict with the interests of those that they study; the members' obligations to the Army may trump their obligations to do no harm, thus contravening the Code of Ethics.

- "Voluntary informed consent" is compromised due to the complicated nature of working in a war zone where refusal to cooperate may not always seem like an open, and ultimately viable option.
- The uncontrolled use of information gathered in the field may pose harm to those they study.
- Non-Human-Terrain-System anthropologists may suffer consequences, possibly going as far as being physically harmed due to perceived association with American Human Terrain System anthropologists (CEAUSSIC, 2009, p. 69-70).

Figure 4.3: Human Terrain Team Meeting with Village Elders, Afghanistan

Original caption: Capt. Duke Reim, 1st Battalion, 12th Infantry Regiment, Charlie Company commander, and Human Terrain Team members talk with a local village elder during a village assessment. As Capt. Reim is finding out, the villagers are more receptive to him and his Soldiers when they see them interacting with them on a personal level, providing consistent security and meeting their needs. The Human Terrain Team embeds anthropologists and other social scientists with combat units in the field to help commanders understand local cultures. Photo by Staff Sgt. Justin Weaver, 1st Battalion, 12th Infantry Regiment. (Creative Commons License: Share, Remix, Attribution.)

The Executive Board of the American Anthropological Association concluded in agreement that the HTS program results in conditions contradicting the Code of Ethics, and that by association it increases risks for non-HTS anthropologists and those they study. They state, "The executive board views the Human Terrain System project as an unacceptable application of anthropological expertise" (CEAUSSIC, 2009, p. 70).

Roberto González argues that anthropologists should never assist the military except in humanitarian missions by vote of the association, somewhat akin to the suggestion by Professor Margaret Walker of Arizona State University for founding a NGO of anthropologists (Stannard, 2007; Lucas, 2009), perhaps modeled on Medecins Sans Frontières, namely, Anthropologists Without Borders. It remains to be established more definitively as to whether subjects participate with HTTs voluntarily, and whether information gathering for targeting is the norm. Nevertheless, the available information suggests that the question of whether Human Terrain System members can practice anthropology in accordance with the Code of Ethics of the American Anthropological Association should currently be answered in the negative. Collective integrity for all anthropologists requires that much work be directed towards rectifying this untenable situation.

References

American Anthropological Association (AAA). (2007). *Final Report of the AAA Commission on the Engagement of Anthropology with the U.S. Security and Intelligence Communities.* Washington, DC: American Anthropological Association.

Batson, D. (2008). *Registering the Human Terrain: A Valuation of Cadastre.* Washington, DC: National Defense Intelligence College.

Commission on the Engagement of Anthropology with the U.S. Security and Intelligence Communities (CEAUSSIC). (2009). *Final Report on the Army's Human Terrain Proof of Concept Program.* Washington, DC: American Anthropological Association.

Human Terrain System (HTS). (2008). *Human Terrain Team Handbook.* Fort Leavenworth, KS: Human Terrain System.

——————— . (n.d.). Frequently Asked Questions. http://hts.army.mil/faqs.html

Gonzalez, R. (2008). "Human terrain": Past, Present and Future Applications. *Anthropology Today*, 24(1), 21-26.

Jean, G. (2010). Human Terrain: "Culture Maps" Becoming Essential Tools of War. *National Defense*, February 1.

Kipp, J., Grau, L., Prislow, K. & Smith, D. (2006). The human terrain system: A CORDS for the 21st century. *Military Review*, September-October, 8-15.

Lucas, George R. Jr. (2009). *Anthropologists in Arms: The Ethics of Military Anthropology.* Plymouth, UK: Altamira Press.

McFate, M. (2005). The Military Utility of Understanding Adversary Culture. *Joint Force Quarterly*, 38, 42-48.

McFate, M., & Jackson, A. (2005). An organizational solution to DOD's cultural knowledge needs. *Military Review*, 85(4), 18-21.

Rhode, D. (2007). Army Enlists Anthropology in War Zones. *The New York Times*, October 5.

Stannard, M. (2007). Montgomery McFate's Mission: Can One Anthropologist Possibly Steer the Course in Iraq? *San Francisco Chronicle*, April 29, CM-11.

Vergano, D. & Weise, E. (2008). Should Anthropologists Work Alongside Soldiers? *USA Today*, September 9.

CHAPTER FIVE

Kosovo, 1979-1999: The Ways and Means of American Empire

Elizabeth Vezina

The bombardment of Kosovo by the North Atlantic Treaty Organization (NATO) military forces and the ensuing ground war in 1999 has been portrayed, and largely accepted, as a humanitarian intervention to stop the ethnic cleansing of the Albanian people by Serbs. However further investigation reveals an orchestrated attempt by European countries, and particularly the U.S., to break up the internationally recognized sovereign state of Yugoslavia and to interfere in what was basically a civil war. Some of the methods used in this endeavour include: the economic and fiscal manipulation of the local economy by the International Monetary Fund (IMF) and World Bank; a propaganda campaign to legitimize the invasion; a travestying of the process of diplomatic negotiation; the ignoring of international laws and treaties; and, the use of overwhelming military power to subjugate a population and to establish a military presence in an area economically and geopolitically strategic for global dominance by the U.S.

Although the events leading up to the creation of a separate country of Kosovo occurred a decade ago, it is revealing to re-examine this situation. With the passing of the Freedom of Information Act, some information, although limited by blackouts, is now available that would not have been at the time. Also, hindsight, a less emotional response to the events, and further research, gives a different perspective. However, it is impossible within the confines of this paper to discuss in detail all of the reasons for the breakup of Yugoslavia. The intent is to highlight some of the many ways in which the U.S. engineered and influenced the events in Kosovo that ultimately were to the advantage of the U.S. and increased its empire.

Figure 5.1: Map of the Former Yugoslavia

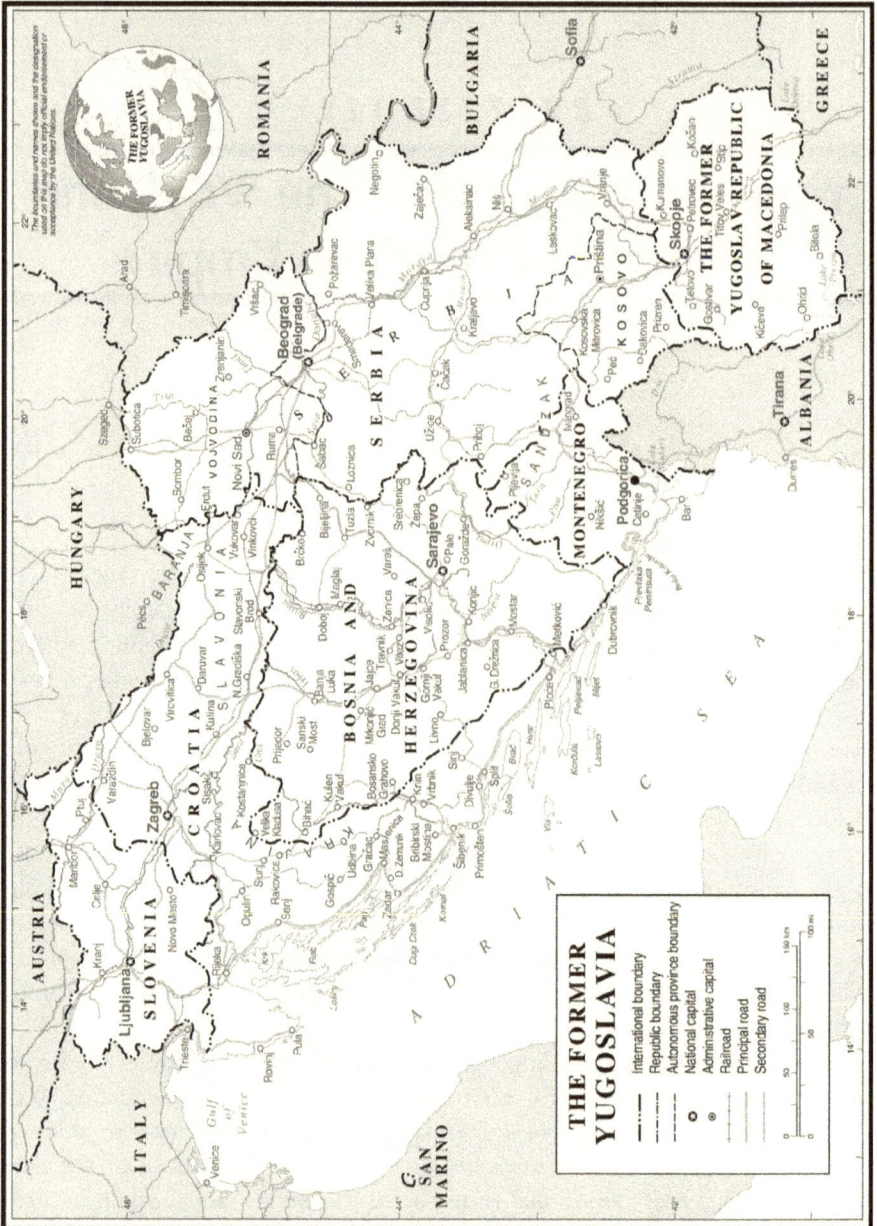

Source: Cartographic Section of the United Nations (CSUN), and the cartographer of the UN, Vladimir Bessarabov. Provided by Wikimedia Commons, as part of the public domain.

Figure 5.2: Map of Kosovo

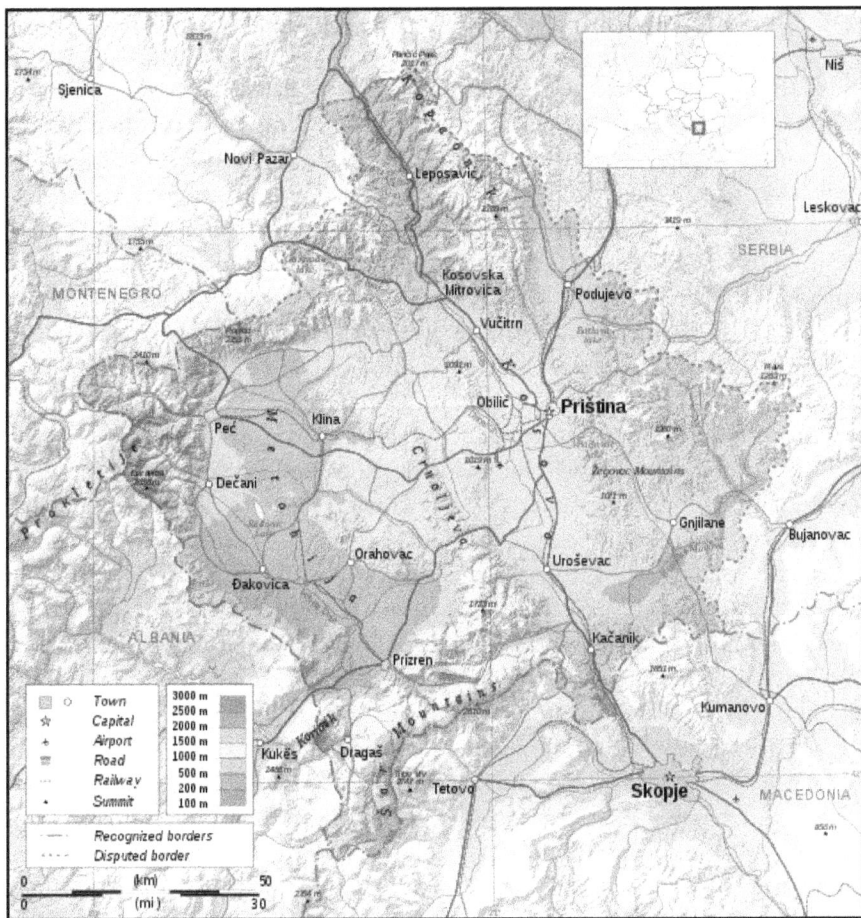

Source: the Wikigraphists of the Graphic Lab, for Wikimedia Commons.

It should be noted that the actions of the U.S. and its affiliate organizations against Yugoslavia, and particularly with regards to Kosovo, were by no means unique in the history of American foreign policy. They had been employed in many previous conflicts with other nations. All of the methods would be used again in more recent episodes contributing to the global spread of American hegemony. However, American efforts to camouflage their true intentions have been more successful in this context than in other conflagrations. To this day, many believe this was a successful venture, waged to stop ethnic cleansing. Kosovo was one of the first violations of local and international rights in which the U.S. and other western powers used the philosophy of "humanitarian intervention" as a justification for furthering the plundering of a country, by way of privatization and divestment of local industries as dictated by the IMF.[1]

IMF, World Bank, *inter alia*:
Fiscal, Political and Economic Destruction

The IMF and the World Bank were originally created in 1944 to bolster the economies of war-torn Europe. They have since become a consortium of several financial organizations with the mandate to lend money and assist in the development of "developing countries." Within these institutions, a weighted voting scheme is used in the approval process for projects. Countries that contribute the most money to the fund have the larger say in which projects are implemented. The U.S. is by far the largest contributor and so has the biggest influence on all decisions. As such, the U.S. has used the IMF, World Bank, the U.S. Agency for International Development (USAID) and other mechanisms to promote and implement its own agenda of world dominance including the creation of new markets for itself and the control of sources of energy.

Based on neoliberal economic theories, these organizations have imposed a variety of "structural adjustments" on borrowing countries that have in many ways reduced their economic, political and social health (Klein, 2007) and, more importantly in the case of Yugoslavia, to open up the economy to private enterprise (Chossudovsky, 1998). Once Yugoslavia became indebted to the IMF and World Bank, the many restrictions imposed by these organizations created the economic collapse of the country, "with the disintegration of the industrial sector and the piecemeal dismantling of the welfare state" (Chossudovsky, 1998, p. 244). This was the cause of the tensions between the many ethnic communities residing in the country (Woodward, 1995; Chossudovsky, 1998; Gibbs, 2009) and not necessarily the differences in ethnic origins and religion, as vividly portrayed by western media. There is evidence to suggest that the adjustments imposed were "intended to dismantle statist economic systems to make them more accessible to multinational investors" (Gibbs, 2009, p.56). A declassified U.S. National Security Division Directive entitled *United States Policy towards Yugoslavia* reiterated a former directive which proposed the reintegration of "the countries of Eastern Europe into a market-oriented economy" (Gervasi as cited in Chossudovsky, 1998, p. 244).

The Propaganda Campaign – Duplicity, and Distortions

During the period from 1979 to 1990 and beyond, economic sanctions and the withdrawal of funding brought tensions, economic hardships, and strife to Yugoslavia, a country already divided by regional economic differences between the various republics. In 1991 Slovenia and Croatia seceded from the country. It took a bloody war for Bosnia to establish its independence from Yugoslavia. The Serbian president Slobodan Milošević was determined to keep together what was left of the country (Gibbs, 2009). Europe and the United Nations (UN) intervened in the Bosnian conflict with the U.S. playing a very secondary role. When Milošević used the Yugoslavian army to quell insurgents in Kosovo, who were led by the Kosovo Liberation Army (KLA), the U.S. was determined to take the lead in any intervention and to take advantage of the situation. To justify a military intervention, the State Department initiated a propaganda campaign against Yugoslavia. This campaign included a demonization of Milošević and the creation of a criminal charge of ethnic cleansing and genocide against him and his army.

A large majority of the American press aided and abetted the official party line. A quick survey of issues published during this period, of only one well circulated newspaper, *The New York Times*, reveals a progressive demonization of Milošević. In 1992, he is described as a "former Communist and former international banker" (Kaufman, 1992), as a Serb nationalist (Kinzer, 1992) and as "Serbia's Czar" (Sudetic, 1993). By 1997 he had become a "combative Serb leader" (Perlez, 1997). Later in 1998, there were stories about him that included terms such as "death chronicles" (Perlez, 1998a) "massacres" (Perlez, 1998b) and "Kosovo terror" (Crossette, 1998). Just prior to the bombing, Milošević was described as a "tyrant", comparing him to Saddam Hussein (Smale, 1999). The problem with demonizing a leader, whether that is Saddam Hussein in Iraq or Salvador Allende in Chile (Gustafson, 2007), is that it greatly simplifies the context of a conflict and leads to the conclusion that regime change will solve all problems within a country (Gibbs, 2009, p. 5). As in most countries experiencing strife and bloodshed, the situation in the Balkans was an extremely complex one, involving social, economic and political issues, all of which were exacerbated by the ethnic composition and the history of that ethnicity within the region.

The charge of ethnic cleansing and genocide was quickly fabricated. U.S Defence Secretary William Cohen claimed "we've now seen about 100,000 military aged [Albanian] men missing...they may have been murdered" (as cited by Pilger, 2002, p. 144). David Scheffer, the U.S. Ambassador at Large for War Crimes, escalated that number to 225,000 (Pilger, 2008).

The "massacre" in Račak is a poignant example of the distortion of truth in the media. The day after a confrontation between Serbian troops and the KLA on 14 January 1999, the Kosovo Verification Mission (KVM) was invited by the KLA to inspect the aftermath of this battle. The KVM had been set up in October 1998, when, under the threat of NATO bombing, U.S. envoy Richard Holbrooke pressured Milošević to sign a unilateral deal to stop all operations against the armed rebels, the KLA, in Kosovo. The agreement was to be monitored by 2,000 foreign "verifiers," the KVM, which were provided under the auspices of the Organization for Security and Cooperation in Europe (OSCE). An American, William Walker, was head of the mission and he personally inspected the site. He quickly reported to the OSCE and the world that a group of villagers had been assassinated in a ditch outside the village of Račak. Although reports are contradictory, later investigation reveals enough evidence to speculate that the entire incident may have been staged by the KLA for the western press (Johnstone, 2000). The then leader of the KLA, Hashim Thaci admitted to this to Canadian Major General Lewis MacKenzie, former UN Protection Force commander in Bosnia (2008). Chatelot, a French journalist who saw the corpses, noticed very little blood in the area and few cartridges around the bodies, indicating that they may have been brought to the ditch (1999). William Walker is best known as an apologist for the death squads in El Salvador (Flaherty & Israel, 2002). In her biography, Helena Ranta, the forensic dentist who performed the autopsies on the same bodies, for the OSCE, reveals that Walker attempted to pressure her to use stronger language in her report that would indict the Serbs for murder (Helsingin Sanomat, 2008, ¶ 12).

After the bombardment, international forensic teams combed Kosovo to verify the extent of the "atrocities." Several weeks later, both the FBI and the Spanish team returned home, having been unable to locate one single mass grave. The International War Crimes Tribunal announced in 2000 that the number of bodies found as a result of skirmishes prior to the bombing in Kosovo totalled 2,788. This total included Serbs, Roma and combatants. The discrepancy between these reports and the media was little reported (Pilger, 2002, p. 145). Although the needless killing of any people is most certainly regrettable, this was a civil war and few would call the number of deaths genocide.

Probably the most flagrant abuse of language was to call this invasion a "humanitarian intervention" or an act of "peace keeping". In an essay in the *New York Times*, Bill Clinton called the confrontation a "just and necessary war" (1999). Clinton added: "We are in Kosovo with our allies to stand for a Europe, within our reach for the first time, that is peaceful, undivided and free. And we are there to stand against the greatest remaining threat to that vision: instability in the Balkans, fuelled by a vicious campaign of ethnic cleansing" (1999).

It may have been deemed *necessary* to establish a permanent American presence in that corner of the world but it is difficult to find the justice in any of it. A more accurate description would be a humanitarian disaster.

Diplomacy - Perversion of the Process

After the Račak incident, U.S. officials organized a peace conference at Rambouillet, outside Paris, to demand an end to fighting. The draft settlement plans included Kosovo's autonomy and an armed peacekeeping force to maintain the accord (Gibbs, 2009, p. 187). Although Europeans had a high profile in this meeting, the U.S. dominated the conference and maintained an underlying threat of air strikes if no agreement was forthcoming. Negotiations were proceeding well until a *Military Annex* ("Annex B") was introduced. This stipulated that:

> "a NATO force occupying Kosovo must have complete and unaccountable political power immune from all legal process, whether civil, administrative or criminal, [and] under all circumstances and at all times, immune from [all laws] governing any criminal or disciplinary offences which may be committed by NATO personnel in the Federal Republic of Yugoslavia....NATO personnel shall enjoy, together with their vehicles, vessels, aircraft, and equipment, free and unrestricted passage and unimpeded access throughout the Federal Republic of Yugoslavia, including associated airspace and territorial waters...[The government of Yugoslavia] shall, upon simple request, grant all telecommunications services...needed....NATO is granted the use of airports, roads, rails and ports without payment of fees, duties, tolls or charge. The economy shall function in accordance with free market principles." (Pilger, 1999)

A proud nationalist such as Milošević, intent on maintaining what was left of Yugoslavia[2] and his own power, would have never accepted such as infringement on sovereign authority. The Yugoslav parliament was willing to have a UN force in Kosovo to monitor a political settlement, but this was ignored by the U.S. Milošević and the parliament refused to sign. Several diplomats and analysts, including Henry Kissinger (as cited in Gibbs, 2009, p. 190), Barry Posen (2000) and John Gilbert, former UK defence minister (as cited in Gibbs, 2009, p.190) have concluded that Annex B was a deliberate provocation for a fight. It was this "failure of diplomacy" that Clinton engineered as justification for the use of force.

Extreme Force

Five days later, on 24 March 1999, NATO began 78 days of aerial bombing. Initially targets were military or quasi military installations. Within three days, having exhausted all such possible targets, NATO turned its sights to civilian structures, resulting in bombings of "50 bridges, 12 railroad lines, 5 civilian airports, 50 hospitals and clinics, 190 educational institutes, 16 medieval monasteries and shrines, and several factories, power plants, water mains, major roadways, media stations, libraries and homes" (Cohn, 2002, p. 98). The 10,000 strikes against the area (Arkin, 2000) resulted in 500-1800 civilian deaths (Cohn, 2002, p. 98). Later, U.S. officials admitted that the goal of demolishing civilian targets ("Phase Three" in military terms) was to make life miserable for the people and to put pressure on Milošević to surrender.

Kosovo was also a testing ground for new U.S. weapons. New, "improved," smart and cluster bombs, such as the CBU-102 (V) 2/B (Arkin, 2000) were used on the country's infrastructure. As in the first Gulf War, depleted uranium was used in bullets and missiles. This type of radioactive material has long been known to be a carcinogen and to affect the DNA of foetuses. This has resulted in an unprecedented increase in Kosovo and Serbia of birth defects and incidents of cancer for which the country will be paying for decades (Vujadinovic, 2010).

To stop the economic ruin of Serbia and Kosovo, with NATO threatening to bomb the factories belong to pro-government industrialists, and not because of military defeat, Milošević finally surrendered (see Hirsh, 1999; PRNewswire, 1999). NATO ground forces then invaded Kosovo. However these NATO forces initially stepped aside and let the KLA[3] attempt to destroy what was left of the Serbian population in Kosovo. The bombings, and the killings and the atrocities perpetrated by the KLA prompted a massive exodus of thousands from the country. Although people had fled Kosovo prior to this, by far the greatest majority of "ethnic cleansing" was completed after the bombing, not before (Chomsky, 2003, p. 55; Johnstone, 2008).

Military force has been an integral component of American foreign policy throughout its history. As early as 1898, U.S. forces slaughtered 250,000 local freedom fighters and civilians in the Philippines (Foster, 2006, p. 124). The conflict in Kosovo gave NATO a raison d'être, which it had lacked since the end of the Cold War, as a global police force. It also reaffirmed U.S. dominance over European affairs and strengthened its position of worldwide dominance (Gibbs, 2009; Cohn, 2002). Nor is it surprising to learn that the KLA was backed and trained by the CIA (Chomsky, 2003, p. 56; Chossudovsky, 1998; Walker & Laverty, 2000) and financed by the sale of heroin (Ruppert n.d.; Chossudovsky, 1999b; Szamuely, 1999; Cottin, n.d.; O'Kane, 2000; Klebnikov, 2000). The CIA has trained and equipped insurgent and entrenched armies in many parts of the world and in many cases drugs have been implicated in these activities (Chossudovsky, 1999b, p. 211; Chomsky, 1993).

Flagrant Disregard of International Law and Treaties

The Kosovo incident gives strong testimony to the U.S.' appreciation for international law and treaties. Article 2(4) of the UN Charter stipulates that all members "shall settle their international disputes by peaceful means and shall refrain from treat or use of force against the territorial integrity of any state" (United Nations [UN], 1945). Point 7 of the same article prohibits states from interfering in "domestic matters of other states, unless authorized by the Security Council" (UN, 1945). Furthermore, Article 33 of the same charter clearly states that prior to the use of force peaceful solutions are to be sought by means of negotiation. The Rambouillet "negotiations" were a sham, as they were conducted under the threat of bombardment and were an "ultimatum, impossible for Milošević to accept" (Cohn, 2002, p. 97). The U.S. deliberately bypassed Security Council approval for its invasion. NATO also violated Article 51 which states that an armed attack is permissible only "in self defence if an armed attack occurs against a Member of the UN" (UN, 1945). All members of NATO are members of the UN and none of them had been attacked (Cohn, 2002, p. 97). These actions were also against NATO's own charter.

NATO also contravened Principle VI of the Nuremberg Tribunal principles which "prohibits the planning, preparation, initiation or waging a war of aggression or war in violation of international treaties, agreements or assurances" (UN, 1950). Walter J. Rockler, a former prosecutor of the Nuremberg War Crimes Tribunal, had this to say on the bombing of Yugoslavia, as originally reported in the *Chicago Tribune* on 23 May 1999 (cited in Ryan, 2005):

> "The bombing war also violates and shreds the basic provisions of the United Nations Charter and other conventions and treaties; the attack on Yugoslavia constitutes the most brazen international aggression since the Nazis attacked Poland to prevent "Polish atrocities" against Germans. The United States has discarded pretensions to international legality and decency, and embarked on a course of raw imperialism run amok.

> "The illegality of the aerial war on Yugoslavia, along with the way in which it was conducted, is a matter of solid documented fact. Yugoslavia's refusal to sign the American-drafted scandalous Rambouillet ultimatum was the technical pretext for the bombing, but to get around the awkward fact of the war's illegality and to get the general public on side, clever propaganda portrayed the war as "humanitarian intervention." Much of this was enabled by shrill reports that Slobobdan Milosevic's military were conducting a campaign of genocide and that at least 100,000 Kosovo-Albanians had been exterminated and buried in mass graves in Kosovo. This deliberate propaganda was so convincing that even progressive-minded people and journals supported this "just war" against the demonic Serbs."

The devastation to Yugoslavia's infrastructure is defined as a "war crime" in both the Nuremberg Tribunal principles and the Geneva Convention. The U.S. and NATO even ignored a 1991 U.S. Nuclear Defence Agency report that condemned depleted uranium weapons as "a serious health threat" (Cohn, 2002, p. 101). As Jeremy Scahill points out, the US is quick to accuse other states of breaking international law but has no qualms of doing so itself (2008). The only "law" to which the U.S. seems to adhere is that of "might is right."

Military Bases: Power and Pipelines

Immediately after the bombing of Yugoslavia, U.S. forces seized 1,000 acres of farmland in southeast Kosovo and proceeded to build a military base—Camp Bondsteel. According to Colonel Robert L. McClure, the planning for this base was done "months before the first bomb was dropped" (as cited in Stuart 2002). Ten years later, the camp is an American settlement with its own sports halls, a chapel, library, hospital and retail outlets as well as a prison. Although the fighting is long over, there are no signs of the 7,000 troops leaving soon. Chalmers Johnson equates the approximately 1,000 American military bases worldwide to the colonies of earlier European Empires (2007, p. 138). Just as colonies were used to extract riches for Europe, the U.S. bases assist in supplying resources for America.

Figure 5.3: Aerial Photograph of Camp Bondsteel

Aerial photo of Camp Bondsteel, KFOR, Task Force Falcon Public Affairs Office. Provided by Wikimedia Commons as part of the public domain.

Camp Bondsteel is the largest in a series of US bases that straddle the Albanian/Macedonian border. The locations of these bases coincide with the site of the Albanian-Macedonian-Bulgarian (AMBO) oil pipeline that links the corridors between the Black Sea and the Caspian Sea basin. The Caspian Sea Basin is estimated to be the repository of 50 billion barrels of oil.[4] The pipeline is essential to transport oil to Europe and America and bypass the congested Bosporus Straits, where tanker size is restricted (Stuart, 2000). With its internal reserves of oil all but depleted and its continued reliance on oil and gas for energy, the U.S. is desperate for new sources and to control the spigots existing in the world (Harvey, 2003).

Figure 5.4: Oil Pipelines in the Balkans

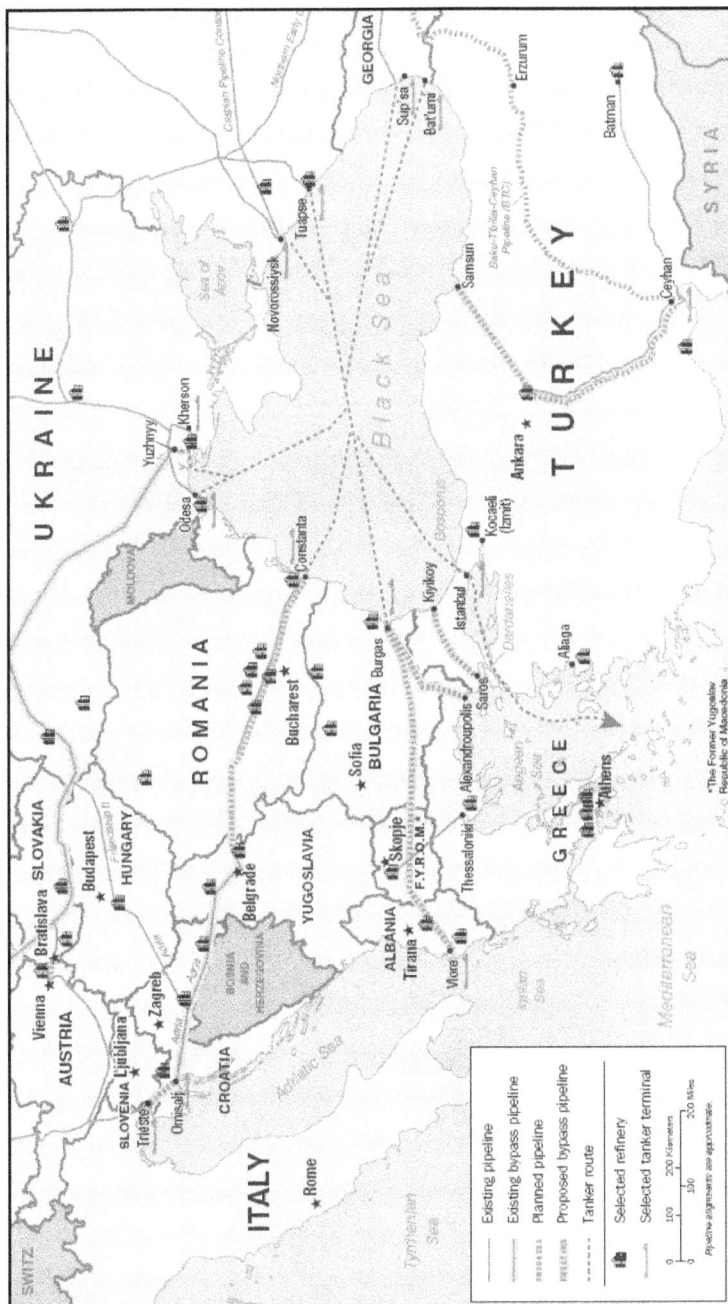

The focus on the Balkan region here is extracted from a larger map of oil pipelines running from north-western Asia through Europe. Source: Energy Information Administration, U.S. Department of Energy, 2007. Provided by Wikimedia Commons as part of the public domain.

Unfortunately, Kosovo is just one example of the continued escalation of American imperialism. In the decade following the invasion of Kosovo, the world has already seen major repetitions of US invasions in Iraq and Afghanistan. There has been little change in IMF and World Bank policies. Although Haiti has collapsed, so far, there is no indication that its huge debt to the World Bank will be erased. A propaganda campaign is currently being waged against Iran and North Korea. The U.S. continues to ignore international treaties and agreements or refuses to ratify them, which accelerates the marginalization and impotency of international organizations. Permanent military bases have been constructed in Iraq and more are under way in Afghanistan. The initial hopes of change under the Obama administration have been dashed with the increased deployment of 30,000 troops to Afghanistan. The demand by American society for fossil fuels and other resources continues to grow. When one examines the covert and overt history of U.S. foreign policy, especially since the end of the Cold War, it becomes evident that America will continue to attempt to increase its global dominance by a variety of means and by *any* means.

Notes

1 A series of structural adjustment laws were passed that destroyed much of Yugoslavia's industry and made it much easier for local companies to be bought by foreign investors. For instance, there was legislation that forced "insolvent" businesses into bankruptcy or liquidation. Under the new law, if a business were unable to pay its bills for 30 days running or for 30 days within a 45-day period, the government would launch bankruptcy procedures within the next 15 days (see Kiss, 1994; Chossudovsky, 1999a). Much of U.S. foreign policy is directed towards controlling resources in the world. Just as in other empires, the periphery is used to maintain the high lifestyle of the centre. Initially Milošević favoured a free market economy but later he began to support a more statist type of economy and was no longer willing to adhere to the dictates of the IMF. Some think this may be why he was no longer in favour with the U.S. General Wesley Clark maintained that not one foreign owned factory or industry was bombed by NATO (see Clark, 2004).

2 Milošević had declared the Republic of Serbia along with the Republic of Montenegro, the new Yugoslavia (1992) with Kosovo and Vojvodina as autonomous provinces. He also tried to convince Macedonia and Bosnia to join but they refused (Gibbs, 2009, p. 120).

3 NATO was aware of the nature of the KLA forces, having previously called it a terrorist organization, and so they were cognizant of the ramifications of allowing them free reign in Kosovo.

4 Caspian oil deposits were estimated at four trillion dollars by U.S. News and World Report, May 10, 1999. The Washington-base American Petroleum Institute, voice of the major U.S. oil companies, called the Caspian Sea region, "the area of greatest resource potential outside of the Middle East" (Cohn, 2002, p. 86).

References

Arkin, W. M. (2000). Smart Bombs, Dumb Targeting. *The Bulletin of the Atomic Scientists*, 56(3), May/June, 46-53.

Chatelot, C. (1999). Where the Racak Dead Really Coldly Massacred? *Le Monde*, January 21. Translated by D. Johnstone.
http://emperors-clothes.com/articles/Johnstone/racakhoax.htm

Chomsky, N. (1993). How the Cold War Worked.
http://www3.niu.edu/~td0raf1/history468/apr2304.htm

——————. (2003). *Hegemony or Survival.* New York: Metropolitan Books.

Chossudovsky, M. (1998). *The Globalization of Poverty: Impacts of IMF and World Bank Reforms.* New York: Zed Books.

——————. (1999a). How the IMF Dismantled Yugoslavia. *Albion Monitor*, April 2. http://www.albionmonitor.com/9904a/yugodismantle.html

——————. (1999b). Kosovo "Freedom Fighters" Financed by Organised Crime. *World Socialist Web Site*, April 10.
http://www.wsws.org/articles/1999/apr1999/kla-a10.shtml

Clark, N. (2004). The Spoils of Another War: Five Years after NATO's Attack on Yugoslavia, its Administration in Kosovo is pushing through Mass Privatization. *The Guardian (UK)*, September 21.
http://www.commondreams.org/views04/0921-05.htm

Clinton, W. J. (1999). A Just And Necessary War. *The New York Times*, May 23.
http://newimperialism.wordpress.com/2010/03/01/speech-bill-clinton-a-just-and-necessary-war-1999/

Cohn, M. (2002). NATO Bombing of Kosovo: Humanitarian Intervention or Crime against Humanity? *International Journal for the Semiotics of Law*, 15, 79-106.

Cottin, H. (n.d.). The Balkan Route and the Contras of Kosovo. *Institute for Media Analysis.*
http://www.covertaction.org/content/view/77/75

Crossette, B. (1998). Serbs Continue Kosovo Terror, Annan Asserts. *The New York Times*, October 6.
http://www.nytimes.com/1998/10/06/world/serbs-continue-kosovo-terror-annan-asserts.html

Flaherty, J. & Israel, J. (2002). William Walker (Alias, Mr. Racak) and His Salvador Massacre Cover-Up. *The Emperor's New Clothes (TENC)*, March 22.
http://emperor.vwh.net/analysis/meetmr.htm

Foster, J. B. (2006). *Naked Imperialism: The U.S. Pursuit of Global Dominance.* New York: Monthly Review Press.

Gibbs, D. N. (2009). *First Do No Harm: Humanitarian Intervention and the Destruction of Yugoslavia.* Nashville, TN: Vanderbilt University Press.

Gustafson, K. (2007). *Hostile Intent: U.S .Covert Operations in Chile, 1964-1974.* Washington, DC: Potomac Books Inc.

Harvey, D. (2003). *The New Imperialism.* Oxford, UK: Oxford University Press.

Hirsch, M. (1999). Nato's Game of Chicken: Victory Over Milosevic—Never Really in Doubt—Was Actually a Pretty Close Call. *Newsweek*, July 26. http://www.newsweek.com/id/89013

Johnson, C. (2007). *Nemesis: The Last Days of the American Republic.* NY: Henry Holt and Company.

Johnstone, D. (2000). Humanitarian War: Making the Crime Fit the Punishment.
http://emperors-clothes.com/articles/Johnstone/crime2.htm

—————. (2008). Independence in the Brave New World Order: NATO's Kosovo Colony. *CounterPunch*, February 18. http://www.counterpunch.org/johnstone02182008.html

Kaufman, M. T. (1992). Yugoslavia Denies Involvement of Belgrade in War in Bosnia. *The New York Times*, June 6.
http://www.nytimes.com/1992/06/06/world/yugoslav-denies-involvement-of-belgrade-in-war-in-bosnia.html

Kinzer, S. (1992). Conflict in the Balkans: Serb Nationalist Claims a Victory; Rival Cries Foul. *The New York Times*, December 22.
http://www.nytimes.com/1992/12/22/world/conflict-in-the-balkans-serb-nationalist-claims-a-victory-rival-cries-foul.html

Kiss, J. (1994). Debt Management in Eastern Europe. *Eastern European Economics*, 32(3) May - Jun., 52-75.

Klebnikov, P. (2000). Heroin Heroes. *Mother Jones*, January-February.
http://motherjones.com/politics/2000/01/heroin-heroes

Klein, N. (2007). *The Shock Doctrine: The Rise of Disaster Capitalism*. Toronto: Alfred A. Knopf.

MacKenzie, L. (2008). War Crimes and the Recognition of Kosovo: Observations on the Current Political Leadership in Kosovo. *Global Research*, April 3.
http://globalresearch.ca/index.php?context=va&aid=8533

O'Kane, M. (2000). Kosovo Drug Mafia Supply Heroin to Europe. *The Guardian*, March 13.
http://www.guardian.co.uk/world/2000/mar/13/balkans

Perlez, J. (1997). Cable Reveals a Combative Serb Leader. *The New York Times*, August 22.
http://www.nytimes.com/1997/08/22/world/cable-reveals-a-combative-serb-leader.html

—————. (1998a). In Kosovo Death Chronicles, Serb Tactic Revealed. *The New York Times*, September 27.
http://www.nytimes.com/1998/09/27/world/in-kosovo-death-chronicles-serb-tactic-revealed.html

—————. (1998b). Massacres by Serbian Forces in 3 Kosovo Villages. *The New York Times*, September 30.
http://www.nytimes.com/1998/09/30/world/massacres-by-serbian-forces-in-3-kosovo-villages.html

Pilger, J. (1999). Revealed: The Amazing Nato Plan, Tables at Rambouillet, to Occupy Yugoslavia. *New Statesman*, May 17.
http://www.newstatesman.com/199905170014

—————. (2002). *The New Rulers of the World*. London: Verso.

—————. (2008). *Don't Forget Yugoslavia. Anti-War.com*, August 16.
http://www.antiwar.com/pilger/?articleid=13303

Posen, B. R. (2000). The War for Kosovo. *International Security*, 24(4), 39-84.

PRNewsire. (1999). Serb President Believed Ground War Imminent. *PRNewswire*, July 18.
http://www.thefreelibrary.com/Newsweek:+Reconstruction+By+Newsweek+Reveals:+Milosevic%27s+Surrender+a...-a055180814

Ruppert, M. C. (n.d.) Kosovo Liberation Army and Albanian Sponsors Have Well Documented Roots in the Heroin Trade. *From the Wilderness Publications*.
http://www.fromthewilderness.com/free/regional/KLA1.html

Ryan, J. (2005). An Honorary Degree in Child Sacrifice? Madeleine Albright and US Foreign Policy. *CounterPunch*, December 10-11.

http://www.counterpunch.org/ryan12102005.html

Helsigngin Sanomat. (2008). Helena Ranta: Foreign Ministry Tried to Influence Kosovo Reports. *Helsingin Sanomat*, May 18.

http://www.hs.fi/english/article/Helena+Ranta+Foreign+Ministry+tried+to+influence+Kosovo+reports/1135240292632

Scahill, J. (2008). Lessons in the Bi-Partisanship of Empire: The Real Story Behind Kosovo's Independence. *CounterPunch*, February 23-24.

http://www.counterpunch.org/scahill02232008.html

Smale, A. (1999). The World; Two Different Tyrants, Very Much the Same. *The New York Times*, March 21.

http://www.nytimes.com/1999/03/21/weekinreview/the-world-two-different-tyrants-very-much-the-same.html

Stuart, P. (2002). Camp Bondsteel and America's Plans to Control Caspian Oil. *World Socialist Website*, April 29. http://www.wsws.org/articles/2002/apr2002/oil-a29.shtml

Sudetic, C. (1993). The World; How Serbia's Czar Holds Fast to Power. *The New York Times*, March 14.

http://www.nytimes.com/1993/03/14/weekinreview/the-world-how-serbia-s-czar-holds-fast-to-power.html

Szamuely, G. (1999). A world safe for kleptocracy. *New York Press*, July 7.

http://www.srpska-mreza.com/Kosovo/occupation/heroin-trade.html0

United Nations (UN). (1945). *Charter of the United Nations*.

http://www.un.org/en/documents/charter

United Nations (UN). (1950). *Principles of International Law Recognized in the Charter of the Nürnberg Tribunal and in the Judgment of the Tribunal.*

http://untreaty.un.org/ilc/texts/instruments/english/draft%20articles/7_1_1950.pdf

Vujadinovic, L. (2010). Depleted Uranium Radiation Resulting from NATO Bombings in Serbia: High Incidence of Cancer. *Global Research*, April 1. http://www.globalresearch.ca/index.php?context=va&aid=18432

Walker, T. & Laverty, A. (2000). CIA Aided Kosovo Guerrilla Army. *Sunday Times*, March 12.

http://www.balkanpeace.org/index.php?index=/content/balkans/kosovo_metohija/articles/kam01.incl

Woodward, S. L. (1995). *Balkan Tragedy: Chaos and Dissolution after the Cold War*. Washington, DC: The Brookings Institution Press.

CHAPTER SIX

The Responsibility to Protect Human Rights

Thomas Prince

The "Responsibility to Protect" (R2P) was adopted by the United Nations (UN) in 2005. This UN policy spells out the responsibilities of the individual state, and the larger international community of all UN member states, to protect and respect the human rights of all citizens around the world. Specifically this doctrine places responsibility on the governments of the world to deter the crimes of genocide, ethnic cleansing, war crimes, and crimes against humanity. To its supporters this is a long awaited victory for the protection of human rights, and limits those who would use national borders to pursue policies endangering these rights. Others cite human rights and other reasons to criticize and condemn the R2P mandate. In this chapter I will explore how protection for human rights is an argument used by both critics and supporters of R2P. The paper is divided into three different sections: introducing R2P, describing the position of its supporters; presenting the arguments of critics; and, elaborating on the international community and its responsibilities with the implementation of R2P.

Before addressing R2P, we need to pause for a moment to discuss "human rights." Human rights are a foundation upon which R2P's supporters and critics defend themselves. The UN formally adopted the Universal Declaration on Human Rights in 1948. Composed of 30 different articles which enshrine the rights to which all people of the world are equally entitled without discrimination or limitation, these rights have been formally defined and ratified by over 180 countries of the world since 1948. By signing on to the UN human rights declaration nations bind themselves to protect these rights for their own citizens, and for the citizens of the world (United Nations [UN], 1948). The UN declaration and all subsequent human rights conventions are non-binding, and the mechanisms in place to protect them have very little power within the UN. Human rights under the UN are overseen by a number of different bodies, including the Human Rights Council, the International Criminal Court (ICC) and other bodies and instruments of the UN, including special rapporteurs and advisors to the Secretary General.

R2P and its supporters

The Responsibility to Protect was adopted by the United Nations at the 2005 World Summit, being endorsed by over 150 nations. This document was the product of a commission started in 2000, the International Commission on Intervention and State Sovereignty (ICISS). The ICISS' publication in 2001, *The Responsibility to Protect*, offered new avenues to discuss the politically charged issues of sovereignty and humanitarian intervention. The recommendations included that nations had a responsibility to protect their own citizens, and that the international community shares responsibility to support nations that are at risk for the outbreak of mass atrocities. The report outlined a series of interventionist steps for the UN to pursue, culminating in military intervention as a last resort. The ICISS report was written based upon Secretary General Kofi Annan's attempts to balance national sovereignty with individual sovereignty as outlined by the UN human rights instruments (Evans, 2008, p. 37). R2P's focus is narrowed to four international crimes which are genocide, ethnic cleansing, war crimes and crimes against humanity. A further caveat has been placed that in order for R2P doctrine to apply the crimes must occur on a large scale, with a high number of fatalities.

For supporters, R2P is a victory for the protection of human rights. While earlier legal documents and international charters had been unable to offer binding and effective protection to human rights, this was a way to ensure their protection. It was a call to arms for the international community to embrace its responsibilities, to not sit passive as atrocities such as the slaughter in Rwanda occur. The ICISS used human rights protections as one of its four core foundations upon which the document was drafted and conceived (ICISS, 2001, p. xi). R2P defenders are quick to note that many different regional organizations, most prominently the African Union, have written similar responsibilities into their own charters. This reflects the broad international consensus on the obligation to protect human rights that exists within the international community (Luck, 2008, p. 2).

Many civil society groups and non-governmental organizations (NGOs) have also given their support to R2P, including human rights organizations such as Human Rights Watch, Oxfam, and other organizations from around the globe. Since the early hearings of the ICISS, and the later creation of the International Coalition for the Responsibility to Protect (ICRtoP) there has been a conscious effort to include the many different regions of the world, and to work collaboratively with non state actors, especially NGOs and civil society groups. By working collaboratively with experts in human rights, international development, and actors on the ground in conflict regions, R2P gains legitimacy and respect from those organizations who share a similar commitment and ensure that human rights protection remain central to the norm.

R2P builds upon existing powers for intervention entrusted to the UN Security Council, by articles VI, VII and VIII that deal with the Security Council's responsibilities to prevent war and protect human rights. As such the ICISS report and the adopted paragraphs 138 and 139 of the 2005 UN Summit highlight that it is the Security Council that is the most legitimate international body to reconcile the demands of R2P, and decide which situations are appropriate for intervention (UN, 2005, p. 30).

R2P Critics

The critics of R2P can at times find themselves in difficult positions. If R2P is designed and implemented to protect human rights, then how can someone protest R2P, especially on grounds of human rights protection? Surely no rational person in the world can condone genocide or other terrible crimes, so how could one argue that prevention and intervention are not appropriate to prevent the deaths of thousands of people? This is the position which confronts the critics of R2P. For the critics of R2P, human rights are framed differently than by R2P's supporters. Rather than utilizing an appeal to morality or obligation, the critics challenge how the human rights discourse can undermine international law, is selectively used, and thus they challenge the positions of some of its strongest advocates.

R2P can be a tool which could cause the UN to send military forces to intervene in the affairs of sovereign nations, and in the lives of sovereign individuals. This completely challenges some of the fundamental roles and obligations of the UN, including respecting territorial integrity and the prevention and ending of war. While R2P may offer war only as a last resort, this is a major question which I feel faces the UN. The UN was created as a vehicle to prevent war, and respect the autonomy of sovereign nations. Some critics argue that human rights are now being used to trump international law, and that despite the assurances of its critics R2P brings us closer to UN sanctioned violations of territorial integrity. One argument of how human rights are being used to undermine the UN charter is offered by Herman and Peterson who remind us of the initial responsibilities of UN members, and its founding principles:

> "Chapter I of the UN Charter states: 'To maintain international peace and security,' all member states shall respect the 'principle of the sovereign equality' of their fellow

members, 'settle their international disputes by peaceful means,' and 'refrain in their international relations from the threat or use of force against the territorial integrity or political independence of any state'." (Herman & Peterson, 2009).

Those who criticize R2P fear that "human rights" has become a loaded term to which there are few defences, and upon whose back all actions can be justified.

Another challenge to using human rights is the problem of selectivity. There are 30 human rights outlined in the UN Universal Declaration, but not all of them are equally protected. Rights such as those to life and political freedoms are enshrined by many different instruments, declarations and covenants. Some of these rights have been advanced by state and non state actors like, including conventions on genocide, torture, and landmines to name a few. But there are many rights that are not always vigorously defended. Bricmont reports that in 1981 the U.S. was the only nation to vote against a UN statement declaring that rights to education, work, healthcare, proper nourishment, and national development were not human rights (2004, p. 100). While protecting people from genocide and other terrible crimes are no doubt human rights, they are not the only ones. Why should some rights take precedence? For this reason the human rights card is difficult to wield for supporters of R2P when many smaller steps can be taken to protect and enshrine a large number of other human rights, for example access to affordable medication to prevent diseases from treatable illness. Francis Deng's work on sovereignty which helped guide the redefining of sovereignty, also includes the importance of protecting all human rights in his influential work. As Rothchild, Deng, Zartman, Kimaro, and Lyons, argue: "[in] the UN Vienna World Conference on Human Rights in 1993 [a] consensus emerged that 'All human rights are universal, indivisible and independent and interrelated. The international community must treat human rights globally in a fair and equal manner, on the same footing, and with the same emphasis'" (1996, p. 19). A further challenge to the use of the human rights argument in support of R2P is Article 30 of the UN Declaration which specifically states: "Nothing in this Declaration may be interpreted as implying for any State, group or person any right to engage in any activity or to perform any act aimed at the destruction of any of the rights and freedoms set forth herein." When viewed from this perspective it becomes more difficult to intervene in foreign countries on the grounds of protecting human rights. If all rights are held equal then death and war can never be solutions to threats against human rights.

There are some voices on the left who criticize human rights organizations for not taking impartial positions in denouncing human rights abuses. Jean Bricmont criticizes Human Rights Watch and Amnesty International for campaigning to protect the rights of non combatants in Iraq, while not criticizing the U.S. government for an illegal war (Bricmont, 2004, p. 146). I think that such a criticism applies to R2P as well. By endorsing R2P human rights organizations are supporting the use of force, as approved by the Security Council, in the name of protecting the rights of all people. But human rights organizations have an obligation to take an impartial position, and to defend human rights without regard to power dynamics. The use of force by the UN, as directed by the Security Council, should not be supported or criticized more than other combatants by impartial human rights observers. Are human rights advocates prepared to sacrifice their position of impartiality, and support military intervention to protect select human rights for some, even at the expense of the human rights of others? This becomes a very slippery slope very quickly in my opinion. While human rights can be a political topic, and advanced or protected at times with political intentions, it can also be a recognition of the dignity and equality that exist between all people. Intervention and fighting on such a behalf does not advance or enshrine these values, it instead moves us further away from them.

R2P Challenges and Progress: Human Rights and International Actors

While supporters of R2P counter criticisms of a return to colonialism, one of the groundings is the central role of the UN Security Council to limit any abuse of power by particular nations. They present R2P as an apolitical tool which the world community uses only to protect innocent lives. But first amongst criticisms by smaller nations is the format of the Security Council, and there have long been calls for reform. Power is divided unequally at the Security Council, with the permanent five members (P5) having veto powers. The U.S. is one the P5 members, and many would argue a very influential nation in the UN, and has been widely criticized for some of its past interventions. I feel it is important to consider the actions of these nations to which are entrusted the additional powers and responsibilities of R2P, and offer a brief glimpse at a fragment of the U.S.'s recent history of intervention.

During the Cold War the U.S. was directly involved in many Latin American conflicts, often backing brutal dictators, or assisting in the overthrow of governments which were deemed unfriendly to American interests. An ever outspoken critic of U.S. foreign policy, Noam Chomsky provides details of some U.S. interventions including its intervention in Nicaragua for which the U.S. was found guilty by the International Court of Justice (ICJ) in 1986 of aggression and war crimes; in 1996 the entire UN General Assembly with the exception of three nations voted against the U.S. embargo on Cuba, which the Inter-American Commission on Human Rights had condemned as violating international law and human rights protection in 1995 (Chomsky, 1999, pp. 73-74). The more recent invasion and occupation of Iraq was not supported by the UN, and many would argue is an illegal war. The U.S. has long supported countries accused of human rights abuses, including Colombia, Israel, and others, that are major recipient of U.S. foreign and military aid. Finally the U.S. has itself been widely criticized for failing to respect international conventions and violating the human rights of detainees in the "war on terror."

The U.S. has become dependent on the use of its military to resolve conflicts. By continually increasing funding to the military while cutting funding to the U.S. Agency for International Development (USAID) and the State Department, which could better assist with negotiation, conflict resolution, reconciliation and other non-military measures to prevent genocide and other crimes, the U.S. has severely limited its capacity to resolve conflicts through non-military means (Kilcullen, 2009, p. 26). If the U.S. does not make serious contributions to show its ability to fulfill its obligations through peaceful mechanisms, and through existing international instruments and agreements, how can outcomes which do not serve U.S. interests or do not require the use of U.S. military influence be expected? If the Security Council is the legitimate actor to entrust effective enforcement of R2P, then what are the restrictions placed upon the P5 to ensure that R2P will never be misused? Interestingly while R2P boasts of support amongst a majority of UN member countries, an equally large number would like to see the Security Council structure revised, and power shared more equally among more nations (Lund, 2009).

While R2P supporters have been outspoken about their work to include the input of non-state actors, I feel it is important for multilateral agencies to also collaborate. The International Monetary Fund (IMF), World Bank, and World Trade Organization (WTO) all wield significant power and influence in the economies of the world, and these have a direct impact on human rights protections. In many respects the UN defers economic decision-making to these bodies, however many past policies have been used to impose limits on government spending for social services, including education, health care, sanitation. These institutions have to abandon policies that prevent the government from intervening in its own economy to protect the well being of its people if R2P is offering international intervention as a solution for human rights protection.

While the UN has yet to address these concerns, it is important that R2P mechanisms and discussions recognize the influence of international forces that can ignite or create conditions for genocide and not to limit the debate to state failure or ethnic conflict as consequences of internal forces only. There are many scholars who have written of these concerns including Yash Tandon who criticized the IMF, WTO and World Bank as agents whose policies may directly or indirectly support and accelerate ethnic killings, and other internal conflicts, and makes specific reference to the case of Rwanda (Tandon, 2004, p. 10). Hopefully these international organizations will work collaboratively in R2P design and implementation to ensure international human rights are protected.

Concluding Remarks

Current challenges facing R2P include designing effective guidelines for when to intervene. Conflicts continue to rage around the globe and innocent victims die in Sir Lanka, the Israel-Palestine region, or in the war torn provinces of Iraq and Afghanistan. As yet the UN has not intervened in any of these conflicts, though they do support the African Union's troops in Darfur, and the UN has sent troops to the Democratic Republic of Congo, and other regions. As yet there have been no R2P interventions, only conversation. If R2P is to work to the best of its potential it should prevent the tragedies from ever reaching such points that military intervention becomes necessary. The ICISS report and supporters of R2P always stress prevention in early stages as desired. But what about the conflict regions where R2P is not applicable? Who will decide which conflicts merit R2P interventions, and which do not? While supporters say that ambiguity is not a reason to do nothing, it should neither be a reason to race in, or ignore the creation of protocols and guidelines. Whatever guidelines and protocols are devised they need to be applied equally, so that allies of the U.S. and other powerful states are subject to the same requirements and obligations as those nations who pursue more independent politics.

Whether we choose to embrace R2P as a good international norm, or challenge the assumptions it is built on and the abuses of power that opens a Pandora's box, the reality is that it has been ratified by the General Assembly, and negotiations and further work to design protocols and criteria will continue. There are many challenges which confront the protection of human rights, and the success or failure of R2P may depend in part on how some of these factors influence, or are influenced by, this emerging norm. Some of the questions and positions raised in this chapter are similarly being debated in the UN General Assembly. Fundamentally, R2P seems here to stay as the 2009 outcome was that R2P was moving forward and the debate as to the legitimacy and legality was resolved (Global Center for the Responsibility to Protect [GCRP], 2009, pp. 4-5). In the latter document the UN has stated its position on why only four rights are to be protected, on why decisions will be made on an ad hoc basis, and also addresses the balance of power between the Security Council, General Assembly and other bodies. This chapter was not written to challenge the morality or legality of R2P. One of the major intentions of this chapter was to instead consider the use of human rights discourse as justification for R2P supporters and critics. Hopefully the voices of the critics will help the supporters ensure that the shared position of human rights creates a responsible development of R2P. The Responsibility to Protect is a new and fast emerging international norm. Hopefully in time it will become the tool which defends human rights, and never becomes the one which violates, undermines or perverts them.

References

Bricmont, J. (2006). *Humanitarian Imperialism: Using Human Rights to Sell War.* New York: Monthly Review Press

Chomsky, N. (1999). *Profit over People.* New York: Seven Stories Press

Evans, G. (2008). *Responsibility to Protect: Ending Mass Atrocity Crimes Once and for All.* Washington, DC: The Brookings Institution Press.

Global Centre for the Responsibility to Protect (GCRP). (2009). Implementing the Responsibility to Protect: The 2009 General Assembly Debate: An Assessment. New York: Global Centre for the Responsibility to Protect, Ralph Bunche Institute for International Studies, The CUNY Graduate Center.
http://globalr2p.org/media/pdf/GCR2P_General_Assembly_Debate_Assessment.pdf

Herman, E. S., & Peterson, D. (2009). The Responsibility to Protect, the International Criminal Court, and Foreign Policy in Focus: Subverting the UN Charter in the Name of Human Rights. *Monthly Review*, August 24. http://mrzine.monthlyreview.org/2009/hp240809.html

International Commission on Intervention and State Sovereignty (ICISS). (2001). *The Responsibility to Protect: Report of the International Commission on Intervention and State Sovereignty.* Ottawa: International Development Research Centre. http://www.iciss.ca/pdf/Commission-Report.pdf

Kilcullen, D. (2009). *The Accidental Guerrilla: Fighting Small Wars in the Midst of a Big One.* New York: Oxford University Press.

Luck, E. C. (2008). The United Nations and the Responsibility to Protect: Policy Analysis Brief. The Stanley Foundation.
http://www.stanleyfoundation.org/publications/pab/LuckPAB808.pdf

Lund, J. S. (2009). Reforming the Working Methods of the Security Council. *Center for UN Reform Education*, November 18. http://www.centerforunreform.org/node/412/

Rothchild, D.; Deng, F. M.; Zartman, I. W.; Kimaro, S., & Lyons, T. (1996). *Sovereignty as Responsibility: Conflict Management in Africa.* Washington, DC: The Brookings Institution Press.

Tandon, Y. (2004). Economic Policy and Conflict in Africa. *Journal of Peacebuilding and Development*, 2(1), 6-20.

United Nations (UN). (1948). The Universal Declaration of Human Rights.
http://www.un.org/en/documents/udhr/

————. (2005). Resolution Adopted by the General Assembly. Paragraphs 139, 139, A/RES/60/1.
http://unpan1.un.org/intradoc/groups/public/documents/un/unpan021752.pdf

CHAPTER SEVEN

Policing the World: Modern Military Humanism and the Responsibility to Protect

Justin De Genova

There has been much debate about what intentions Western democratic superpowers, particularly the U.S., have when they intervene to provide humanitarian assistance. While often these efforts appear to solely assist people in need, in an alarming number of cases humanitarian intervention furthers Western hegemonic power in vulnerable Third World regions. Noam Chomsky (1999b) popularized the phrase "new military humanism," which describes the exploitation of humanitarian missions in order to further Western military domination abroad. This chapter looks at the U.S. as a primary example of how a Western nation can disregard the harm it causes within the international community when it intervenes in another sovereign state's affairs, using the excuse of humanitarian issues to further its worldwide influence. The main points covered herein draw from the warfare waged during the first Bush administration (that of the 41st president, George H.W. Bush, 1989-1993, sometimes referred to as "Bush 41"), the intervention in Kosovo during the Clinton Administration, and the "war on terror" waged in Iraq during the second Bush administration (the 43rd president, George W. Bush, or "Bush 43").

The recently adopted concept known as the Responsibility to Protect (R2P) is a policy stating that all nations have a duty to protect their own people and those of other nations if possible, to uphold basic human rights. This chapter will thus also focus on the issues of international foreign policy related to R2P, and the request for more stringent restrictions by international critics. Before R2P, international foreign policy only allowed for a limited international inquiry before violent interventions by Western democracies were waged on Third World states for purposes deemed to be strictly humanitarian in nature.

Finding a New Enemy

The end of the Cold War came with the dissolution of the Soviet Union in 1991, and this posed problems for the U.S. government, particularly because it had to figure out how to continue to exert U.S. power, opting for a continued strong military presence throughout the world. The first Bush administration proposed a new National Security Strategy that began to focus on both real and imagined threats that could arise from Third-World conflicts in vulnerable regions throughout the world (Chomsky, 2008). Concerns such as rampant terrorism, drug trafficking, and inhumane dictators took centre stage and were named as issues that were complicating U.S. diplomacy. George H. W. Bush's administration decided that new approaches would be required in order to suppress various illegal and inhumane acts occurring abroad, as defined by Western law and society. The concept that the National Security Strategy outlined was that the U.S. could sustain a large military presence either within or surrounding hostile environments such as the Middle East and South America (Chomsky, 2008). The military presence in the developing world inspired the new term "military humanism," which describes the use of violence or force for purely humanitarian purposes (Chomsky, 1999b). The rise of military humanism sent a clear message to the world that the U.S. plans to police the planet, and that they have the power to do so.

While U.S. intervention might seem beneficial to developing states at first, in many cases the reality is different from the promise. The protection of Western interests usually comes before those of the country in need. The invasion of Kuwait by Iraq, and the subsequent humanitarian intervention with U.N. authorization, is a prime example of the new military humanism that was practiced during the first Bush administration. The changes and military presence in the area, which was allegedly beneficial to the people who inhabited the region, quickly became advantageous to the U.S. and the Western world in general (Peters & Deshong, 1995).

The post-Cold War conflict in Kuwait during August 1990 exercised this new kind of military humanism by creating international allies and turning the Western-influenced coalition against a Middle Eastern power (Peters & Deshong, 1995). The intimidating military intervention that the U.S. spearheaded against the Iraqi military in Kuwait was one of the first bricks laid in creating a path toward an increased U.S. military presence in the Middle East. These bombings were described by Bush I as a "wholly defensive" mission, aimed specifically at restoring the Kuwaiti government to power and ousting the Iraqi military.

The first Bush administration instantly demonized Saddam Hussein as a vicious dictator, who would attempt to capture Saudi Arabia, and attempt to gain control of the world's largest reserves of oil (Bush, 1990, and Chomsky, 2008). Bush I stated in his 11 September 1990 address to a joint session of the U.S. Congress: "Saddam Hussein is literally trying to wipe a country off the face of the Earth. We do not exaggerate" (Bush, 1990, ¶ 9). Americans renamed Hussein "The Butcher of Baghdad," compared him to Adolf Hitler, and cartoons depicted him as a voracious spider (James, 2003, ¶ 34). These personifications of Hussein helped to justify the invasion of Iraq. It quickly became obvious that the nation of Kuwait and the basic rights of its people were not the first priority of the U.S. military when it came to protecting that particular region. The primary goal of the mission was to protect the interests of the developed world that has become ever more reliant on oil, and the safe passage of that oil through the Persian Gulf. In his 1990 address, Bush I referenced oil 14 times. As he stated, "Vital economic interests are at risk as well. Iraq itself controls some 10 percent of the world's proven oil reserves" (Bush, 1990, ¶ 9). The idea of Hussein controlling one of the most demanded resources on the planet was perceived as a huge threat to the developed world, so it was quickly agreed upon that action against this regime must be taken and that "international interests' (i.e. Western interests) should be protected. This became a blueprint of sorts for future missions. While the threat of communism was used in the past as an excuse to invade, now humanitarian concerns are the justification for military force abroad.

When planning humanitarian missions using the concept of new military humanism, increased harm toward civilians is virtually inevitable. The way that the first Bush administration dealt with the ousting of Iraq in Kuwait caused unnecessary civilian casualties due to the low-risk (to U.S. forces), high casualty warfare such as air raids. These military strategies saved American dollars and soldiers, but at the cost of lives on the ground. During the U.S. bombings aimed at the Iraqi military prior to the ground invasion of Kuwait, it was reported that an estimated 3,500 Iraqi civilians were killed as a result of these bombings, including one incident where stealth planes bombed a civilian bunker, killing between 200 and 400 innocent Iraqis (Conetta, 2003). Although these casualties were often classed as "collateral," this type of warfare illustrates how inhumane the so called humanitarian efforts end up being, while the U.S. continues to find places to raise their Star-Spangled Banner in the Middle East.

Trying To Make Right With Another Wrong

Continuing into the next administration under President Clinton, warfare deemed humanitarian continued to be as unjust in providing humanitarian relief as in the first Bush era—even more unjust when considering that no action was taken in places such as Rwanda in 1994, that might have seemed more suitable for intervention on humanitarian grounds (Chomsky, 1999b), but which received no such attention from the U.S. at all. A huge problem with the system of military humanist intervention at this time is the fact that the military superpowers are entitled to pick and choose who they wish to help. It is possible for Western nations to evaluate the benefits of providing aid based on, geographical military placement, investment of capital, and lack of desirable resources to protect, instead of openly helping anyone who requests or needs it.

The Clinton Administration, like its predecessors, continued to increase military presence throughout the world in what was avowedly an effort to protect human rights and equality for the greater good of all humankind (Chomsky, 1999b). Again, the problem with this picture is that the U.S. usually causes more harm than good by intervening in forceful humanitarian efforts rather than first trying to work to find peaceful solutions. Noam Chomsky looks for the answer to the question of "How should we react when bad things happen in unimportant places?" He deduces that the U.S. will "react by helping to escalate the atrocities," or in some cases by not reacting at all, such as the failure to respond to the violent genocide in Rwanda in 1994 that saw hundreds of thousands of Tutsis killed by the dominant Hutu government (see also Chomsky, 1999a). This ethnic cleansing continued for weeks before NATO intervention was even considered (Dallaire, 1999).

While the Clinton administration failed to provide aid for Rwanda during the genocide, it was quick to jump at the opportunity to intervene in the conflict in Kosovo between Albanian rebel guerillas and the Federal Republic of Yugoslavia in 1999. Albanian nationalists desperately needed assistance, but all that the U.S. military did was air bomb the land, displacing innocent Serbian civilians. The air strikes intended to hit both military and civilian infrastructure in use by the regime, but international opinion began to turn sour as NATO inadvertently killed thousands of refugees during this process, some of them Albanian. Internationally influential targets such as the Chinese Embassy in Belgrade were also bombed under the pretense of an accident, but it was later found to be deliberate due to the testimony from at least three NATO officers who explained that transmissions were intercepted from within the Chinese Embassy, suggesting that it had leaked information to the Yugoslav government, based in part on Chinese monitoring of cruise missile attacks (Sweeney, Holsoe, Vulliamy, 1999, ¶ 2, 3). The irresponsible intervention of NATO and their bombing campaign against the Federal Republic of Yugoslavia not only escalated the atrocities, but also furthered the power of the wealthy NATO nations, and allowed them to exert control further afield worldwide (Chomsky, 1999). These displays of power and authority did nothing to help the estimated one million displaced people, but rather placed them in immediate danger. The situation quickly escalated to the accelerated exile of the Albanian refugees and even mass murder of Serbian civilians as a result of the increased bombings. While innocent civilians were placed in compromising situations, NATO, headed by the U.S., continued to propagate its ideals as to what they believed was right for these people, even if it meant taking action that resulted in more negative consequences for locals, in order to gain prestige and respect in the Balkan area of Southeastern Europe.

These lessons from modern warfare as seen in the NATO bombings in Kosovo and Serbia present military humanism as a mere mechanism that fulfills a sense of self-perceived righteousness that the Clinton Administration enacted (Chomsky, 1999b). This was followed by the narrative that the U.S. helped solve the crisis in Kosovo by means of humanitarian intervention, when in actuality they were creating more of a problem for both international law as well as the refugees as the bombings continued to increase in intensity (Chomsky, 1999). Whether one perceives these actions as irresponsible intervention rather than NATO having not participated at all, the U.S. military once again has used the international spotlight to display its ultimate power with ever-quickening response, making sure that "evildoers" know that Uncle Sam and his strong arm are watching over the world with god-like powers to ensure that no individuals or states can come between Western power and its advance toward what it believes to be fundamental goals. When Clinton exited office and Bush II replaced him as the new President in 2001, the blowback of the increased hegemonic power and presence of the U.S. military in the Middle East was finally felt at home. It arrived via four commercial jetliners headed for New York City, Washington and Arlington, Virginia.

What Lies Are Ahead

As powerful as the U.S. is, there is no better example than the terrorist attacks in September of 2001 to display just how vulnerable any country can be to the disastrous effects of increased hegemonic influence worldwide. This desperate act of terrorism on U.S. soil sparked an international manhunt aimed at dismantling all terrorist groups that posed a major threat to the U.S. This U.S. led "War on Terror" declared on 07 October 2001 claimed to have the "support by the collective will of the world" (Bush, 2001).

This proclaimed war on terror did not offer any geographic, demographic, or systematic guidelines, but it did foreground many problematic themes. This war offered no clear definitions as to who is a terrorist, or what is or is not an act of terrorism. As easy as it was for the second Bush administration to become caught up in a public demand for a military campaign in reaction to these atrocities, it capitalized on public opinion in seeking more political and military control in the Middle East (Goodman, 2006). Although these missions in Iraq and Afghanistan are deemed to be part of a war, the main point of the war on terror is made to sound like a humanitarian effort that will provide relief to the Middle East, a region claimed to harbor the most terrorists currently active.

One of the most controversial uses of the war on terror theme was in serving as a pretext for the 2003 invasion and occupation of Iraq, a country that had not engaged in any international aggression since the 1980s, when Hussein worked alongside the U.S. to deter Soviet expansion in the Middle East. The U.S. invaded Iraq on the claim that Iraq had Weapons of Mass Destruction (WMD), and it was these devices that the U.S. focused on, rather than capturing terrorist cells that were supposedly harbored within the country. One cannot help but wonder if the U.S. government was determined to create a major subordinate authority in the Middle East at any cost. Setting up a "democratic government" in Iraq seems to be the next step in doing so after the massive increase in U.S. military presence within Afghanistan, Pakistan, and Kuwait over the last decade.

This new type of military humanism was a partially effective way of gaining both American public support and the collaboration of some governments, as a means of justifying entering a war with Iraq. Judging by the U.S.' concentration on the development of a stable democratic Iraq, this so called "war on terror" seems to be a puppet show, while an operation to militarize the Middle East ensues.

Maintaining International Law and Order

During the 2005 United Nations World Summit, the Heads of State and their respective governments collectively decided that, "each individual State has the responsibility to protect its populations from genocide, war crimes, ethnic cleansing, and crimes against humanity" (United Nations General Assembly [UN], 2005b, p. 31). If a state is considered to be "manifestly failing" to protect its population from these violations, the international community will be "prepared to take collective action in a timely and decisive manner" (United Nations General Assembly [UN], 2009, p. 1, 4, 22). This concept, known as the Responsibility to Protect (R2P), is a UN strategy aimed at providing basic human rights and equality for all humankind, ultimately discouraging the misuse or mistreatment of people around the world. Whether it is one's own government, or a government that uses humanitarian intervention as a means of imposing violence or authority on another state, R2P is a new approach that requires UN Security Council approval in order to intervene legally by force, and states can willingly choose to follow a set of guidelines mandated by the UN Charter of rights (UN, 2009).

The R2P doctrine involves a three-pillar strategy that is intended to prevent atrocities such as war crimes or crimes against humanity from happening, an issue that has been long suspended from international policy until the twenty-first century. Pillar One set outs the responsibilities that each State has to protect their own population from mass atrocities, while Pillar Two outlines the international assistance in case a state cannot protect its population by itself. Finally, Pillar Three ensures that response to these crimes, whether by internal or external intervention, shall be timely and decisive as outlined by the UN Security Council (UN, 2005a). These pillars are adopted in order to detract a state from falsely intervening for its particular gain, however there is still debate regarding the military intervention of states that cannot or will not abide by R2P.

There is controversy between the states that see humanitarian intervention as an infringement of their sovereignty, and other states that argue that R2P can be implemented as a last resort in preventing mass atrocities. A main focus of R2P that will hopefully help discourage the increased practice of new military humanism by hegemonic superpowers is the "responsibility to prevent" clause, which helps to prevent crimes before they actually exist. Another prevention to violent intervention is the process of intervening itself, which graduates through stages from diplomacy to coercive action, and finally as a last resort, forceful intervention (Bellamy, 2009). R2P also includes what is called a threshold of intervention (International Commission on Intervention and State Sovereignty [ICISS], 2001), in which forceful intrusion can only be fulfilled if there is just cause, right intention, final resort, legitimate authority, proportional means, and reasonable prospect (UN, 2005a). All these guidelines are implemented to try to discourage any exploitation that one country may have over another via forceful occupation.

Conclusion

Military humanism has considerably transformed the landscape of humanitarian relief efforts into one that more manifestly creates an opportunity for wealthy Western countries to exert their power by intervening in conflicts and broadening their influence worldwide. The U.S. has served as a formidable example in exercising this notion of new military humanism, as they have projected their presence into some of the most vulnerable regions on the planet. Throughout the course of two decades, and three different presidential administrations, the U.S. has continued efforts to put itself in the middle of conflicts that they can benefit from, whether economic or political. The U.S. experience in various unstable environments such as Kuwait, Kosovo, and the present wars in Iraq and Afghanistan prove that they are bent on becoming the supreme global authority during the twenty-first century. In the pursuit of power and profit, the U.S. has used public relations in its foreign policy to create an image of a country that is all about doing right, yet continues to do wrong. Critics of R2P hope to curb these interventions premised on a hollow humanitarianism, and are thinking of new policies that will hold countries more accountable for the negative repercussions of their actions on peripheral states, thus providing a more level playing ground for countries of the periphery to stand up for themselves against wrongful interventions in their lands.

References

Bellamy, A. J. (2009). *Responsibility to Protect: The International Commission on Intervention and State Sovereignty.* Cambridge, MA: Polity.

Bush, G. H. W. (1990). Address Before a Joint Session of Congress (September 11, 1990). University of Virginia, Miller Center of Public Affairs.
http://millercenter.org/scripps/archive/speeches/detail/3425

Bush, G. W. (2001) Presidential Address to the Nation. Washington, DC: The White House.
http://georgewbush-whitehouse.archives.gov/news/releases/2001/10/print/20011007-8.html

Chomsky, N. (1999a). Kosovo Peace Accord. *Z Magazine*, July.
http://www.chomsky.info/articles/199907--.htm

Chomsky, N. (1999b). *The New Military Humanism: Lessons from Kosovo.* Monroe, ME: Common Courage Press

Chomsky, N. (2008). Humanitarian Imperialism: The New Doctrine of Imperial Right. *Monthly Review*, September. http://www.chomsky.info/articles/200809--.htm

Conetta, C. (2003). The Wages of War: Iraqi Combatant and Noncombatant Fatalities in the 2003 Conflict: Appendix 2, Iraqi Combatant and Noncombatant Fatalities in the 1991 Gulf War. Project on Defense Alternatives Research Monograph No. 8, October 20.
http://www.comw.org/pda/0310rm8ap2.html

Dallaire, R. (2004). *Shake Hands with the Devil: The Failure of Humanity in Rwanda.* Toronto: Vintage Canada.

Goodman, R. (2006). Humanitarian Intervention and Pretexts for War. *The American Journal of International Law*, 100(1), pp. 107-141.

International Commission on Intervention and State Sovereignty (ICISS). (2001). The Responsibility to Protect: Report of the International Commission on Intervention and State Sovereignty. Ottawa: Human Security and Human Rights Bureau, Foreign Affairs Canada.
http://www.iciss.ca/report2-en.asp

James, M. S. (2003). Demonizing the Enemy: A Hallmark of War. *ABC News*, January 29.
http://abcnews.go.com/International/story?id=79071

Peters, J. E., & Deshong, H. (1995). *Out of Area or Out of Reach?: European Military Support For Operations in Southwest Asia.* Santa Monica, CA: RAND

Sweeney, J., Holsoe, J., & Vulliamy, E. (1999). Nato Bombed Chinese Deliberately: Nato hit Embassy on Purpose. *The Observer*, October 17.
http://www.guardian.co.uk/world/1999/oct/17/balkans

United Nations General Assembly (UN). (2005a). In Larger Freedom: Towards Development, Security and Human Rights for All: Report of the Secretary-General. (March 21, A/59/2005). New York: United Nations General Assembly.

http://www.responsibilitytoprotect.org/index.php/publications?module=uploads&func=d
ownload&fileId=103

————. (2005b). Sixtieth Session: World Summit Outcome (September 15, A/60/L.1). New
York: United Nations General Assembly.

http://www.who.int/hiv/universalaccess2010/worldsummit.pdf

————. (2009). Implementing the Responsibility to Protect: Report of Secretary General
(January 12, A/63/677). New York: United Nations General Assembly.

http://www2.ohchr.org/english/bodies/chr/special/docs/17thsession/SG_reportA_63_67
7_en.pdf

CHAPTER EIGHT

Torture and the Global War on Terror

Nageen Siddiqui

"The power you gave them to torture me, rape me...search me naked to present me in court, I am dead...I was dead the first time I was raped ... I do not consider you a Judge, a Court!...this country leave me alone or send me back to my country Pakistan."—Dr. Aafia Siddiqui during court hearing (WitnessToIt, 2010).

These were the words spoken by Dr. Aafia Siddiqui during her trial in the court. Her mother and sister described in an interview how Dr. Siddiqui underwent various forms of torture at the hands of U.S. agents.[1] It is not only Dr. Siddiqui who experienced torture, there are many more who experience it, and in different forms.

Historically, efforts were made through The Hague and Geneva conventions to limit cruelty suffered by detainees. However, 9/11 brought a drastic change in the world with the "War on Terror"—the label assigned by the Bush administration to its national security policy (Reese & Lewis, 2009, p. 778). The U.S. government sought the help of psychologists in designing interrogation techniques. The interrogation process can include various forms of torture. There are different forms of torture that will be discussed in this chapter. One is that suffered by Dr. Siddiqui, who in her court hearing revealed being raped; other suspects such as like Khalid Sheikh Mohammad and Abu Zubayda were water boarded; Moazam Begg was subjected to sleep deprivation; and, Maher Arar faced beatings when he went through forced extraordinary rendition ("extraordinary rendition is the practice of transporting suspected foreign terrorists or other individuals suspected for crimes, to third countries for interrogation and imprisonment" [Zalman, 2010, ¶ 10]). Moreover, there are many detention centres where suspects are interrogated and tortured against international law governing humanitarian treatment of detainees. The prominent detention centres have been in Guantánamo Bay, Cuba; Abu Ghraib, Iraq; and, Bagram Air Base, Afghanistan.

The 1949 Geneva Convention's three main goals were protecting civilians in wartime, protecting the victims of non-international armed conflicts, and to support the provision of aid to nationals of warring states by granting the International Committee of the Red Cross (ICRC) the right to offer its services (ICRC, 2009; Bugnion, 2000, p. 42). In 1984 the United Nations (UN) General Assembly adopted a *Convention against Torture and Other Cruel, Inhuman or Degrading Treatment or Punishment* which entered into force on 26 June 1987 and was ratified by 20 States (UN, 1984). This built on previous treaties, such as the United Nations' *International Covenant on Civil and Political Rights* (1966), and before that, what was known as *Common Article 3*, common to all four of the 1949 Geneva Conventions, which specifically prohibited torture (ICRC, 2009).

These conventions were created to guard against inhumane treatment, and to protect war victims, military personnel, civilians, and so forth. According to the Geneva Conventions, basic human rights must be guaranteed to all captives (Mayer, 2008, p. 120). In 2000 the UN reaffirmed that such actions that can be deemed cruel and inhumane constitute a criminal attempt to destroy a fellow human being physically and mentally, which can never be justified under any circumstances, by any ideology or overriding interest, including a state of war (Cole, 2005, ¶ 2).

As Ripley (2004, p. 44) explained, torture techniques such as, sleep deprivation, physical, and sexual abuse, are all illegal under international law: "The *Convention against Torture and Other Cruel, Inhuman or Degrading Treatment or Punishment* is perhaps the most relevant legal baseline, and it was interpreted by the first Bush Administration to mean that detainees should be protected from cruel and unusual punishment". Moreover, the 1949 Geneva Conventions clearly stated that, "Prisoners of war who refuse to answer may not be threatened, insulted, or exposed to any unpleasant or disadvantageous treatment of any kind [and] be paid a daily wage" (Ripley, 2004, pp. 44-45).

Changes after 9/11

However, things changed after 9/11, Bush administration declared a worldwide "war on terror". President Bush in his speech said that, "justice will be done" (Bush, 2001). What followed opened up the very question of the meanings of justice. John Yoo, an official in the Department of Justice, Office of Legal Counsel, under G. W. Bush, revealed that CIA personnel told him "we're going to have some real difficulties getting actionable intelligence from detainees" if the Agency's interrogators "were required to respect the limits for treatment demanded by the Geneva Conventions" (Mayer, 2008, p.120). In Yoo's version of events, "the impetus to break out of Geneva's strictures thus came from the

CIA. Many at the agency however saw this differently suggesting it was Cheney and his lawyer, Addington, who pushed the agency to take the path toward torture" (Mayer, 2008, p.120).

Under international humanitarian law, none of the "harsh interrogation" techniques used after 9/11 fell inside the limits set in the Geneva Conventions. As indicated in Torturing Democracy (Jones, 2008): "on February 7th 2002…President Bush declared that the United States would not be constrained by Geneva's prohibitions against cruel and inhumane treatment. None of the prisoners in U.S. custody would be protected by the laws of war." This was the first time, however, that the rules of the Geneva Conventions would not be respected by the U.S. (Bugnion, 2000, p. 43). Ironically, as Mayer (2008, p. 238) mentions, on 26 June 2003, on the UN International Day in Support of Victims of Torture, George W. Bush addressed called on "all governments to join with the United States and the community of law-abiding nations in prohibiting, investigating, and prosecuting all acts of torture and in undertaking to prevent other cruel and unusual punishment." Bush further said that the "suffering of torture victims must end, and the United States calls on all governments to assume this great mission" (Mayer, 2008, p. 238). Clearly, actions differed from words spoken in public. According to Ripley (2004, pp. 44-45), "since 9/11 the U.S. has ignored the conventions when convenient".

The Role of Psychologists

Katherine Eban (2007, ¶ 13) reported that, "psychologists, working in secrecy, had actually *designed* the tactics and trained interrogators in them while on contract to the CIA". Furthermore, according to Benjamin (2007, ¶ 1), they "helped the CIA exploit a secret military program to develop brutal interrogation tactics". According to Amrit Singh, the staff attorney of the American Civil Liberties Union, "psychologists and medical personnel played a key role in sustaining prisoner abuse—a clear violation of their ethical and legal obligations" (quoted in Burghardt, 2008, ¶ 2).

Psychologists were hired to design a program called SERE (Survival, Evasion, Resistance and Escape), which was to "reverse engineer" techniques "originally designed to train U.S. soldiers to resist torture if captured, by exposing them to brutal treatment" (Benjamin, 2007, ¶ 1). Benjamin finds that there are "striking similarities between descriptions of SERE training and the interrogation techniques employed by the military and CIA since 9/11"—for example, "soldiers undergoing SERE training are subject to forced nudity, stress positions, lengthy isolation, sleep deprivation, sexual humiliation, exhaustion from exercise, and the use of water to create a sensation of suffocation" (Benjamin, 2007, ¶ 10) Two psychologists, James Mitchell and Bruce Jessen, were employed in the SERE program, hired by the CIA after 9/11, whose work "likely violated the Geneva Conventions on the treatment of prisoners" (Benjamin, 2007, ¶ 2). Jessen specialised in the effects of isolation (Benjamin, 2007, ¶ 12). According to Jane Mayer, Mitchell, "was neither an expert in fighting Islamic terrorism nor an interrogator but he was experienced in designing testing, implementing and monitoring illegal torture techniques" used by the U.S. (2008, p. 157).

The reverse engineered version of SERE was applied to captives held by the U.S. in Iraq, Afghanistan, and Guantánamo Bay, Cuba (Burghardt, 2008, ¶ 1). Brad Olson, president of the Division for Social Justice within the American Psychological Association, noted the irony and the tragedy in the application of SERE techniques, "specifically designed to protect our soldiers from countries that violated the Geneva Conventions," which when reverse-engineered and used by the U.S. against foreign detainees, "made us the country that violated the Geneva Conventions" (quoted in Benjamin, 2007, ¶ 9).

From early on in the debate about the use of "harsh interrogation techniques" such as those described, serious questions emerged not just about the legality of their use, but also about whether one could argue that they generated any useful information, which many say they did not. The CIA itself generally refused to either confirm or deny the reports produced by journalists. (Ross & Esposito, 2005).

Detention Centers and Torture

Labelled by George W. Bush as "unlawful combatants" and by Donald Rumsfeld as "the worst of the worst," detainees in Guantánamo have been met with these remarks by their captors: "You are in a place where there is no law-we are the law" (Herbert, 2006, ¶ 6). According to the Center for Constitutional Rights the prisoners are kept in deplorable conditions. For example, they are kept in cages with their heads covered with hoods and their eyes covered with sensory deprivation goggles which prohibit them from seeing. Prisoners hear soldiers screaming insults and dogs barking near them. James Yee, a former Guantánamo chaplain, was quoted as stating in a recent lecture: "Guantánamo Bay's secret weapon,'... is the use of Islam against prisoners to break them." He also said that female interrogators "exploit conservative Islamic etiquette" by undressing before interrogating detainees and "giving lap dances" to unnerve them (Crawford, 2007, ¶ 6, 7).

Similarly, Abu Ghraib, was where the prisoners of the U.S. "war on terror" were placed after the fall of Iraq. Images presented in Mayer's book *The Dark Side* shows the extreme cruelty visited upon detainees at Abu Ghraib. For example, in chapter 8, a smiling female soldier posing in front of Manadel al-Jamadi's body who died within an hour of interrogation. Pathologists reported this case as a homicide but no further investigations were made. The news media have shown many more images, and many more graphic ones, than the ones shown below, which have been viewed around the world. President Barack Obama's administration asked a federal court to block the release of previously unseen images of the detainees in Iraq and Afghanistan.

Figure 8.1: Thumbs Up over a Prisoner Beaten to Death in Abu Ghraib, Iraq

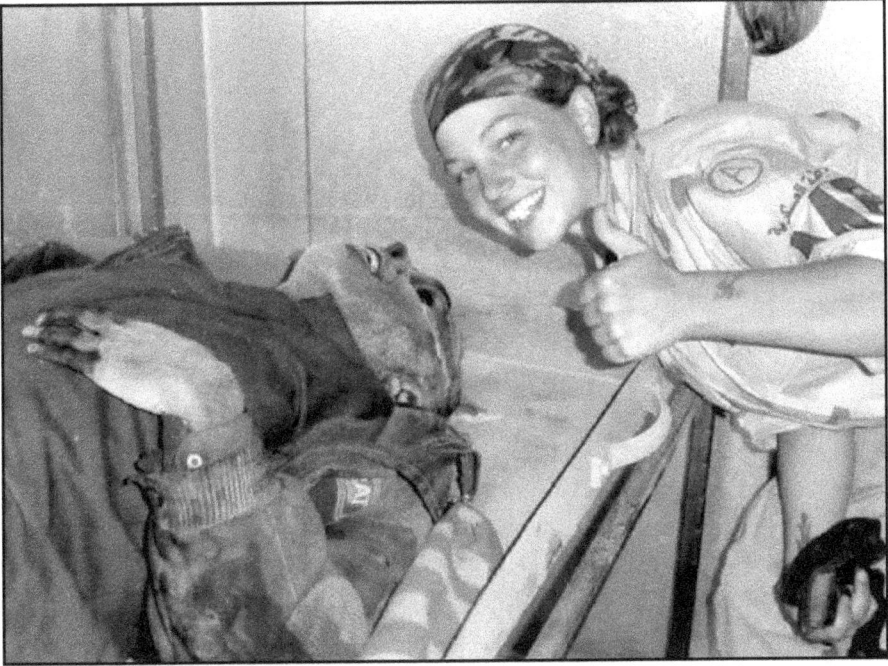

One of the American female military captors serving in Abu Ghraib, posing for a photo over the body of a murdered prisoner. (This image is in the public domain because it is ineligible for copyright. This applies worldwide. Pictures taken by U.S. military personnel on duty are ineligible for copyright, unless the photographer successfully claims that the photographs were not taken as part of his or her official duties. The photographers of the Abu Ghraib prisoner abuse photos have denied this under oath.)

Figure 8.2: Mock Electrocution

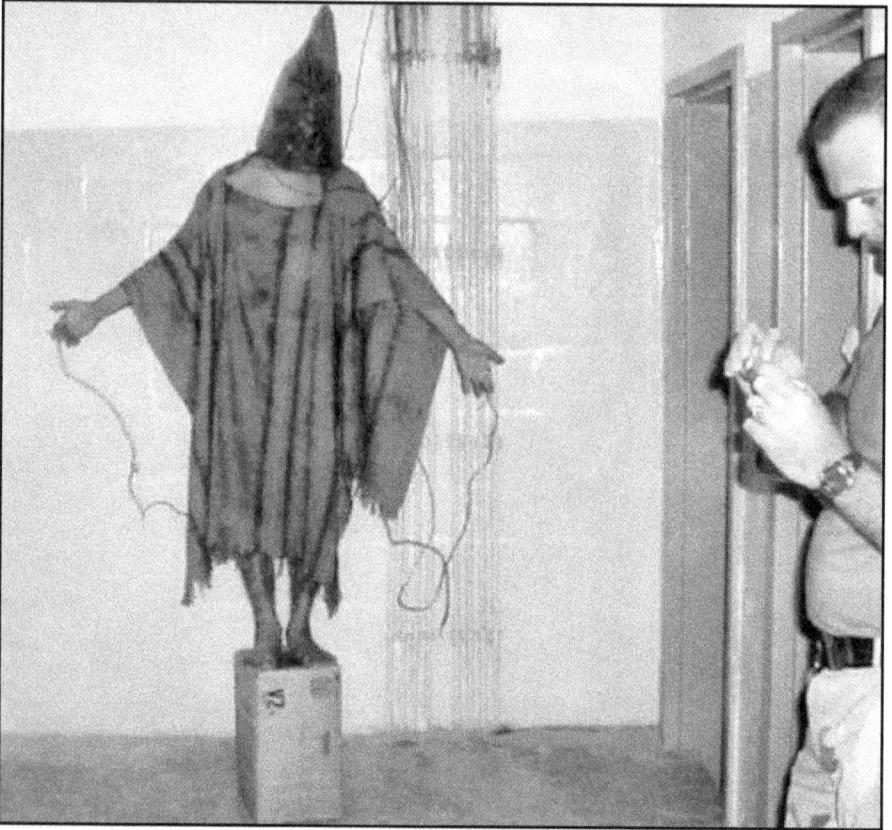

Staff Sergeant Ivan "Chip" Frederick told a Baghdad court martial that he hooked up wires around a hooded detainee in a mock electrocution, on the commands of military and civilian intelligence officials. (This image is in the public domain because it is ineligible for copyright. This applies worldwide. Pictures taken by U.S. military personnel on duty are ineligible for copyright, unless the photographer successfully claims that the photographs were not taken as part of his or her official duties. The photographers of the Abu Ghraib prisoner abuse photos have denied this under oath.)

Figure 8.3: Using Dogs to Terrorize an Inmate in Abu Ghraib

An example of how dogs were used to either threaten or intimidate victims, this one denuded, in Abu Ghraib prison. (This image is in the public domain because it is ineligible for copyright. This applies worldwide. Pictures taken by U.S. military personnel on duty are ineligible for copyright, unless the photographer successfully claims that the photographs were not taken as part of his or her official duties. The photographers of the Abu Ghraib prisoner abuse photos have denied this under oath.)

Figure 8.4: Punching Hooded and Handcuffed Prisoners

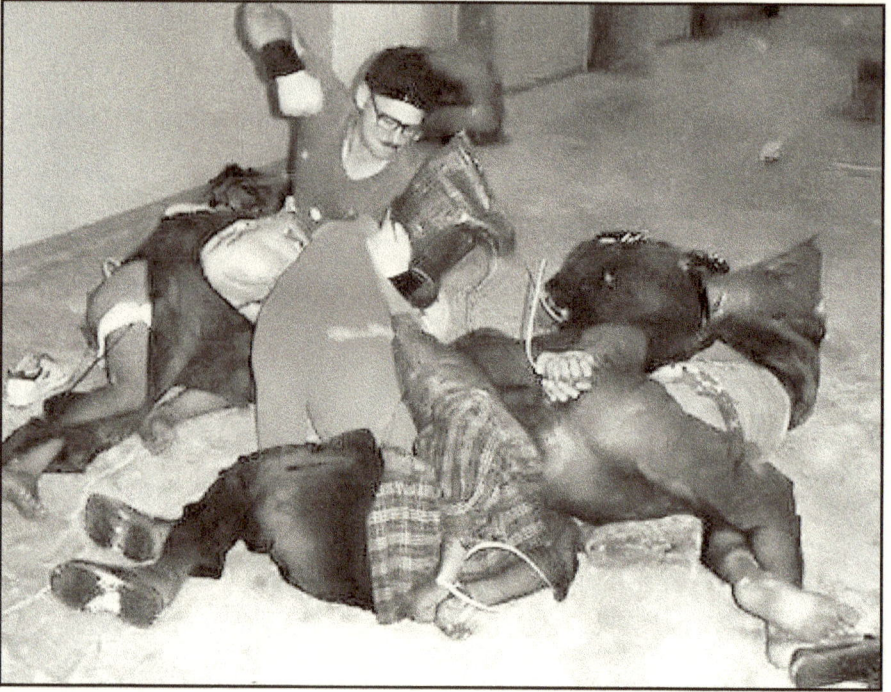

Specialist Charles Graner punches hooded and handcuffed detainees on the floor of Abu Ghraib prison.

In these detention centers many detainees have been tortured without being given any reason for their captivity and were forced to confess for crimes that they had not committed. For example, Emad Al-Janabi, a prisoner of Abu Ghraib, narrated how he was punched, slammed into walls, hung from the bed frame and kept naked and handcuffed in a "stress position" in a filthy cell. No reason was given to him for detention and abuse, but during interrogation the Americans told him that he was a terrorist and that he was trying to attack the U.S. forces. Al-Janabi was forced by the interrogators to confess (Associated Press, 2008; Kolker, 2008).

Types of Torture

There are several torture techniques that have been used. The following consists of some of the better known techniques.

Water Boarding

Water boarding is one of the many in the list of the interrogation techniques. Mayer reported that, "in 2008 the Bush Administration acknowledged publicly that it had in fact, as had been reported, used what is often considered the most notorious of the U.S. interrogation tactics—water boarding—on three high value terror suspects," those being Abu Zubayda, Khalid Sheikh Mohammad, and Abd-al Rahim al Nashiri (Mayer, 2008, p. 171). Some in the Bush administration made light of the severity of the technique, most notably the Vice President. Benjamin (2010, ¶ 1) tells us that "self-proclaimed water boarding fan Dick Cheney called it [the technique] a no-brainer in a 2006 radio interview: Terror suspects should get 'a dunk in the water'."

Recently released internal documents reveal the nature of water boarding, even as seen from the perspective of those applying the technique. A water boarding session would typically last two hours:

> "Interrogators were instructed to start pouring water right after a detainee exhaled, to ensure he inhaled water, not air, in his next breath. They could use their hands to 'dam the runoff' and prevent water from spilling out of a detainee's mouth. They were allowed six separate 40-second 'applications' of liquid in each two-hour session—and could dump water over a detainee's nose and mouth for a total of 12 minutes a day. Finally, to keep detainees alive even if they inhaled their own vomit during a session—a not-uncommon side effect of waterboarding—the prisoners were kept on a liquid diet. The agency recommended Ensure Plus." (Benjamin, 2010, ¶ 3).

Khalid Sheikh Mohammad was water boarded for 183 times in a month (Finn & Tate, 2009, ¶ 16). Abu Zubayda (whose actual name is Zayn al-Abidin Muhammed Hussein) was water boarded 83 times (Finn & Tate, 2009, ¶ 5). Zubayda was "the first person ever to be water boarded at the command of the President of the United States" (Mayer, 2008, p. 171). In addition to water boarding, Zubayda was denied basic medical treatment, such as painkillers, having been shot several times during his capture (Natta, 2003, ¶ 3)

Extraordinary Rendition

Extraordinary rendition involved extraditing "criminal suspects" from one country to another outside of the recognized legal process. It would be cited by President Bush and CIA Director George Tenet as among the most valuable weapons in the war on terror (Mayer, 2008, p. 102). To understand how rendition works Kerry Pither quotes Robert Baer, a former CIA case officer in the Middle East: "We pick up a suspect or we arrange for one of our partner countries to do it. Then the suspect is placed in a civilian transport to a third country where, let's make no bones about it, they use torture. If you want a good interrogation, you send someone to Jordan; if you want them to be killed, you send them to Egypt or Syria" (Pither, 2008, p. 101). Sending detainees to a country where torture is known to occur, and is expected to occur, is a clear violation of Article 3 of the UN *Convention Against Torture and Other Cruel, Inhuman or Degrading Treatment or Punishment*:

> "No State Party shall expel, return or extradite a person to another State where there are substantial grounds for believing that he would be in danger of being subjected to torture. For the purpose of determining whether there are such grounds, the competent authorities shall take into account all relevant considerations including, where applicable, the existence in the State concerned of a consistent pattern of gross, flagrant or mass violations of human rights." (UN, 1984).

The case of Maher Arar offers us Canadian example of extraordinary rendition. Arar held dual Syrian and Canadian citizenship. He was deported to Syria from New York where he was detained and tortured for more than a year (Siddiqui, 2006, p. 18; Cohen & Corrado 2005, p. 105). There he was "whipped by a two-inch-thick, two-foot-long black twisted metal cable" on different parts of his body. He was insulted and yelled at (Pither, 2008, p. 186). He was kept in a body-sized slot of a windowless underground cell—his was "Cell No. 2"—which he likened to being buried alive in a casket (Mayer, 2008, p. 131). According to Arar, the prisoners over there went through "psychological torture" as they did not know what would happen to them next (Pither, 2008, p. 195). Although he initially tried to assert his innocence, he eventually confessed to anything his tormentors wanted him to say. "You just give up," he said. "You become like an animal" (Mayer, 2008, p. 131).

Sleep Deprivation

Mayer writes that there have been reports that CIA's high value detainees were deprived of sleep. They were deprived of sleep intermittently for up to three months. They were bombarded by bright lights, and eardrum-shattering sounds 24 hours a day for weeks on end (2008, p. 169). Mayer further adds that according to the SERE program scientists "noise stress" was often more difficult for trainees to endure than anything else, including water boarding (2008, p. 170). According to SERE personnel, the most stress inducing sound for many was that of babies crying inconsolably (Mayer, 2008, p. 170).

Moazam Begg, a former Guantánamo detainee, British citizen was picked up from Islamabad, is an example of someone who experienced sleep deprivation during his imprisonment. According to Begg, he was interrogated at any time of the day or night, unannounced; his cell was floodlit 24 hours a day (Jones, 2008, pp. 19-20). Mayer indicates that the "cells were bombarded with deafening sounds 24 hours a day for weeks" (2008, p. 274). Mayer adds that "usually the sounds were music" but Begg describes "hearing hysterical female screams from an unseen woman who he was led to believe was his wife"

(Mayer, 2008, p. 274). An interrogator might also threaten to harm the prisoner's family if the prisoner does not cooperate (Jones, 2008, p. 20)

As with Cheney's "dunk in the water" interpretation, military officials were not likely to condemn the techniques. Colonel Roger King, spokesman for the American-led force in Afghanistan, said in 2003 that it was "legitimate to use lights, noise and vision restriction, and to alter, without warning, the time between meals, to blur a detainee's sense of time," and that sleep deprivation was "probably within the lexicon" (Natta, 2003, ¶ 31). At the same time, however, Holly Burkhalter, the U.S. director of Physicians for Human Rights, emphasized: "They don't have a policy on torture. There is no specific policy that eschews torture" (Natta, 2003, ¶ 11)

Conclusion

We now know that few of the prisoners taken to these detention centers were guilty of any crime. Many more were imprisoned in CIA detention centers worldwide, and the number of those detained in such centres has not been identified. The reasons for detention, and the treatment the detainees receive(d), are being debated by many. Maher Arar was never charged with any crime, and was denied the rights of a Canadian citizen (Siddiqui, 2006, p. 19).

In an interview with Harry Kreisler (2008), Jane Mayer held up a mirror to our governments: "we were copying the methods of the people that we have labelled Imperial States and the states we call the torture states and enemy states."

Notes

1   Some of these were discussed on the Sunni Forum, a web discussion board, in a thread titled "Aafia Siddiqui Forced to Walk Naked Over the Quran!" which began on 30 March 2010. It was accessed at http://www.sunniforum.com/forum/showthread.php?57201-Aafia-Siddiqui-Forced-to-Walk&p=469439.

References

Associated Press. (2008). Iraqi Man Sues, Alleging Torture. *Los Angeles Times*, May 7.
    http://articles.latimes.com/2008/may/07/local/me-briefs7.S5
Benjamin, M. (2007). The CIA's Torture Teachers. *Salon*, June 21.
    http://www.salon.com/news/feature/2007/06/21/cia_sere/print.html
—————. (2010). Waterboarding for Dummies. *Salon*, March 9.
    http://www.salon.com/news/feature/2010/03/09/waterboarding_for_dummies

Bugnion, F. (2000). The Geneva Conventions of 12 August 1949: From the 1949 Diplomatic Conference to the Dawn of the New Millennium. *International Affairs*, 76(1), 41-50.

Burghardt, T. (2008). Psychologists Collaborated with "War on Terror" Torture Program. *Global Research*, May 3. http://www.globalresearch.ca/index.php?context=va&aid=8884

Bush, G. W. (2001). Address to a Joint Session of Congress and the American People. Washington, DC: The White House.
http://georgewbush-whitehouse.archives.gov/news/releases/2001/09/20010920-8.html

Cohen, I. M., & Corrado, R. R. (2005). State Torture in the Contemporary World. *International Journal of Comparative Sociology*, 46(1-2), 103-131.

Cole, D. (2005). Intolerable Cruelty. *The Nation*, 281(17), November 21, 5-6.
http://www.thenation.com/article/intolerable-cruelty-0

Crawford, F. (2007). Former U.S. Army Guantánamo chaplain James Yee Warns of Living in "Very Dangerous post-9/11 Era". *Cornell University Chronicle Online*, April 6.
http://www.news.cornell.edu/stories/April07/JamesYee.html

Eban, K. (2007). Rorschach and Awe. *Vanity Fair*, July 17.
http://www.vanityfair.com/politics/features/2007/07/torture200707?currentPage=all

Finn, P., & Tate, J. (2009). CIA Mistaken on 'High-Value' Detainee, Document Shows. *Washington Post*, June 16.
http://www.washingtonpost.com/wp-dyn/content/article/2009/06/15/AR2009061503045.html

Herbert, B. (2006). The Law Gets a Toehold. *The New York Times*, July 13.
http://query.nytimes.com/gst/fullpage.html?res=9D04EFDF1E30F930A25754C0A9609C8B63&sec=&spon=&pagewanted=all

International Committee of the Red Cross (ICRC). (2009). The Geneva Conventions of 1949.
http://www.icrc.org/web/eng/siteeng0.nsf/html/genevaconventions

Jones, S. (Producer). (2008). Torturing Democracy [Motion Picture]. Transcript:
http://www.pbs.org/moyers/journal/05292009/transcript1.html

Kolker, C. (2008). Former Abu Ghraib Prisoner Accuses CACI, L-3 of Torture in Suit. *Bloomberg*, May 6.
http://www.bloomberg.com/apps/news?pid=newsarchive&sid=aN5bbh5efPOA

Kreisler, H. (2008). Conversations with History: How the War on Terror Turned into a War on American Values [Video]. Berkeley, CA: Institute of International Studies, University of California at Berkeley. http://www.youtube.com/watch?v=J19uEOrO7go

Mayer, J. (2008). The Dark Side: The Inside Story of How the War on Terror Turned into a War on American Ideals. New York: Doubleday.

Natta, D. (2003). Questioning Terror Suspects in a Dark and Surreal World. *The New York Times*, March 9.
http://www.nytimes.com/2003/03/09/international/09DETA.html?pagewanted=all

Pither, K. (2008). *Dark Days*. Toronto: Penguin Group Canada.

Reese, S. D., & Lewis, S. C. (2009). Framing the War on Terror: The Internalization of Policy in the U.S. Press. *Journalism*, 10(6), 777-797.

Ripley, A. (2004). The Rules of Interrogation. *TIME*, 163(20), 44-46.

Ross, B., & Esposito, R. (2005). CIA's Harsh Interrogation Techniques Described: Sources Say Agency's Tactics Lead to Questionable Confessions, Sometimes to Death. *ABC News*, November 18. http://abcnews.go.com/Blotter/Investigation/story?id=1322866

Siddiqui, H. (2006). *Being Muslim*. Toronto: Groundwood Books/ House of Anansi Press.

United Nations (UN). (1966). International Covenant on Civil and Political Rights. New York: United Nations General Assembly. http://www.hrweb.org/legal/cpr.html

—————. (1984). Convention against Torture and Other Cruel, Inhuman or Degrading Treatment or Punishment. New York: United Nations General Assembly. http://www.hrweb.org/legal/cat.html

WitnessToIt. (2010). Justice for Aafia Siddiqui! JFAC Trailer [Video]. *Justice for Aafia Coalition*, March 30. http://www.youtube.com/watch?v=1eNAp95S1Pg

Zalman, A. (2010). Extraordinary Rendition. *About.com: Terrorism Issues*. http://terrorism.about.com/od/e/g/Renditon.htm

Lies, Damn Lies and Afghanistan: What Do Canadians Really Know About Our Military Role?

Kate Roland

Brand Canada: Peacekeepers, negotiators, humanitarians, non-aggressors—Canadians cherish this reputation of our nation and our military. When we travel to foreign countries with our backpacks and suitcases, we proudly display the Canadian flag labels. A signal, perhaps, of our "non-American" status, but probably and more significantly, our justifiable pride in our global "good guy" reputation.

Afghanistan is proving to be the mirror that is sending back a somewhat distorted view of our reputation—reflecting actions not "in synch" with Canadian values. As the sad motorcades wind their way along the "Highway of Heroes" we repeat by rote that we support the troops, and almost in the same breath, increasingly question the mission that caused these deaths.

The Afghanistan "mission" is a political football and photo-op. Truly arrogant and egregious behavior by our politicians and the military commanders have made Canadians increasingly uncomfortable with our military role. Most recently, this was exemplified in the bullying behavior against a credible and respected Canadian diplomat who spoke up about our military's handling of Afghan detainees.

Our vote in a general election apparently means "carte blanche" for politicians to play high-handed "Russian roulette" with our brave military. With a collective sigh of relief, heard more loudly as more controversial issues arise about our actions in Afghanistan, Canadians welcome the decision to bring the troops home in 2011.

For now, there appears to be a huge "disconnect" between Canadians' values and expectations, and the evolution of our foreign policy with respect to our military—specifically the practical impact and consequences this has on Canada's reputation and Canadians-at-large. Canadians and politicians need to understand that re-engagement on decisions about our role in Afghanistan and the conditions for any subsequent military commitment to the U.N. and NATO, is vital to our national well-being and world image we wish to project.

In this chapter I examine what Canadians "know" about the use of the military in Canadian foreign policy, and specifically how it applies to Afghanistan. Underscoring this inquiry is the reasonable level of information owed to Canadians when politicians assume the moral authority to act in their names. I am interested in bringing to the surface how and why this Canadian "brand" contradiction came about; who can be held accountable; how this colors our thinking about Afghanistan; and what, if anything, Canadians can do to have our military actions more aligned with our thinking.

My focus will be on three factors that likely contribute to the disparity between the valued Canadian brand and Canadians' perception of our Afghanistan mission: 1) Canada's power structure and foreign policy with respect to our military in Afghanistan; 2) what Canadians were/are told about the Afghanistan mission and their reactions to it; and, 3) one example of off-brand "un-Canadian" military behavior to examine the dynamics.

Figure 9.1: Map of Afghanistan, 1993

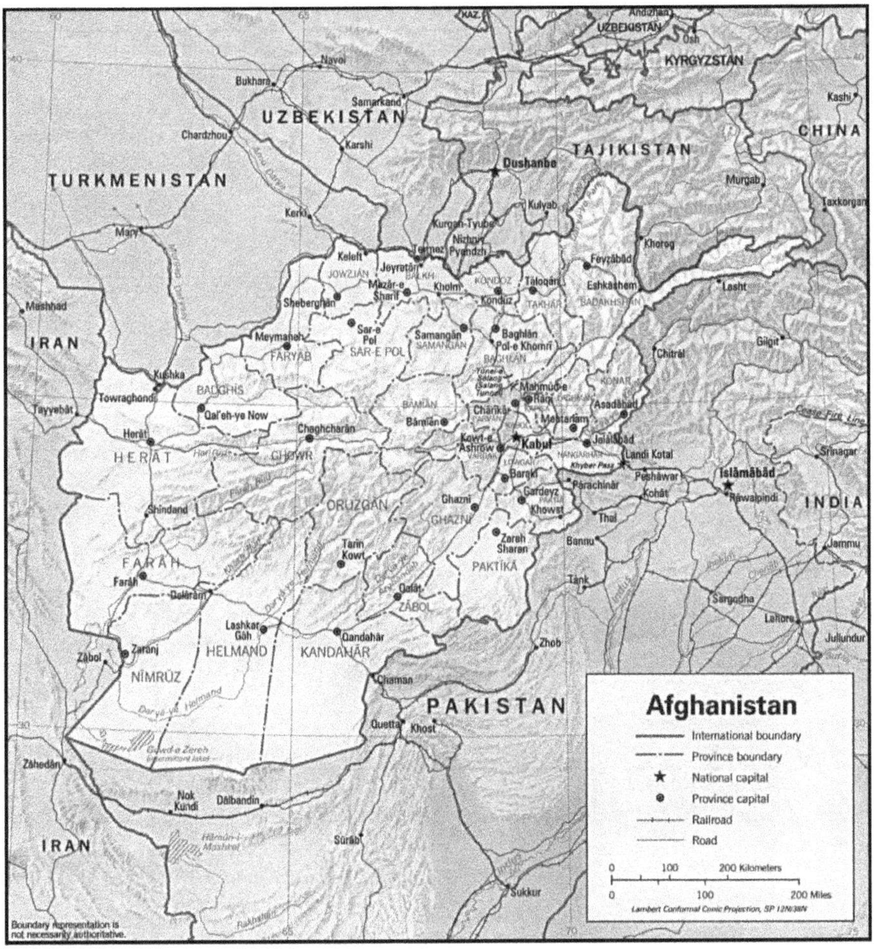

Produced by the U.S. Central Intelligence Agency, presented by the Library of Congress Geography and Map Division Washington, D.C. 20540-4650 USA, as part of the public domain.

Figure 9.2: 2006 Map of Distribution of NATO Forces forming the International Security Assistance Force

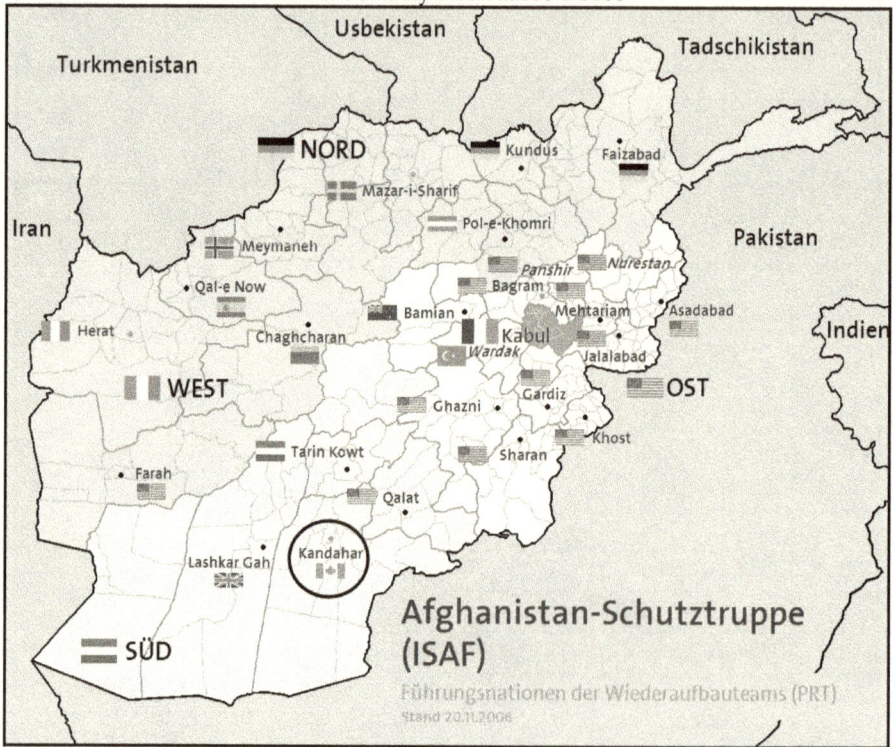

Source: CedricBLN, Wikimedia Commons (Creative Commons License: Share, Remix, Attribution).

Canadian Foreign Policy and the Military

Power Structure

The Governor General is the Commander-in-Chief of Canada.[1] Under the Westminster system's parliamentary custom and practice, the Prime Minister of Canada holds de facto decision-making ability over the deployment and disposition of the Canadian forces.[2] The Cabinet officer in charge of the Canadian forces is the Minister of National Defence (MND) who answers to the Prime Minister.[3] The Minister of Foreign Policy and International Trade reports to the Prime Minister and is largely responsible for Canada's role in the United Nations (U.N.) and the North Atlantic Treaty Organization (NATO) (Foreign Affairs and International Trade Canada [FAITC], 2010).[4] Reporting to the Prime

Minister, the Cabinet Committee on Afghanistan considers diplomatic, defence, development and security issues related to Canada's mission in Afghanistan (Government of Canada, 2010a).[5] The military head of the Canadian Forces is the Chief of Defence Staff (CDS), the highest-ranking military officer in the nation.[6]

Foreign Policy and Military Impact

The Canadian military has a stellar reputation based on its contributions to U.N. peacekeeping missions, and it is this reputation that Canadians cherish. Canadian foreign policy has long pursued the path of "peacekeeper" and "honest broker," a noteworthy contribution made through the U.N., following wars between nations. Today's reality is that global conflict has mainly shifted to internal conflict within nations, and includes humanitarian intervention when a sovereign nation and its government cannot guarantee the well-being of its citizens. This re-framing of military engagement brings with it new terminology: "peace making;" "peace building;" "peace enforcement;" "nation building;" "humanitarian intervention" and a host of others. They sound somewhat similar to the "peacekeeping" label familiar to Canadians, but all entail a more seriously aggressive combat focus than the "self defence" of peacekeeping.

The trend in the past decade has been for Canada to move away from U.N. peacekeeping missions and toward peace enforcement. Canada now ranks 56th amongst troop contributing countries to U.N. peacekeeping missions (Peace Operations Working Group [POWG], 2009). A more significant Canadian military presence is with NATO, whose purpose is to safeguard the freedom and security of all its members by political and military means. This pledge of collective defence requires NATO members to assist in responding to any armed attack on another ally in Europe or North America. On 14 October 2001, following the terrorist attacks in the U.S., Canada and the other NATO member countries, responded positively to the U.S.' request for troops and implemented measures to contribute direct military support to the campaign against terrorism (CTV, 2008).

Afghanistan Mission

Afghanistan is not a U.N. peacekeeping mission, nor could it be labeled peace enforcement—there is no peace to keep or enforce. This is a combat mission. Canada is "one of 41 countries participating in the International Security Assistance Force (ISAF), a NATO led formation that operates under the authority of the U.N." (Government of Canada, 2010b). Our military role today includes combat—fighting the "war on terror"—training and mentoring the Afghan National Police (ANP), along with diplomacy, development and humanitarianism initiatives. This is very far afield from our traditional peacekeeping role, and yet it is from this former role our perception of Canadian military engagement is derived.

Figure 9.3: Canadian Forces on Patrol in Kandahar City, Afghanistan

Official caption: Kandahar City, Afghanistan. Corporal Adam Naslund watches his arcs as other members of the patrol stop to speak with locals. Members of Stab A from the Kandahar Provincial Reconstruction Team (KPRT) conduct a foot patrol in District 9 of Kandahar City on 2 February 2010. Source: National Defence Canada, Master Corporal Matthew McGregor, Image Tech, JTFK Afghanistan, Roto 8, in accordance with government rules for reproduction.

In October 2001, former Prime Minister Jean Chretien responded with Canadian troop commitments to the U.S. and NATO, and thus the Canadian military entered Afghanistan (Chretien, 2001). In April 2004, former Prime Minister Paul Martin pledged troops until 2005 (CBC, 2006). In February 2005, (then) Defence Minister Bill Graham agreed to a major expansion of the NATO mission, and deployment of Canadian troops to the front lines of the counter insurgency in Kandahar to relieve the departing U.S. troops (CBC, 2006).

In 2008, the Manley Report (Independent Panel on Canada's Future Role in Afghanistan, 2008) provided Parliament with an argument and conditions that enabled an all-party Parliamentary agreement to keep Canadian troops in Afghanistan, with a decisive end date of 2011 to bring the troops home. Prime Minister Harper repeatedly states there will be no extension to Canada's military mission beyond 2011 (Canadian Press, 2010). Suspicion lingers that the U.S. influence on our economy, and President Obama's wish that Canadian military stay in Afghanistan to suit the United States' foreign policy, might persuade the government to yet again extend this mission (CTV, 2010a, 2010b).

Statistics show that Canada has contributed seven per cent of all non-US troops to this Afghan mission and suffered 24 per cent of all non-US casualties (O'Neill, 2010, ¶ 4). To date, 146 Canadian soldiers have lost their lives in Afghanistan. Estimates have the severely wounded at 10 times that amount (CBC, 2010).

Figure 9.4: Bringing Home the Dead from Afghanistan

Official caption: Kandahar, Afghanistan, 12 April 2010. A ramp ceremony was held for Private Tyler William Todd. Private Todd, 26, was killed by improvised explosive device near the town of Belanday on 11 April 2010. Joint Task Force Afghanistan (JTF-Afg) is the Canadian Forces (CF) contribution to the international effort in Afghanistan. Its operations focus on working with Afghan authorities to improve security, governance and economic development in Afghanistan. JTF-Afg comprises more than 2,750 CF members. Source: National Defence Canada, Master Corporal Matthew McGregor, Image Tech, JTFK Afghanistan, Roto 8, in accordance with government rules for reproduction.

Information Flow and Public Opinion about the Afghanistan Mission

Context

No discussion of public information about Afghanistan would be relevant without the tumultuous context of the time frame in which it was delivered.

The mind-numbing pictures of the twin towers and the Pentagon, layered with the horrific screams and gentle last words of those about to die, will forever be emblazoned on our minds. The terrorist attacks in the U.S. on 11 September 2001, set the stage for a U.S. led NATO retaliation in Afghanistan that no ally would refuse. In that emotionally-charged context, Prime Minister Jean Chretien said in his televised speech to Canadians on October 7, 2001, that "our troops would do us proud" (Chretien, 2001, ¶ 8).

In the subsequent nine years, Canadians were faced with three Federal elections, each producing a minority government; two new Prime Ministers; three new leaders of the Liberal Party; government scandals that rocked government stability; emergence of the Chief of Defence Staff—in particular General Rick Hillier—to the spotlight about Afghanistan due to this instability; Parliamentary investigation of a former Conservative Prime Minister; subsequent terror attacks in London; heightened terror alerts world-wide and stringent new personal travel restrictions; discovery of a Canadian-based terrorist plot; a massive economic failure in the U.S. that directly impacted the Canadian and world economies; election of a (then) popular new U.S. President; two prorogations of the Canadian Parliament requested by Prime Minister Harper; bankruptcies and unemployment in key economic sectors; hosting the Winter Olympics; massive devastation in Haiti and other world locales; an attempted terrorist attack on an aircraft bound for Detroit; currently, a new lobbying scandal involving a (now former) Cabinet member and her husband; and, whatever local and personal concerns arose for each individual Canadian. Any news about Afghanistan is played out against the backdrop of this "new normal" post-9/11.

Public Opinion

Given the context of any message delivery, public interest and reaction tends to peak when the media put specific information and issues in the spotlight, and when the bodies of Canadian soldiers are returned home. Military fatalities mounted when troops deployed to Kandahar in 2006, peaking at 37 that year due to the font line nature of that mission, and have remained at a steady 30+ in subsequent years (CTV, 2010c; iCasualties, 2010).

Table 9.5: Canadian Troop Deaths by Year in Afghanistan

YEAR	2002	2003	2004	2005	2006	2007	2008	2009	2010
FATALITIES	4	2	1	1	36	30	32	32	8*

* To 24 May 2010; Sources: CTV (2010c); iCasualties (2010).

Two things are clear from current polls: Canadians want the troops home; Canadians have no patience and little trust in their politicians. According to the latest Ekos Politics Poll, consistent with numerous other polls over the past eight years, when it comes to current Canadian involvement in Afghanistan, 49 per cent of Canadians oppose the war, 36 per cent support it, and 14 per cent are undecided; as for an extension of Canada's mission in Afghanistan, 60 per cent oppose an extension, 28 per cent support one, and 14 per cent are undecided (Ekos, 2010). In an Angus Reid poll, also published in April 2010, 56 per cent opposed the war in Afghanistan (Angus Reid, 2010).

The Ekos Politics report also shows that 46.5 per cent of Canadians believe that, overall, the government is moving in the wrong direction. At the same time, however, none of the political parties would muster over a third of voters if an election were held today. The Harris Decima/Canadian Press poll also completed in April 2010, as was Ekos', suggests that Canadians have little confidence in the two main parties, the Conservatives and the Liberals, to manage the economy, or to adequately reflect the values of Canadians (Canadian Press & HarrisDecima, 2010).

Government

A beleaguered Canadian public that is in almost total ennui and suspicion of their politicians needs the catalyst of the media to focus issues and express their views on Afghanistan. Among others, the Angus Reid (Vision Critical) Public Opinion poll, published 21 April 2010, shows a majority of respondents believe the federal government has provided too little information about the conflict. Just one in four Canadians (27 per cent) think the federal government has provided the right amount of information about the war in Afghanistan, while more than half (53 per cent) claim it has been too little (Angus Reid, 2010).

Media

In stark contrast, this same poll shows Canadians remain content with the way the country's media have covered the Afghanistan conflict. A majority of respondents (51 per cent) claim the media has provided the right amount of information about the war in Afghanistan, 22 per cent think it is too little, 15 per cent say it has been too much (Angus Reid, 2010). It is also a fact that little information on the number of troops injured, the number of Taliban attacks against Canadian forces, and the number of Afghan detainees held by Canada, are either not released at all (the latter two), or released at a snail's pace to diminish the impact of the war on public opinion (see Stewart, 2010).

Diplomacy

Little is heard of Canada's diplomatic successes in Kabul, nor governance and development efforts in Kandahar province through our civilian presence, under the direction of the Representative of Canada in Kandahar (RoCK), Ben Rowswell, except through the media. Canada has a rapidly growing cadre of "combat diplomats," and according to Rowswell, "there is a sense that this is what the future of Canadian diplomacy looks like and that those of us who are cutting our teeth here will be able to apply what we've learned to further Canada's interests in other conflict settings" (Fisher, 2010, ¶ 1, 3).

Canada's senior diplomats may have a different view. One of Canada's most distinguished diplomats, Canadian envoy Robert Fowler, recently stated that Canada's international reputation has been wantonly squandered by politicians of all stripes who have descended to propagating a "small-minded, mean-spirited, me-first , little Canada, whatever the Americans want, foreign policy" (Bauch, 2010, ¶ 5). Fowler's words carry some weight: Fowler has been a foreign policy adviser to three Canadian prime ministers; he served as deputy minister of national defence; and, was Canada's longest serving ambassador to the U.N. Fowler also emphasized: "The bottom line is that we will not prevail in Afghanistan" (Bauch, 2010, ¶ 2). In addition, he was critical of the mission as colonialist, and a squandering of precious resources:

> "They say look at the number of little girls we have put in school—at a cost of 146 Canadian lives and an incremental cost of $11.3 billion. My, think of the number of little girls we could put in school throughout the Third World—particularly in Africa— with that kind of money. And without having to kill and be killed to get that worthy job done." (Bauch, 2010, ¶ 13)[7]

Military

The "unmuzzled" clarity and directness in the memoir comments of former Chief of Defense Staff, General Rick Hillier (Retired), in his 2009 book, *A Soldier First: Bullets, Bureaucrats and the Politics of War*, crystallize the dichotomy between the Canadian military and public perception of Canada's military role. In his review for the *The Globe and Mail*, Granatstein says that Rick Hillier's aim in his role as Chief of Defence Staff from 2005 to 2008, was to change how Canada "played the game," proclaiming the military's job is to kill people (quoted in Granatstein, 2009, ¶ 3, 4). As Granatstein puts it, "the popular idea that Canadians were peacekeepers first, last and always had to be smacked between the eyes" (2009, ¶ 3). Hillier's remarks began the process of "changing the mindset of the Canadian forces to a war-fighting culture" (Granatstein, 2009, ¶ 4). Granatstein acknowledges that Hillier had less impact in changing the peacekeeping mindset of the public. Huge numbers still think Canada is doing peacekeeping in Afghanistan. Hillier's comments about the world context in which Canada lives were also squarely on the side of brute force: "soft power— peacekeeping and values—is well and good. But without the capacity to deploy effective, well-trained, well-led hard power when needed, no one will pay attention to Canada" (Granatstein, 2009, ¶ 5, 12).

Off-Brand Action

The Afghan Detainee Issue

One example that demonstrates how the current dynamics produce this brand disparity for Canadians is the Afghan detainee issue. As far back as 2006 allegations were put forward that the Canadian military knowingly turned over Afghan detainees to almost certain torture. In late 2009, respected Canadian diplomat, Richard Colvin, presented damaging evidence supporting these allegations (see Chase, 2009). He also revealed a pattern of indifference and obstruction to his attempts to warn higher-ups of what was happening. Repeated attempts were made to discredit Mr. Colvin and his claims by the government during Question Period and the all-party Commons Committee review. Almost entirely blacked-out documents were waved about by the opposition, incensed by the government's claim of security concerns. Those government suppression tactics did not work, nor did the military's bluster. Mr. Colvin stands vindicated in the court of public opinion through massive, public support by his colleagues in the diplomatic corps.

In the larger scheme of things, Mr. Colvin has done Canadians the important service of telling us the consequences of mistreating these detainees—it cost Canada the trust of locals in Kandahar, certainly what we needed to have to facilitate any military mission. He also clearly demonstrated the failings of the Canadian Department of Foreign Affairs who remonstrated with him, and told him not to put his statements into written documents (Chase, 2009).

Prime Minister Harper asked Governor General Michaelle Jean to prorogue Parliament in early January 2010, ostensibly to allow time for budget preparation and the Olympics. The opposition parties and many Canadians thought this was really to avoid answering questions about the detainee issue. Liberal Member of Parliament, Derek Lee, is now challenging the Harper government to deliver documents it has been ordered by Parliament to produce, or face a charge of contempt of the institution. According to Queen's University political studies professor Ned Franks, "Both sides should be able to find a satisfactory middle road, but from the way that both opposition and government are behaving on this issue, they do not appear to want to compromise their rigid and opposing views. Canadians deserve better from their politicians and Parliament" (Queen's University, 2010, ¶ 3).

Who's the Boss – Who's to Blame?

Controversial issues and sadness over Canadian casualties, are the hallmark of the Canadian military mission in Afghanistan. The context is one consisting of:

a minority government with its own agenda, to not only stay in power but leverage that power base to a majority position; the political opposition parties clamoring to increase their share of Canadian support; a newly invigorated military in the spotlight of combat; whistle-blower diplomats clamoring to be heard; and, all of these played out against a panoply of domestic Canadian urgencies and scandals, as well as tumultuous world events. This has clearly not proven to be a successful recipe for engagement, understanding and support of the Canadian public for any new military role. Canadians have "tuned out" the political circus and tend to focus only when a significant event, such as the death of a soldier, or any discussion about an extension to the mission, is surfaced in the media.

The result has been an out-of-balance scenario in which the key players in Afghanistan – the military and the diplomats—have been silenced by their political masters, except when needed to deflect blame. Canadians deserve better. General Hillier for all his military wisdom is not an elected official, and the military is only one contributor to the image and values Canadians wish to present. Rather than learning about our new military stance—and at our expense through the purchase of Hillier's memoirs, not to mention the lives of our soldiers—we need to be asked for our support in a general election.

The politicians' claims of "national security" insult Canadians' intelligence and Canadians are doing the only thing they can do: massively and overwhelmingly support the move to bring the troops home. But this will not change the potential for disparity between the cherished Canadian brand and the next political decision for any new military mission—for that we need transparency, education and open discussion.

The U.N. and NATO are highly valued by Canadians and politicians, as a means of global engagement, defence against common enemies, and a means to provide our contribution on the world stage. Reform and modernization of both of these institutions is long overdue and appear to be moving at glacial speed. General Hillier and others deride their effectiveness, and possibly they are right. We need to task our politicians with public education of the issues involved, and the options available to Canada to improve them. "Pleasing" our NATO and U.N. allies cannot be the goal of Canadian foreign policy, especially when it means ignoring Canadian values.

The Way Forward

No reasonable person would argue that everything must be known by the Canadian public about our military activities—there is some level of national security involved. This does not mean Canadians abdicate their responsibility at the polling station but it does mean the government has an obligation to transparently inform them of important strategic changes in military and diplomatic ac-

tivities. The media have proven they can do their job of ensuring public awareness. Reconciliation of known facts to their perceived Canadian image will
cause Canadians to adjust their thinking—or adjust the political direction by exercising their right to have this on the ballot agenda for the next Federal election.

Canadians and politicians need to understand that re-engagement on decisions about our role in Afghanistan and the conditions for any subsequent military commitment to the U.N. and NATO, is vital to our national well-being and
world image we wish to project. Canadians bear the responsibility to vote for
representatives who will work in the best interests of Canada and Canadians,
and part of that responsibility is to protest when politicians hold them in contempt. This time it is through their overwhelming support of the mandate to
bring the troops home. Given the current political circus, it is unlikely an election will be called—Canadians have expressed their contempt for their political
leaders in the public opinion polls.

Canadian politicians need to understand, however, that the way to secure
and possibly improve their political future is to pursue the path Canadians support for their military following transparent disclosure and debate. In a minority
parliament, where the will of the people is not fully expressed by the party in
power, there needs to be a mechanism by which privileged information is
shared with the leader(s) of the opposition, and the appropriate shadow cabinet
ministers, and a consensus reached. This worked with the Manley Report, with
arguably the most fractious Parliament Canada has experienced. For the balance
of the Afghanistan mission, this would quell the public posturing and force
consensus—or an election. Parliament should put its efforts to encouraging a
credible, well-supported intelligence network, with respected and motivated en-
voys and diplomats, working in synch with our military and government leaders,
and create the plan to bring home our troops in 2011—with honor—from a
highly unpopular, sketchily understood mission. Respect for Canadians, even if
motivated solely by political self-interest, should make a statesman-like approach on this issue a remedial priority for Prime Minister Harper's agenda.

Given the current stalemate with the Canadian public, continuing the same
behavior while expecting a different outcome and possibly a majority, is mad-
ness for Canadian politicians. Mr. Harper would be well-advised to immediately
invite the leaders of the opposition parties to join the Cabinet Committee on
Afghanistan, and work toward consensus. He should make a commitment to
the Canadian people that no military engagement will be undertaken without
full disclosure and debate in Parliament. He should not only apologize to Mr.
Colvin, he should invite the Canadian diplomatic corps to join at full level with
the military, his government and opposition leaders, to jointly define the best
way home from Afghanistan, and begin the work of articulating a foreign policy
and military activity, that Canadians can support. Canada's exit plan from Af-

ghanistan in 2011 should inspire re-engagement by Canadians and their elected representatives to better align Canada's foreign policy and military contributions with the values and expectations implicit in the Canadian brand—who we are and who we aspire to be.

Notes

1   "The Governor General of Canada: Roles and Responsibilities" (http://www.gg.ca/document.aspx?id=13288).

2   "The Prime Minister of Canada" (http://www.pm.gc.ca/eng/default.asp).

3   "National Defence and the Canadian Forces" (http://www.forces.gc.ca/site/home-accueil-eng.asp).

4   "Foreign Affairs and International Trade Canada" (http://www.dfait-maeci.gc.ca/international/index.aspx).

5   See "Government of Canada: Canada's Engagement in Afghanistan" (http://www.afghanistan.gc.ca/canada-afghanistan/index.aspx?lang=en).

6   See "National Defence and the Canadian Forces: About the Canadian Forces" (http://www.forces.gc.ca/site/acf-apfc/index-eng.asp), and "Chief of Defence Staff" (http://www.cds-cemd.forces.gc.ca/index-eng.asp).

7   The full text of Robert Fowler's address, apparently a copy of his reading notes, is available at: http://davidakin.blogware.com/100328.Fowler.Can150.pdf

References

Angus Reid. (2010). Support for Afghanistan Mission Falls Markedly in Canada; Half of Respondents Believe the Federal Government has not Provided Enough Information about the War. Angus Reid Public Opinion, April 21.

> http://www.visioncritical.com/wp-content/uploads/2010/04/2010.04.21_AfghanCAN.pdf

Bauch, H. (2010) Envoy savages Liberals, Tories on foreign policy. *The Gazette* (Montreal), March 29, A10.

> http://www.montrealgazette.com/news/Envoy+savages+Liberals+Tories+foreign+policy/2737969/story.html

Canadian Press. (2010). PM Stresses Security, But Holds Firm on Afghan Withdrawal. *The Star*, March 30.

> http://www.thestar.com/news/canada/article/787453

Canadian Press & HarrisDecima. (2010). Liberals and Conservatives Remain Stuck. Canadian Press/Harris Decima Public Opinion Poll, April 6.
http://www.harrisdecima.com/sites/default/files/releases/2010/04/07/hd-2010-04-07-en616.pdf

CBC. (2006). In Depth, Afghanistan: Timeline of Canada's Involvement from 2001-2006. *CBC News*, November 9. http://www.cbc.ca/news/background/afghanistan/timeline.html

————. (2010). In the Line of Duty: Canada's Casualties. *CBC News*, May 24.
http://www.cbc.ca/news/background/afghanistan/casualties/list.html

Chase, S. (2009). Canada Complicit in Torture of Innocent Afghans, Diplomat Says. *The Globe and Mail*, November 18.
http://www.theglobeandmail.com/news/politics/canada-complicit-in-torture-of-innocent-afghans-diplomat-says/article1369069/

Chretien, J. (2001). Chretien: Cdn Troops "Will Do Canada Proud" [transcript of speech]. *CTV News*, October 7.
http://www.ctv.ca/servlet/ArticleNews/story/CTVNews/1025062429054_20471629

CTV. (2008). Afghanistan: A Timeline of Canadian Involvement Post-9/11. *CTV News*, March 7.
http://www.ctv.ca/servlet/ArticleNews/story/CTVNews/1123179692508_118588892

————. (2010a). U.S. Wants Canada to Stay in Afghanistan Past 2011. *CTV News*, March 29.
http://montreal.ctv.ca/servlet/an/local/CTVNews/20100329/afghanistan_canada_100329/20100329/?hub=MontrealHome

————. (2010b). After 2011, Canada May Mentor Afghan Police. *CTV News*, April 10.
http://www.ctv.ca/servlet/ArticleNews/story/CTVNews/20100410/canada_afghanpolice_100410/20100410?hub=TopStoriesV2

————. (2010c). Canadian Casualties in Afghanistan. *CTV News*, May 26.
http://www.ctv.ca/war/

Ekos. (2010). Political Landscape Frozen; Canadians Continue to Oppose Both the Afghanistan Mission and an Extension. Ekos Politics Public Opinion Poll, April 8.
http://www.ekos.com/admin/articles/cbc-2010-04-08.pdf

Fisher, M. (2010). Canada's ROCK in Afghanistan. *Canwest News Service*, March 18.
http://www.ottawacitizen.com/news/Canada+ROCK+Afghanistan/2695450/story.html

Foreign Affairs and International Trade Canada (FAITC). (2010). Canada in the North Atlantic Treaty Organization (NATO). http://www.international.gc.ca/nato-otan/canada.aspx

Government of Canada. (2010a). Cabinet Committee on Afghanistan.
http://www.afghanistan.gc.ca/canada-afghanistan/approach-approche/ccoa-ccsa.aspx

————. (2010b). Canadian Forces Operations.
http://www.afghanistan.gc.ca/canada-afghanistan/approach-approche/cfo-ofc.aspx?menu_id=66&menu=L

Granatstein, J. L. (2009). Making War to Keep the Peace. *The Globe and Mail*, October 30.
http://www.theglobeandmail.com/books/review-a-soldier-first-by-rick-hillier/article1345304/

iCasualties. (2010). Coalition Deaths by Nationality: Canada. *iCasualties.org*, May 26.

http://www.icasualties.org/OEF/Nationality.aspx?hndQry=Canada

Independent Panel on Canada's Future Role in Afghanistan. (2008). Ottawa: Minister of Public Works and Government Services.
http://epe.lac-bac.gc.ca/100/200/301/pco-bcp/commissions-ef/independent_panel_afghanistan-ef/final_report-e/pdf/Afghan_Report_web_e.pdf

O'Neill, J. (2010). NATO Needs Retooling: Canadian Study. *Canwest News Service*, March 24.
http://www.montrealgazette.com/story_print.html?id=2722002&sponsor=

Peace Operations Working Group (POWG). (2009). Canada & UN Peacekeeping. Ottawa: Peace Operations Working Group.
http://www.peacebuild.ca/documents/POWGcanada&UNPK.pdf

Queen's University. (2010). Contempt of Parliament. *Queen's University News Centre*, May 6.
http://www.queensu.ca/news/media/hottopic/contempt-parliament

Stewart, B. (2010). What Our Military Isn't Telling Us. *CBC News*, March 18.
http://www.cbc.ca/canada/story/2010/03/17/f-vp-stewart.html

CHAPTER TEN

Canada's Changing Military Role Demonstrated through War in Afghanistan

Rosalia Stillitano

S ome might ask: so what if Canada's military is changing, becoming more integrated with the American military, and that as a result the Canadian military can better protect Canadian national interest abroad? Well, in a sense they are right to ask. The fact that Canada's military is undergoing a transformation is not really a problem and it can be interpreted as both a positive or negative achievement for Canada. The problem lies more in what the Canadian government is using the military for, which is primarily counterinsurgency warfare through the militarization of humanitarian aid. The problem is that the Canadian army is becoming Americanized; we are slowly but surely loosing our identity as neutral peace-keepers.

From the 1950s onward, the Canadian army has been undergoing changes regarding its role. Canada's military has gone from United Nations (UN) mandated peacekeeping missions to U.S. and North Atlantic Treaty Organization (NATO) mandated counterinsurgency missions. Prime Minister Chrétien entered Afghanistan as an escape to avoid the war in Iraq while retaining good relations with our neighbour, the U.S. However the Canadian government feels destroying terrorist bases in Afghanistan has become a matter of national security (Kowaluk & Staples, 2009, p. 34; Jockel & Sokolsky, 2008, p. 106). Integration between the American and Canadian military has been steadily increasing since the 1990s, to the point where it has become dangerously "natural" for Canada to support the U.S.; this no doubt also influenced the decision to send troops to Afghanistan. In the 1990s Canada began to withdraw from peacekeeping operations in order to commit more to better structured NATO operations. In 1994 Canadian UN troops accounted for around 2,700, this number has now decreased to 179. Canada has sent 2,800 troops to Afghanistan under NATO (Charbonneau & Cox, 2008; Coulon & Liégeois , 2010, p. 42).

Understanding Afghanistan

Afghanistan exploded into civil war at the same time as aid flows decreased. Once aid ended completely, the state collapsed (Rubin, 2006, p. 178). The Taliban largely recentralised control over coercion. In 2001 Afghanistan was proclaimed a failed state by the U.S and coalition forces (Windsor, Charters & Wilson, 2008, p. 19). In an interview, Rory Stewart (who was deputy governor of Maysan Province in Iraq between 2002 and 2004, Harvard professor, and chairman of the Turquoise Mountain Foundation which provided development work in Afghanistan) stated that Afghans are "quite suspicious of foreigners. They don't know a great deal about the outside world….most of these people we're dealing with can barely read or write. They live very limited lives where, in the winter, they're basically holed-up in their houses. They're often three hours walk from the nearest village….They couldn't find the United States on a map" (Sherr, 2009, ¶ 13). Afghanistan is a multi-ethnic society, and although a common identity as Afghans exists, loyalties tend to lie with their respective tribes, limiting the authority of the national government (Windsor et al., 2008, p. 16). They are nearly all Muslim with a Sunni majority and Shi'i minority (Ayub & Kouvo, 2008, p. 642). Human rights groups had been warning the international community about the repressive rule of the Taliban from before 9/11. Governments of "failed states," from the Canadian government's perspective, are those that are unstable, lacking in centralized political authority, security, and other basic services, making them potential "breeding grounds" for "terrorism" (Charbonneau & Cox, 2008, p. 316).

The Pakistani Inter-Service Intelligence (ISI) played a role in training the Taliban who managed to take over the capital and much of the countryside by the mid-1990s. As interest grew in Caspian oil, violence erupted between the Taliban and opposition factions. During this timeframe Osama Bin Laden united his base in Afghanistan while channelling aid funds through the Taliban government (Ayub & Kouvo, 2008, p. 643). U.S. intervention brought the fall of the Taliban regime. After the fall of the Taliban regime, the CIA and U.S. military should have engaged in peace building activities in the countryside but instead they funded regional warlords to act as militia against the Taliban and chose to ignore the drug economy in order to avoid compromising their relationships with the local power holders. Warlords hold economic interest in the continuation of conflict. Afghans are vulnerable; much of the economy is illegal, forcing Afghans to engage in some form of violence to secure a livelihood.

Peace building should start by understanding market distortions and systems created around organised crime (Rubin, 2006, p. 180; Goodhand, 2002, p. 839).

Ayub and Kouvo argue that Afghanistan was ignored after the Cold War and that "the international community failed Afghanistan in not staying involved, and virtually disregarded it at a time when the UN and its member states were concluding that something had to be done in other similarly violent contexts" (2008, p. 646). State building is increasingly becoming a way to fit "rogue states" into the international community (2008, p. 649). As Ayub and Kouvo maintain, "peace does not hold without justice, and…legitimate political leadership and functioning government institutions cannot be established without promoting accountability and the rule of law" (Ayub & Kouvo, 2008, p. 656) Afghans are dependent on humanitarian assistance in order to return to their homes and survive. International organizations have created a number of mechanisms to enhance the standard of living for Afghans, such as the Afghan Reconstruction Trust Fund (ARTF), administered by the World Bank, which provides support for the development of basic infrastructure (Rubin, 2006, p. 183). State building consists of interdependent mobilization of three types of resources: coercion (security institutions); capital (economic institutions); and, legitimacy (citizen acceptance, enabling the state to exercise power). State-building depends on the development of a legal economy, and the capacity to mobilise, allocate and spend resources, which is important to the success of peace building. Strengthening fiscal capacity ensures funding, enhances security, and enables the state to provide basic services, furthering state legitimacy in the eyes of Afghans (Rubin, 2006, p. 178; Goodhand & Sedra, 2010, pp. S80-S81).

Canada's Integration with the U.S. Army

Since the early 1950s, Canada-U.S. defence integration has steadily increased. Canadian Generals Mackenzie and Dallaire experienced the failures of UN peacekeeping in extreme conflict zones and the Canadian government also began to think about traditional peacekeeping as outdated (Coulon & Liégeois, 2010, p. 41). Prime Minister Chrétien sketched the "multi-purpose, combat capable armed forces" which would commit around 4,000 personnel, however due to financial difficulty and defence budget cuts this project was never realised (Jockel & Sokolsky, 2008, p. 103). The Canadian forces (CF) often see their interest to be the same as those of their American counterparts. In addition, 60 percent of Canada's armed exports are to the U.S. Defence dollars are spent on the development of weapons designed purposely to be integrated with the American weapons system (Warnock, 2008, p. 75). The war in Afghanistan has sped up the transformation of the Canadian military which was first pressed by Chief of Defence staff General Rick Hillier to include "more personnel and equipment, improved infrastructure and changes to training and the command structure" (Jockel & Sokolsky, 2008, p. 108).

Conducting military operations with the Americans became more politically acceptable after 9/11. Unlike the war in Iraq, Canada was able to support war in Afghanistan because it was recognized internationally as legitimate and by associating counterinsurgency with Canadian ideals of democracy and development, and with important values such as freedom, justice, and human rights (Rubin, 2006, p. 184; Charbonneau & Cox, 2008, p. 319). Moreover Canadian engagement as part of NATO ensures U.S. participation and deploys considerable military power to deal with international crisis, unfortunately much more so than the UN. The majority of our troops in Afghanistan are clearly fighting "terrorists" in peace enforcement missions or wars, which is not peacekeeping, a subject that has caused confusion among the Canadian electorate (Coulon & Liégeois, 2010, p. 42, 44).

The 3D Approach and the Responsibility to Protect

The 3D approach, which stands for defence, diplomacy, and development finds its roots in Axworthian international security operations in "failed states" and is also known as "three-block war" and a "whole-of-government approach".. Since the end of the Cold War the Canadian military has been playing a variety of roles on the battlefield. The war in Afghanistan is Canada's first time deploying this approach, meaning the Canadian military has to be prepared to perform humanitarian relief, stabilization and combat almost simultaneously (Jockel & Sokolsky, 2008, p. 107; Charbonneau & Cox, 2008, p. 319; Coulon & Liégeois, 2010, p. 43). The newly adopted Canadian military doctrine of three-block war is based on an originally developed by General Charles Krulak of the U.S. Marines: "It holds that the military must be prepared for a spectrum of challenges and may be called upon in a given conflict, sometimes simultaneously, to fight, to peacekeep and to provide humanitarian relief. The Canadian version of the three-block approach has its roots largely in the international security operations in failed states, in which the Canadian military was involved between the end of the Cold War and the start of the War on Terror; during these conflicts Canadian troops often were called upon to play a variety of roles." (Jockel & Sokolsky, 2008, p. 107)

Figure 10.1: Building Security Relations

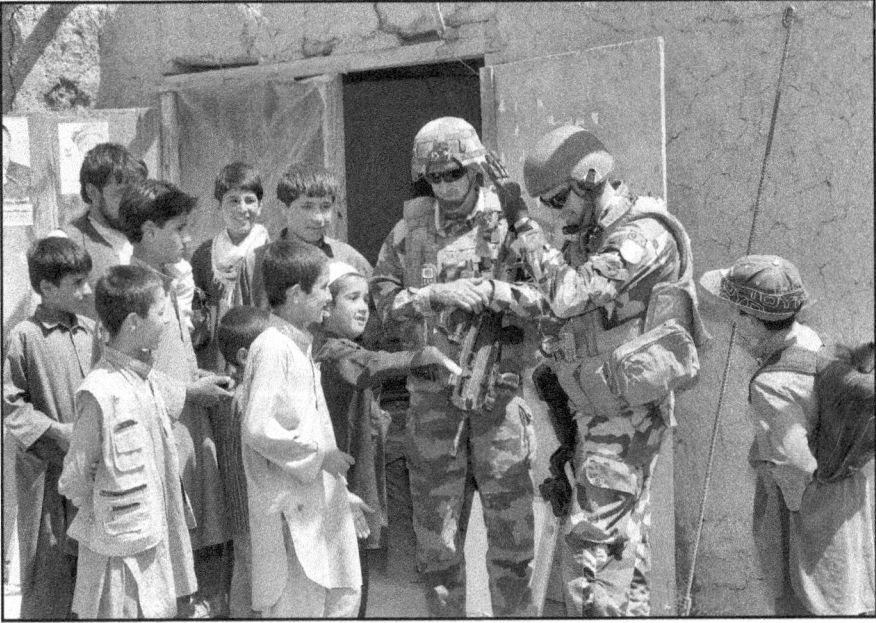

Logar, Afghanistan—A photo op for the "humanitarian" side of counterinsurgency. Members of the Afghan National Army (ANA) and French Operational Mentoring and Liaison Team (OMLT) conduct a security patrol, "to build relations with Afghan civilians and ensure security in the region". The French OMLT are mentors to the ANA, training them in engineering, artillery and medical practices. Official photo by Lance Corporal Ita Joosten, ISAF HQ Public Affairs.

The war on terror created confusion, legal constraints, and political justification for humanitarian interventions. The International Commission on Intervention and State Sovereignty (ICISS) was created in 2000 by the Canadian government and backed by UN secretary general Kofi Annan. The ICISS came up with the doctrine of "Responsibility to Protect" (R2P). R2P includes responsibility to prevent, react, rebuild, and employs a "just war" framework. There are operational principles guiding the decision of a humanitarian intervention. For example all non-military options should be explored before military force is used; the scale, duration, intensity of the intervention should be stated; and, the operation should have a reasonable chance of success (MacFarlane, Thielking & Weiss, 2004, pp. 978-979).

The ICISS argues that sovereignty is a conditional right that depends on respect for a minimum standard of human rights, and the protection of citizens. If states are unable or unwilling to protect their citizens then the responsibility would fall on the international community. Critics argue that the criteria have the potential to facilitate intervention rather than make it more accountable as is the case in Afghanistan. For example in 2007, "the strategic council advised the

Harper government to present the military intervention in Afghanistan in a manner that placed it within the Canadian peacekeeping tradition. It suggested avoiding 'negative' expressions and using more positive words such as 'peace-keeping', 'reconstruction', 'stability', and helping 'women and children'" (Coulon & Liégeois, 2010, p. 46) as positive public opinion is important for gathering the political will needed to intervene in the affairs of another sovereign state (MacFarlane et al., 2004, p. 988).

Canada's Role in the War on Terror

Canada has six objectives set for a five-year period in Afghanistan: to maintain a secure environment and establish law and order; provide jobs, education and basic needs; enhance the management of security of the Afghan-Pakistan border; help build democratic institutions in Kandahar; contribute to Afghan-led political reconsolidations; and, fostering a sustainable peace (Foreign Affairs and International Trade Canada, 2010). The CF have been waiting for a mission like Afghanistan to demonstrate that Canada can conduct combat operations (Coulon & Liégeois, 2010, p. 43, 50).

A month after 9/11, Canadian Naval Task Group 307.1 set sail for the Arabian Sea constituting the naval component of operation Apollo Canada's initial contribution to the war on terror. In November of 2001 the task group was charged with protecting of the entire U.S. Amphibious Ready Group, this included placing American ship under Canadian command. The Task group was relived two months later after the Americans succeeded at establishing bases in Afghanistan (Charbonneau & Cox, 2008, p. 311, 312). The U.S. military appreciates the participation of the Canadian Navy in the war on terror: "the technological and operational flexibility of Canadian warships is something that the American navy does not have" (Charbonneau & Cox, 2008, p. 313). Canada entered Kabul in 2003 in order to provide assistance, security, and stabilization to the transitional Karzai government, under the International Security Assistance Force (ISAF). The majority of funds for security sector reform, including building an uncorrupted Afghan national Army and police force, came from the international community rather than the national government (Warnock, 2008, p. 7; Rubin, 2006, p. 179).

When the international community decided to back the U.S. and intervene, it was on the basis of a military intervention, rather than any projected humanitarianism (Ayub & Kouvo, 2008, p. 646). The CF were repositioned to the southern province of Kandahar under Operation Enduring Freedom (OEF), an American led counterinsurgency mission. In 2006 Canada fell once again under ISAF authority and is the third largest contributor of forces to Afghanistan under ISAF (Jockel & Sokolsky, 2008, p. 102). Since establishing bases in Afghanistan, Canada's military spending has hit $17.5 billion in 2008, and is expected to reach 2 percent of annual GDP in 2011 representing $12 billion in increases over 20 years. Much to the approval of Canadian citizens, Canada's combat role in Kandahar is slowly decreasing due to a parliamentary motion dictating Canada's withdrawal from Afghanistan in 2011. The CF will focus more on reconstruction to help erode the Taliban's sway over the Afghan people (Munroe, 2009; Mulero, 2008).

Nation-Building and Peace-Building: A Facade for Military Intervention

Globalization has connected matters of national security in Canada with the "stabilization" of "failed states" abroad. One core task of security provisions is peace-building, which is becoming the new approach to human security. Officially the records state that the intervention in Afghanistan is based on self-defence, and counterterrorism. In this context humanitarian intervention is not concerned with human rights abuses but with nation-building, the process of preventing an area from becoming a security threat, in short serving the interests of the West (Ignatieff, 2003a, p. 306; Ayub & Kouvo, 2008, p. 641, 647). Nation-building is not about the interest of Afghans as it should be: it is an exit strategy. Rebuilding institutions serves the interest of the international community. Nation-building works when locals are convinced to take a non-violent approach to their future (Ignatieff, 2003b, p. 22, 106; Windsor, Charters & Wilson, 2008, p. 22, 25; Rubin, 2006, p. 179, 183). The Americans, followed by the Canadians, are in Afghanistan to do counterinsurgency; nation-building serves as a counterinsurgency strategy. Humanitarian intervention therefore is an excuse to legitimize military interventions to ensure Afghanistan can no longer be a source of insecurity to the West. Afghans are concerned about getting by on a daily basis they experience high inflation, fear of the police and do not trust their government. They need basic services. According to Rory Stewart, if we're lucky in 20-30 years Afghanistan will maybe look like Pakistan (2009, ¶ 73).

Conquering Hearts and Minds through the Militarization of Aid

Winning hearts and minds is "based on the assumption that reconstruction can, under the shadow of force protection, stabilise communities and build networks of support through partnerships with local elites, communities, and NGOs" (Goodhand & Sedra, 2010, p. S93) this strategy is known as "soft power" and is supposed to lessen Afghans vulnerability to Taliban interest, and more generally keep the Taliban away from Afghan citizens. The main task of all Canadian units is framework patrolling including meeting community leaders, mayors, and village heads, providing security, developing structural awareness, intelligence gathering, community relations, and tactical diplomacy—in short winning the hearts and minds of the local populations. This is believed to cause a sort of butterfly effect where intervention and influence at local levels of governance can influence and affect political decisions at the national level of government (Windsor & Charters & Wilson, 2008, p. 24).

Since 2004 U.S. aid accounted for more than half of donor assistance to the Afghanistan government budget. In order to maintain current costs and provide core services, the Afghan state will continue to depend on foreign aid. Revenues are slowly increasing although they are still extremely low accounting for eight percent of GDP. Aid donors have the responsibility of minimizing effects associated with aid dependency, so that eventually Afghanistan can stand on its own. Unfortunately donors are increasingly shifting resources to projects perceived as capable of winning hearts and minds (Goodhand, 2002, p. 853).

Figure 10.2: Winning Hearts and Minds with Military-Disbursed Foreign Aid

Bareek-Aub, outside Kabul: Members of the headquarters of NATO's International Security Assistance Force (ISAF) hand out donations to a SOZO International Village. According to ISAF Media: "SOZO is a U.S. organization that helps people in need throughout Afghanistan. Because of their good work these Afghans have a home and are provided with schooling and medical care. Photo by Ita Joosten, ISAF HQ Public Affairs.

Winning hearts and minds can be understood as part of international intervention, and it can foster high expectations from the local population, to the point where failure to deliver is a source of frustration among Afghans. The international presence in Kabul has created negative economic and social impacts. For example inflation has increased the cost of housing and living, causing humanitarian projects to be viewed with resentment, as when the resulting negativity manifested itself through the 2006 riots in Kabul that targeted aid agencies (Goodhand & Sedra, 2010, p. S94). When Afghans lead development projects they are more effective than those led by foreigners. Winning hearts and minds is only furthering the militarization of aid, making the job of real aid workers extremely difficult (Munroe, 2009, ¶ 25). Paul O'Brien, of Oxfam America, who formerly worked for the Afghan Ministry of Finance from 2002 to 2007, stated: "When we worked through local systems, I saw effective development happening all over the country. Whereas if we go in with soldiers and build schools, those schools are a political statement, a flag from the international community. [With the addition of more soldiers] the risk is that you're going to see increased militarization of development. Our fear is that decisions are going to be made, not based on whether it's the best development outcome for Afghans, but whether it's the best short-term political outcome for the security effort" (Munroe, 2009, ¶ 28, 29).

Canada and Its Future Role in Afghanistan: Concluding Thoughts and Comments

Public opinion in Canada is widely supportive of a peacekeeping role. There was never any indication that the public was willing to support a counterinsurgency war. Should Canadian causalities increase, public support for the war will continue to decrease (Jockel & Sokolsky, 2008, p. 111). The daily violence imposed on Afghans is rarely mentioned by our political leaders and ignored in our mass media. More than 5,500 people, the majority being Afghan military personnel, have been killed in war-related violence in 2008 (Mulero, 2008, ¶ 19). The CF have been in Afghanistan for eight years; it is time to think about other available options because in five to six years everyone will be fed up and eventually there will be no money, resources, troops, or the will to continue in Afghanistan. With proper Afghan leadership it is possible to stabilize the state. "Fixing failed states" will never guarantee national security; rebuilding institutions will not necessarily end terrorism (Zakaria, 2010; Sherr, 2009; Ignatieff, 2003b, p. 91).

Under the terms of the House of Commons withdrawal is to begin June 2011, and should be completed by the end of that year. Canada will focus on a diplomatic, development, and aid role, a few military members will stay behind as advisors and work with the Karzai government on issues from law to reconstruction. The U.S. wants Canada to stay in Afghanistan past 2011, secretary of state Hillary Clinton asked Canada not to withdraw. Canada has asked coalition countries if they would provide security for civilian workers in south Afghanistan, this could end up making the country a burden to its partners. Obama has sent 30,000 more troops, and NATO plans to have 7,000 more by August of 2010 (Munroe, 2009; CTV, 2009; Woods, 2010).

Projects started by Canada such as the Dahla dam will be completed by June 2011 (Fisher, 2010). Scott Gilmore founder and director of Peace Divided Trust Fund states the Department of Foreign Affairs spends a lot of money, time and energy training civilians to be safe "they now give them hostile environment training, they've got the body armour, and they've got the experience and the protection" (Payton, 2010). Contrary to popular opinion, aid groups do not rely on the CF, they do their own security assessment, make their own security plans and are not concerned with the military pull out, but claim to in fact are ready for it (Payton, 2010).

In 2011 Canada will pull out of Afghanistan much to the delight of the Canadian public. Personally I am not completely against a stronger military. If properly trained to respond to humanitarian needs, I believe our military can do a lot of good on a global scale. However unfortunately it looks as though our military is going the other way. Our military is becoming Americanized as they integrate with their American counterparts, and participate in operations which include counterinsurgency. The Canadian military is forgetting the importance of keeping peace, and they are using aid to advance their goals. Personally I do not believe that counterinsurgency will in the end be effective. The international community needs to step back and let Afghans take the lead, and decide for themselves how they want to live and what kind of government they want.

References

Ayub, F., & Kouvo, S. (2008). Righting the course? Humanitarian intervention, the War on Terror, and the Future of Afghanistan. *International Affairs*, 84(4), 641-657.

Charbonneau, B., & Cox W. S. (2008). Global Order, U.S. Hegemony and Military Integration: The Canadian-American Defense Relationship. *International Political Sociology*, 2(4), 305-321.

CTV. (2009). U.S. Wants Canada to Stay in Afghanistan Past 2011. *CTV News*, March 29. http://www.ctv.ca/servlet/ArticleNews/story/CTVNews/20100329/afghanistan_canada_100329/20100329?hub=SEAfghanistan

Coulon, J., & Liégeois, M. (2010). Whatever Happened to Pecaekeeping? The Future of a Tradition. Calgary, AB: Canadian Defence and Affairs Foreign Institute. http://www.cdfai.org/PDF/Whatever%20Happened%20to%20Peacekeeping%20The%20Future%20of%20a%20Tradition%20-%20English.pdf

Fisher, M. (2010). Troops Won't Protect Workers in Afghanistan Past 2011. *Canwest News Service*, February 24. http://www.canada.com/news/Troops+protect+workers+Afghanistan+past+2011+General/2607943/story.html

Foreign Affairs and International Trade Canada. (2010). Canada in Afghanistan. http://www.dfait-maeci.gc.ca/nato-otan/afghanistan.aspx?menu_id=44&menu=R

Goodhand, J. (2002). Aiding Violence or Building Peace? The Role of International Aid in Afghanistan. *Third World Quarterly*, 23(5), 837-859.

Goodhand, J., & Sedra, M. (2010). Who Owns the Peace? Aid, Reconstruction, and Peacebuilding in Afghanistan. *Disasters*, 34(S1), S78-S102.

Ignatieff, M. (2003a). State Failure and Nation-Building. In J. L. Holzgrefe & R. O. Keohane (Eds.), *Humanitarian Intervention Ethical, Legal, and Political Dilemmas* (pp. 299-322). Cambridge, UK: Cambridge University Press.

—————. (2003b). *Empire Lite: Nation-Building in Bosnia, Kosovo, and Afghanistan*. London, UK: Vintage Books.

Jockel, T. J., & Sokolsky, J. J. (2008). Canada and the War in Afghanistan: NATO's Odd Man Out Steps Forward. *Journal of Transatlantic Studies*, 6(1), 100-115.

Kowaluk, L., & Staples, S. (2009). *Afghanistan and Canada: Is there an Alternative to War?* Montreal: Black Rose Books.

MacFarlane, N. S.; Thielking, J. C., & Weiss G. T. (2004). The Responsibility to Protect: Is Anyone Interested in Humanitarian Intervention? *Third World Quarterly*, 25(5), 977-992

Mulero E. (2008). Canada Steps Up In Afghanistan. *National Journal*, December 6, 30.

Munroe, I. (2009). What's the Real Plan for Canada's 2011 Exit Strategy? *CTV News*, December 25. http://www.ctv.ca/servlet/ArticleNews/story/CTVNews/20091223/afghanistan_2011_09 1225/20091225?hub=TopStoriesV2

Payton, I. (2010). Civilians in Afghanistan Prepare for Military Pull-out. *Embassy*, January 13. http://www.embassymag.ca/page/view/civilians-01-13-2010

Rubin, B. R. (2006). Peace Building and State-Building in Afghanistan: Constructing Sovereignty for Whose Security? *Third World Quarterly*, 27(1), 175-185.

Sherr, L. (PBS). (2009). Interview with Rory Stewart. *Bill Moyers Journal*, September 25. http://www.pbs.org/moyers/journal/09252009/transcript1.html

Warnock, J. (2008). *Creating a Failed State: The U.S. and Canada in Afghanistan*. Winnipeg: Fernwood Publishing.

Windsor, L.; Charters, D., & Wilson, B. (2008). *Kandahar Tour: The Turning Point in Canada's Afghan Mission*. Mississauga: Wiley Canada.

Woods, A. (2010). Full Afghan Withdrawal "Wrong," Top Tory Says. *The Star*, March 30. http://www.thestar.com/news/canada/afghanmission/article/787578--full-afghan-withdrawal-wrong-top-tory-says

Zakaria, F. (2009). Afghanistan: CNN's Fareed Zakaria. http://www.youtube.com/watch?v=VtQRclOyIM8

CHAPTER ELEVEN

The True Mission in Haiti

Katelyn Spidle

The more than 3,000 nongovernmental organizations currently operating in Haiti are being described as "a republic of NGOs," (United States Institute of Peace, 2009); "a Mafia," and "an arm of imperialism" (Engler, 2009, ¶ 6, 9). The devastation in Haiti due to the 7.0 magnitude earthquake which struck Port-au-Prince on January 12, 2010, is ongoing and seemingly unmanageable. This is leading global spectators to question why, with the immense presence and budget that these NGOs have, the infrastructure and social welfare of the country is not improving. As Yves Engler, Canadian foreign policy critic, noted, "most progressive minded Canadians see NGOs as part of the solution to global poverty yet where these groups are 'helping' out the situation is quite different," (Engler, 2009, ¶ 9). The popular assumption is that the goals and intentions of NGOs are selfless and humanitarian. There is increasing concern, however, that NGOs are the new face of imperialism in the country. As the world becomes more globalized and, consequently, more interconnected, so too, it seems, do our social institutions. What we are seeing is the spreading of military activity into territories whose borders it traditionally would not cross. This phenomenon is being described as the militarization of aid.

Military collaboration with NGOs in countries devastated by war or natural disaster has become something of the norm, and there is much skepticism about whether the two ought to collaborate or remain separate entities. This chapter will demonstrate how the presence of NGOs mirrors the presence of the U.S. military in Haiti, because both are backed by the same entity: the U.S. government. The pervasive presence of both NGOs and the U.S. military in Haiti is part of a strategy to keep the U.S. in its leading global economic position. By preventing Haiti's independent development, the U.S. may continue to profit from its cheap labour and dependence on U.S. food imports. The earthquake hit Haiti particularly hard, and to truly understand why this is so we must first acknowledge how the U.S. government has strategically hindered Haiti's development in the past decades. We must then consider how both NGOs and the military are used as an instrument of imperialism by the U.S. government. Having taken this all into consideration, we may be able to predict if, in light of the recent natural disaster, the presence of NGOs and the U.S. military is intended to ensure that the U.S. will maintain its stronghold on the country's government. If so, this will mean that the true mission in Haiti is to ensure that the U.S. may continue to profit from the weak and vulnerable position in which the country has been placed in the international community. In conclusion, I offer some possible alternatives to this seemingly inevitable scenario.

Figure 11.1: Map of Haiti

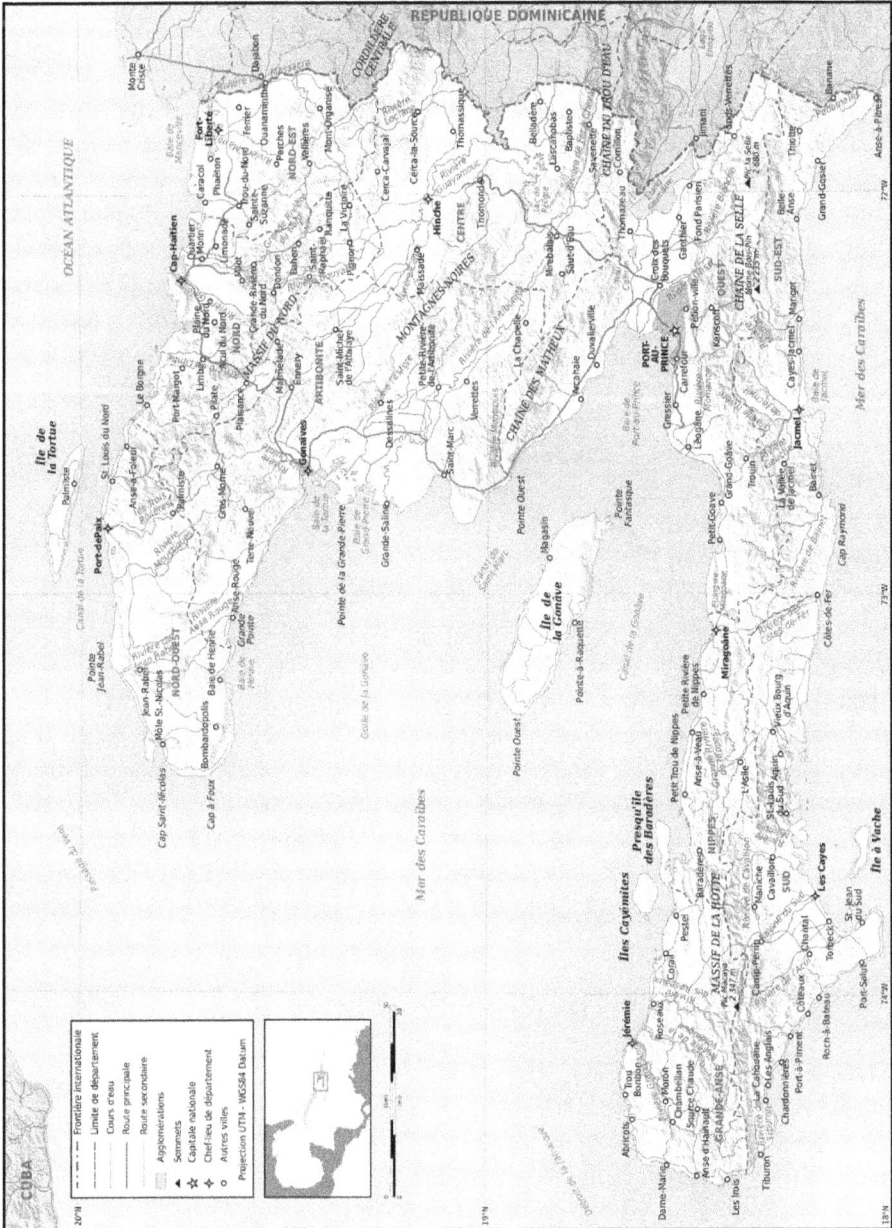

Source: produced by Rémi Kaupp for Wikimedia Commons.

An Inevitable Tragedy?

Since 1915, Haiti has experienced an on-again/off-again relationship with the U.S. from which the people of Haiti have only suffered. In the past century, the U.S. has exerted its control over Haiti both economically and militarily. It has invaded and occupied the country three times; first, from 1915 to 1934; second, from 1994 to 1995 for Operation Uphold Democracy; and, third, following this year's earthquake, in 2010. Between the years 1957 and 1986, the U.S. funded the regimes of Papa Doc and Baby Doc Duvalier (Cockburn, 2010) dictators who violated human rights by killing thousands of Haitians for political reasons, and opened the Haitian market up to U.S. capital—destroying peasant agriculture and forcing mass migration to Port-au-Prince (Smith, 2010).

With the resulting urbanization, caused by the undermining of peasant agriculture, conditions in Port-au-Prince were created for the tragedy this year. As Mark Schuller points out, "Port-au-Prince grew up from 500,000 people (only built for 250,000) in 1980 to an estimated 2.5 million in 2005" (Schuller, 2010, ¶ 9). The city was built with poor infrastructure, and most people took low paying jobs in sweatshops, perpetuating both poverty and dependence on foreign aid. Living in the city also created a situation where people, rather than growing their own food, became reliant on imported rice from the U.S. As well, a U.S. backed UN peacekeeping force was installed in 2004 following the removal of President Aristide. As we can see, the U.S. has assumed and maintained a strong presence in Haiti. This presence has perpetuated and worsened the weak economic and social conditions in the country, and has directly affected the Haitian government's inability to independently and efficiently manage the country post-earthquake.

The Republic of NGOs

Haiti has had a long history of external debt and investment, and this has resulted in the country relying heavily on foreign aid—in the form of food, medical supplies, and jobs. NGOs receive and control copious amounts of dollars worth of foreign aid money from both private sector foreign direct investment (FDI) and public sector "overseas development assistance" (ODA) (Schuller, 2010, ¶ 3, 4), and consequently maintain a very influential position within the country. As Yves Engler noted, "by one estimate, Haiti has the most development NGOs of any country per capita and the vast majority of the country's social services are run by domestic or foreign NGOs" (Engler, 2009, ¶ 6). This has undermined the government's ability to exert adequate control over the influx and distribution of aid money and donations to the population. What this means is that the U.S. is also presently occupying Haiti indirectly, by funding the U.S. run NGOs which operate there such as CARE, the Red Cross, and OXFAM America. In an episode of Riz Khan entitled "Rethinking Humanitarian Aid," aired by Al Jazeera, it was said that, "in Haiti the NGOs have been running the country for the past decades" (Khan, 2010). It is accurate to state that Haiti is completely dependent on NGOs in order for the country to function, and it is no accident that this is the case.

Haiti is not alone in its dependency on NGOs. In fact, "Many of the world's trouble spots are heavily dependent on the work of NGOs, and critics often say that there is a disconnect between their intentions and their actions" (Khan, 2010). This dependency is created and perpetuated by the NGOs themselves. Therefore, "they often create dependency, and allow governments to get away with misguided policies instead of enacting serious reform" (Khan, 2010). NGOs, rather than acting as a crutch in times of need, integrate themselves into the actual social and political fiber of the country as a permanent actor. Consequently, "NGOs fill a gap that governments cannot or will not do themselves" (Khan, 2010). Although they do act to fill the gap left by weak and corrupt governments, the work they do resembles more a weak patch job than a long term solution. In other words, "they only do half a job" (Khan, 2010). Many critics claim that NGOs are as corrupt as the governments they are trying to improve. "It is not only a corrupt government—you can also speak of corruption among the NGOs," said Linda Polman, author of *War Games: Aid and War in Modern Times*. She continued: "the NGOs and their international donors have kept the government in a very weak position by bypassing the government for decades and not doing anything about building the government and strengthening the government" (Khan, 2010). The harsh reality is that the determining factor in much of the activities of NGOs comes down to one thing: money. NGOs, rather than working with the population to develop long term solutions which they themselves control, make the population dependent on their services to keep receiving more government grants (Khan, 2010). Since NGOs operate as autonomous organizations, there is little oversight for how the aid money and donations are distributed. The CEO of the Red Cross, for example, has an annual salary of $7,000,000 U.S. (Sekou, 2010). NGOs engage in fierce competition with one another to receive aid money and donations, a large sum of which of which does not even reach the people (Khan, 2010). One reason for this is because NGOs must negotiate with local authorities to operate in certain areas. In Somalia, for example, up to 80 per cent of aid disappears into the pockets of war lords, as a sort of entrance tax (Khan, 2010). In this sense, NGOs are feeding the corruption.

NGOs must serve the interests of their international donors before they serve the interests of the people in need because they are dependent on external funding. Thus, rather than cooperating in pursuit of a higher purpose, NGOs function as separate agents. This leaves individual NGOs extremely vulnerable to manipulation, and results in less aid reaching the people who need it (Khan, 2010). Many American NGOs operating in Haiti serve the interests of the U.S. government, because it is the U.S. government that funds or otherwise supports their activities. The U.S. government supports these NGOs for one purpose: to keep Haiti in the weak and vulnerable economic position that it has been in since independence. NGOs which distribute food aid make the population dependent on U.S. rice, for example. In this regard, the NGOs operating in Haiti are simply an instrument of capitalism, turning in more profits for the U.S. by depriving the Haitian people of any autonomous control over their basic services, jobs, and agriculture.

Figure 11.2: Military Support, Adventist Development, and Rice

Local Haitians working with Adventist Development Relief Agency unload bags of humanitarian aid rations during a humanitarian aid distribution in Carrefour, Haiti, 12 February 2010. Marines of Battalion Landing Team, 3rd Battalion, 2nd Marine Regiment, 22nd Marine Expeditionary Unit, provided security for a local non-government organization as they supplied local Haitians with 50 pound bags of rice. (Photo: U.S. Marine Corps.)

The Militarization of Aid

Figure 11.3: U.S. Global Response Force Deploying to Haiti

Paratroopers of Bravo Troop, 1-73 Cav, 2nd Brigade Combat team, 82nd Airborne Division board onto a C-130 Hercules aircraft at Pope Air Force Base early Thursday morning 14 January 2010 to deploy in support of the earthquake that occurred in the capital of Port-au-Prince, Haiti. The 2nd BCT is the 82nd Airborne Division's Global Response Force that has been training for real world emergency response missions. These are the first group of paratroopers going to Haiti to provide Humanitarian Aid. (Photo: U.S. Army.)

Within days of the earthquake, U.S. president Obama announced the deployment of more than 10,000 troops to aid in the relief effort in Haiti (Chossudovsky, 2010, ¶ 10). The U.S. military then took control of the airport in Port-au-Prince on 13 January 2010. This meant that the U.S. military dictated who landed in the capital and when. In other words, the U.S. military took direct control of the influx and distribution of the millions of international donations in money, food, shelter, and medical supplies. This immediately undermined the Haitian government's ability to react to the disaster. The Pentagon appointed itself to the leading role in the relief effort—not by the Haitian government, but by that of the U.S. (Chossudovsky, 2010). Ironically, however, as well equipped as the U.S. military is, it has proved incompetent in meeting the immediate needs of the Haitian people. What the world has seen is a relief effort that has been highly disorganized and inefficient. With over 200,000 people dead and 1.5 million people displaced (Khan, 2010), the relief effort was, and still is, immense. In spite of this, the military initially decided to give landing preference to planes containing troops and weapons, rather than aid (Pate,

2010). Planes containing food, medical supplies, and tents, rather, were being redirected to the Dominican Republic—significantly delaying the influx and distribution of these much needed supplies (Villamizar, 2010). This is not the extent of the problem, however. Once on the ground, aid distribution is a slow, complicated process, with the military directing aid vehicles containing aid to various checkpoints determined by security zones around set up Port-au-Prince (Villamizar, 2010). It took weeks for basic aid to reach more remote villages in Haiti, and thousands of people are still waiting for temporary shelter (Villamizar, 2010). The U.S. military, rather than helping to make the distribution of aid more efficient, has instead encroached upon the activities of NGOs, and stripped away civilian control over any decision making processes.

Figure 11.4: Implied Threats of Mob Violence to Justify Heavy Militarization of Aid Distribution

In the original caption, the U.S. Marine Corps described an innocuous gathering of Haitians, some of whom we see here standing and smiling, as a "mob-like crowd" that "surges," implying a threat of violence and chaos. People scavenging for supplies to ensure their survival under desperate conditions were described in some U.S. mainstream media commentaries as "looters," a suggestion with which even CNN's correspondents took issue.

Original caption: A Sri Lanka soldier attached to the United Nations forces in Haiti watches as a mob-like crowd surges to the check point where Haitians presented a food voucher to receive rations at a distribution point in Carrefour, Haiti. 24th Marine Expeditionary Unit Marines, with a handful of UN soldiers, kept the distribution process orderly and free of disruption. (Photo: U.S. Marine Corps.)

Countless media reports have shown how Haitians and the international community alike are concerned with such a large military presence in the country. For example, "The militarization of relief operations will weaken the organizational capabilities of Haitians to rebuild and reinstate the institutions of civilian government which have been destroyed. It will also encroach upon the efforts of the international medical teams and civilian relief organizations" (Chossudovsky, 2010, ¶ 45). The militarization of aid further dislocates the Haitian people from any decision making process, and consequently increases their dependency on foreign aid. Furthermore, a military presence sends the wrong message to civilians, who will see it more as an occupation than as help. Chossudovsky warns that "the entry of ten thousand heavily armed US troops, coupled with the activities of local militia could potentially precipitate the country into social chaos" (Chossudovsky, 2010, ¶ 39). We have seen this happen before, when humanitarian aid workers started to become the targets of attacks after the military began involving itself in humanitarian aid efforts in Afghanistan. The result of the militarization of aid in Haiti, many fear, will be what is known as disaster capitalism. The U.S. has been indirectly occupying Haiti in recent years by funding NGOs, and now the earthquake has given it a reason to directly occupy the country—under the guise of humanitarian assistance.

Figure 11.5: Missionaries to Marines

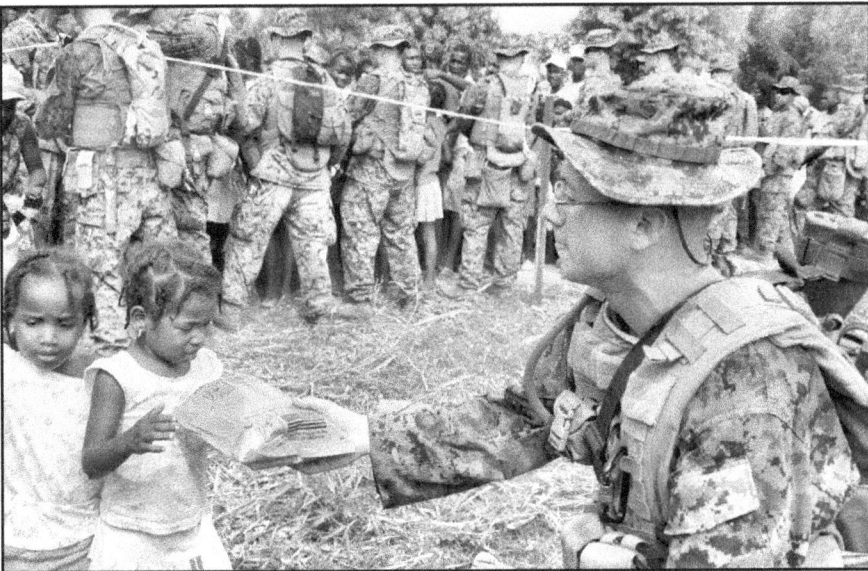

Original caption: A Marine with Battalion Landing Team, 3rd Battalion, 2nd Marine regiment hands humanitarian ration at an aid distribution site near a landing zone in Leogane, Haiti, 26 January 2010. Marines flew into the area on 24 January establishing a new humanitarian aid receiving area for Haitian earthquake victims at a missionary compound. (Official Marine Corps photo by Cpl. Bobbie A. Curtis.)

Conclusions

Haiti's development has been stunted by precisely the powers, both foreign and domestic, which have been entrusted with the major decision making processes. Unfortunately, the severity of the devastation to infrastructure and social integrity caused by the earthquake was the inevitable result of a long history of U.S. occupation whose intention it has been to profit from Haitians' cheap labour and dependence on U.S. imports of rice. The U.S. has, in past decades, maintained its stronghold over Haiti by either indirectly occupying the country through its funding of NGOs, or directly occupying the country through military invasion. The NGOs operating in Haiti do not improve the social, political or economic situation in the country; rather, they create and perpetuate a dependency on foreign aid for its basic services, jobs, and food. In light of the earthquake, military intervention, justified as humanitarianism, has only strengthened that dependency: first, by hindering the activities of NGOs and thus rendering them less effective, and second, by undermining the Haitian government's ability to react or respond to the disaster. The U.S. government has essentially overthrown the Haitian government by installing a military force in the country which has assumed nearly all of its government functions; it dictates the activities of NGOs, controls the airport and ports, and patrols to maintain stability and order. The U.S. government uses NGOs and the military as arms of imperialism in Haiti. Through these two parties it acts in its own economic interests, which aim to keep Haiti in the weak and vulnerable position it holds in the international community. Human rights have, until now, been the justification for U.S. backed NGO and military occupations in the country— but clearly the U.S occupation of Haiti has nothing to do with human rights.

At the time of this writing, it has been nearly four months since the earthquake, and the focus is now shifting from immediate relief to plans for the long term rebuilding of Haiti. Considering Haiti's past, it can be predicted with some clarity that the rebuilding process will be carried out by the U.S. military and U.S. funded NGOs, and private contractors. This means, essentially, that Haiti will be rebuilt to serve the economic interests of the U.S. So long as the Haitian population is kept dependent on foreign aid and leadership, it will exert no control over its own destiny. Three important factors must be considered in the rebuilding of Haiti if it will, in fact, be done in the interests of the Haitian people: better infrastructure, investment in local business, and redevelopment of rural agriculture. Time will only tell, however, whether these are the main concerns and intentions of the U.S. government. Realistically, however, the U.S. does not engage itself in projects from which it does not benefit financially. In this sense, the U.S. would benefit more by exploiting Haiti's vulnerable post-earthquake state, and strengthening its dependency on foreign aid and governance. This would mean three things: prolonging the presence of NGOs to maintain Haiti's dependence on U.S. imports of rice; rebuilding the city of Port-au-Prince with the intention of keeping a high concentration of people living in the city; and, welcoming in foreign investors to create large amounts of low paying sweatshop jobs for the people of Port-au-Prince.

This does not have to be the result, however. Haitians make their voices heard by means of protests, which happen frequently and often make the news, but this does not guarantee that anyone who ought to is listening. This is because it is not the Haitians who are presently in control of the decision making processes in their own country. It is up to the West, right now, to ensure that the rebuilding of Haiti is done in the interests of Haitians, and not in the economic interests of the U.S. government. With the public eye meticulously focused on Haiti, there is arguably a good chance that this may be possible. Finally, the process of handing over power to the Haitian government must start from the level of U.S. foreign policy which directly affects Haiti. If the West wants to ensure that Haiti does begin to develop and prosper, we ought to exercise our democratic rights by making our voices heard—be it out loud through protests, or written down in articles such as this.

References

Chossudovsky, M. (2010). The Militarization of Emergency Aid to Haiti: Is it a Humanitarian Operation or an Invasion? *Global Research*, January 15.
http://www.globalresearch.ca/index.php?context=va&aid=17000

Cockburn, P. (2010). Crushing Haiti, Now as Always: When Haitian Ministers Take a 50 Percent Cut of Aide Money It's Called "Corruption," When NGOs Skim 50 Percent It's Called "Overhead". *CounterPunch*, January 15-17.
http://www.counterpunch.org/patrick01152010.html

Engler, Y. (2009). Haiti. *Z Space*, February 28. http://www.zcommunications.org/haiti-by-yves-engler

Khan, R. (2010). Rethinking Humanitarian Aid. *The Riz Khan Show: Al Jazeera English*, March 31.
http://english.aljazeera.net/programmes/rizkhan/2010/03/201033164114623624.html

Pate, S. (2010). Disaster Imperialism in Haiti. *Monthly Review Magazine*, January 17.
http://mrzine.monthlyreview.org/2010/pate170110.html

Schuller, M. (2010). Clearing the Rubble, Including the Old Plan for Haiti. *Huffington Post*, March 8.

Sekou, O. (2010). NGOs Not Helping in Haiti. *GritTV with Laura Flanders*, March 10.
http://www.youtube.com/watch?v=5D2SnjPIrrk

Smith, A. (2010). Catastrophe in Haiti. *Socialist Worker*. January 10.
http://socialistworker.org/2010/01/14/catastrophe-in-haiti

United States Institute of Peace. (2010). Haiti: A Republic of NGOs?
http://www.usip.org/events/haiti-republic-ngos

Villamizar, M. (2010). Logistical Delays Plague Haiti Aid. *Al Jazeera*, January 29.

http://english.aljazeera.net/news/americas/2010/01/2010129482740401.html

CHAPTER TWELVE

Soft Power in the Information Age: Whose Story Wins

Zoe Dominiak

"Promoting democracy, human rights and development of civil society are not best handled with the barrel of a gun. It is true that the American military has an impressive operational capacity, but the practice of turning to the Pentagon because it can get things done leads to an image of an over-militarized foreign policy."—Joseph S. Nye, Jr. (2007, ¶ 3)

Still the world's military monolith, America's imperial immunity is being challenged to respond flexibly to a rapidly changing global climate that dictates new opportunities for influence. Through contrasting American and Iranian bids for influence this paper explores the interaction between soft power techniques in use today: foreign policy in international relations, and public diplomacy that mitigates the agency of populations to direct global dynamics. As an alternative to conventional warfare, and in addition to economic and political measures, both countries exercise soft power to control the circulation and influence of stories within a worldwide context. Competing narratives of a unified Muslim world and a capitalist democracy respectively promoted by Iranian and American governments interface with international and local dialogues. A nation without kinetic resources equivalent to America's, Iran exemplifies the patience and consistency required for applying soft and smart power to advance strategic relations and shape global opinion.

Narrative, for the sake of this chapter, refers to a series of conventions that are subjectively meaningful and instructive to a community of people. The line between making meaning from coercion or attraction, between manipulated desire and need, is often indistinguishable. As the voices, content, and context of narratives keep changing, it is difficult to evaluate influences outside of the qualitative aspects of political, economic, and cultural relationships.

Soft power, as an instance of competing narratives, is not easily quantifiable. While some nations successfully apply soft power to building regime alliances, they may be losing the allegiance of emerging generations. Other nations engaged in the persistent creation of new scenarios, interpret and reframe social and environmental signals as meaningful referents for future trajectories (Maleki, 2007, slide 21).

Staging Soft Power

Professor Joseph Nye coined and introduced the term "soft power" in his 1990 publication, *Bound to Lead: The Changing Nature of American Power*. However, the concept was not new to academia. Instead, Nye extended earlier discussions of scholars Morton Baratz and Peter Bachrach (1963) on "the second face of power" (referenced in Rugh, 2009, p. 2). Following 9/11, Nye published further refinements of his concept and its interface with public diplomacy. Coinciding with the Bush administration's reliance on hard power to bring about regime change in Iraq, *The Paradox of American Power*, was published in 2002, outlining the maturation of the soft power concept. In ongoing discussions between Nye and colleagues, soft power has been further fine-tuned in the conception of smart power (Rugh 2009:3).

"Power," according to Nye is the ability to influence the behavior of others to get the outcomes one wants. He distinguishes three ways to affect the conduct of others: "you can coerce them with threats, you can induce them with payments, or you can attract them or co-opt them" (Nye, 2004a, ¶ 3). The first two rely on hard power—the "sticks" or "carrots" of military or economic power. The third is the way of soft power: "the ability to affect others to obtain what one wants through attraction rather than coercion or payment" (Nye, 2004a, ¶ 15).

Nye and former Deputy Secretary of State Richard Armitage co-chaired a Commission on Smart Power at the Center for Strategic and International Studies (CSIS), which produced a report defining smart power as "developing an integrated strategy, resource base and tool kit to achieve American objectives, drawing on both hard and soft power" (Armitage & Nye, 2007, p. 7). This approach emphasizes the importance of a strong military, while investing in alliances, partnerships and institutions at all levels to extend a nations influence and establish the legitimacy of its action.

Conventional political power definitions have emphasized concrete and predictable capabilities. In this sense a country is powerful if it possesses a large population and territory, extensive natural resources, strong economy, military force and social stability (Maleki, 2007, slide 4). Yet, beyond geography, most of these factors are dynamic by nature. Nye describes the struggle against international terrorism as an effort of "hearts and minds" (2008, p. 108) for which there is no finite boundary between soft and hard power. Despite its relative inefficacy as a forecasting tool, and lack of numeric precision, soft power, though contingent on modes of communication and dynamics of human relations, affects the definitive success of force.

Requiring a delicate balance, hard power can equally help or harm soft power's effectiveness. In the context of unrivaled American military capabilities, it is important to understand how the potential impact of military action generates either positive or negative "soft power," that directly informs international opinion towards the U.S. Taking the current case of Iran, there are links between the narratives of democracy and well-educated Iranian youth thirsting for change. The use of hard power in Iran could alienate the younger generation, driving them into the arms of that regime through nationalistic reactions to Western actions (Nye, 2010, p. 15).

The American argument for soft power leans on the fact that hard power is increasingly insufficient to support national interests. Hard power asymmetries between Iran and America do not constitute a strategic advantage for America. Chalmers Johnson (2000) is explicit in outlining how military and economic forces backfire. Roger Cohen (2010) makes use of the concept of blowback for understanding what has happened in Iran:

Because the United States and Europe armed Iraq in that war, and Saddam then gassed the Iranians, resentment runs deep: I've often been shown war wounds in Tehran on arms and legs as a single word is uttered, "America." The generation of young officers in that war, like Ahmadinejad, now runs Iran and constitutes the New Right. (Blowback is not limited to Afghanistan.) But most Iranians are under 35 and drawn to the United States.

The Importance of Context

Power resources cannot be judged before knowing the context (Maleki, 2007, slide 6). Soft power is about changing other people's opinions, even if you have to inculcate your own youth to carry the message. Nye lists three sources of soft power: "in international politics, the resources that produce soft power arise in large part from the values an organization expresses in its culture, in the examples it sets by its internal practices and policies, and in the way it handles relations with others" (2008, p. 95). Whether soft power results from any of these sources, the degree of its impact depends on context and credibility.

As credibility may be highly culturally subjective, context is the crucial common denominator for at least partial understandings of how one's values, actions, and relations may be perceived. Neither time, ample resources, nor evident avenues of soft power can predict success—however, timing is critical. Contingent on circumstances, capabilities, and policies, soft power can equally repel or attract others (Rugh, 2009, p. 7). According to Nye (2004b, p. 11):

The soft power of a country rests primarily on three resources: its culture (in places where it is attractive to others), its political values (when it lives up to them at home and abroad), and its foreign policies (when they are seen as legitimate and having moral authority)....When a country's culture includes universal and its policies promote values and interests that others share, it increased the probability of obtaining its desired outcomes because of the relationships of attraction and duty that it creates.

Endorsed by a new Iranian authoritarian class, the narrative of a New Caliphate challenging the domination of Western norms (Maleki, 2007, slide 29) speaks to "extreme" factions around the world, who may perceive themselves as largely disenfranchised by the ideology of Pax Americana, a hegemonic universalism.

Globalization and Power

Profound change means organizational changes connecting internal shifts in people's values, aspirations, and behaviors, with larger external shifts in processes, strategies, practices, and systems (Maleki, 2007, slide 7). In the contemporary globalization and communication revolutions, soft power, able to integrate both levels of change, has increasing significance. Globalization, fuelled by the information revolution, directly correlates to the rise of nongovernmental organizations (NGO) and the international organization of other groups. Current usages of the term "public diplomacy" apply to a host of international actors—governments, NGOs, commercial entities, and individuals (Rugh, 2009, p. 13). Even as the state controls its foreign policy, other aspects of soft power are largely beyond the immediate management of the state (Rugh, 2009, 12). While 9/11 was considered a turning point in modern history, the cataclysmic event obviates the increasing degrees of change in the international arena through information revolutions and forces of globalization. These two factors, Rugh argues, have improved America's ability to project soft power (2009, p. 6). Though greatly influencing the spread of globalization, Nye (2004b, p. 30, 146) contends the U.S. must also acknowledge how globalization challenges its place in the world order in which nearly any organized entity or individual may exert both hard and soft power.

American Sources of Soft Power

Paramount to the Obama administration's diplomatic agenda is incorporation of asymmetrical strategies that respond to the changing nature of global influence, which embrace soft power as key to future ambitions. In this climate, scholarship is publicly accrediting and encouraging a political shift away from dependence on American military force, to tactics that are the de facto constituents of political relations around the world.

During the Cold War, both soft and hard power were central factors in Russian and American relations. However, with the end of the Cold War, some experts criticized the U.S. for virtually eliminating its soft power resources (Matthews, 2009, ¶ 16-25). Following both of the Bush administrations' campaigns of isolation, which alienated the possibility of communication, Obama is challenged to rebuild diplomatic initiatives and foreign policy—with limited resources. Defense Secretary Robert Gates has spoken to the absence of soft power funding—$40 billion in comparison with the $700 billion spent on military defense in 2009 (Matthews, 2009, ¶ 20). Unsurprisingly, rallying behind the term "soft power" has served to distinguish all that is new about the Obama presidency from the unpopularity of Bush-lead initiatives. Secretary Clinton champions a vision of soft power—and its mid-way application smart power—as strategies to reinstate America's global leadership.

If a culture is admired and respected abroad it has positive soft power potential. "Culture" in this sense refers to literature, art, performing arts and music, including both "high culture" and popular culture, and education. Hollywood, Harvard, Microsoft, and Michael Jordan are national brands epitomizing American cultural influence and its fit within the dominant cultural norms of other countries (Maleki, 2007, slide 18). American education institutes, at home and abroad, garner much international admiration. The aspirations of parents to send children to study in the U.S., or follow an American-style curriculum, have been advanced by U.S. support for student exchanges, traveling academic conferences, etc. Nevertheless, these media forms, while passing local censorship, may still be found offensive to a conservative minority, and be taken as further evidence of American immorality (Rugh, 2009, p. 8). Rugh (2009, p. 9) regards the most important sources of U.S. soft power as deriving from political values of democracy and the American political system that protects private and corporate interests. The reputation of America as a land of opportunity, originating from the historical context of a merit system in which anyone has a chance to succeed in a profession or activity of his/her choosing, wields considerable soft power (Rugh, 2009, p. 10). However, political views only have value if a country is seen to live up to them at home and abroad. Foreign media attention to American elections and political activity can both promote American accountability and diminish soft power. For example, Rumsfeld garnered points for his honesty when forced to publicly address difficulties in Abu Ghraib. Concurrently, enhanced security measures, in the form of new visa screenings following 9/11, were largely seen to diminish soft power potential of the U.S. as a country that defends individual rights according to a non-discriminatory system of law (Rugh, 2009, p. 10). When seen as legitimate, and having moral authority, foreign policy generates positive soft power. Understanding the consequences of American foreign policy requires consideration of the priorities and concerns of each foreign group and whether American policy is congruent or incongruent with their interests.

Iranian Uses of Soft Power

While U.S. foreign policy is stalling in the Middle East, Iran is employing all media of influence at its disposal to generate goodwill and strategic partnerships throughout the Muslim world and beyond, building international relationships into an anti-Western network aimed at contesting American interests, engaging the instruments of soft power—trade, media, cultural ties, and local assistance—to further its international agenda (Chorin & Malka, 2008). Since 2001, Iran has been expanding beyond its traditional allies to seek unexpected partnerships: Central Asia, North Africa, and Latin America are leading targets of Iran's soft power (Chorin & Malka, 2008).

Through key agreements in trade, energy, and transport Iran has aggravated discord between the U.S. and its allies. Concern for oil is but one element in the complexity of Iran's far-reaching trade relations. In the competing narrative of a unified Muslim world, soft power derived from Iranian culture and political values, particularly religious affinities, has been used as a calling card for business. As the largest carmaker in the Middle East, Iran is collaborating with Turkey and Malaysia to design and assemble cars for an expanded Islamic market (Chorin & Malka, 2008). In central Asia, Iran signed trade and cooperation agreements in 2008 with Afghanistan and Tajikistan. Linking Iran with the Central Asian Republics and extending to China and Russia, these agreements suggest efforts to restore Silk Road connections. Expanding local development assistance against the Taliban, Iran has supported local *madrasas*, lower-level clerics, and village leaders: efforts that aid local notables who do not benefit from better-funded U.S and UN programs due to regional interceptions of funds (Chorin & Malka, 2008).

Criticisms of Iran's nuclear program are being mitigated by, and mediated through, these cultivated relationships: "Iran has sought, in effect, to buy political friendship that the Islamic Republic can then translate into security agreements and alliances, including political support for the Iranian nuclear program" (Farrar-Wellman, 2009, ¶ 2). In such instances numerous countries benefitting from Iran's generosity have deepened their affiliation with Tehran. While trade relations do not by themselves indicate a more "sinister" alliance, extensive trade often creates strong interconnections or even economic dependence, inclining Iran's trading partners towards increasing political support for Tehran. It is when these partnerships develop into military collaborations or security agreements that they become especially hazardous, from an American geopolitical perspective: "The most benign of these security agreements prevent signatories from participating even passively in any military actions that Iran deems hostile to its interests" (Farrar-Wellman, 2009, ¶ 4).

Iran has become ever more adept at sending signals to its Arab neighbors, and beyond, that its influence runs wide and deep. Iran's significant influence on regional stability is evident in its diverse actions of allegedly arming the Hezbollah in its war with Israel in 2006, brokering ceasefires, and influencing regional reportage (Chorin & Malka, 2008). Able to breach significant obstacles, Iran is "winning the hearts and minds" on the "Arab street", a region historically averse to Persian influence, as well as identifying strategic partners in far corners of the globe.

Chorin and Malka contend that while "the U.S. has developed great talents in reducing issues to black and white conflicts, Iran has become master of both subtle and non-subtle manipulation" (2008). Then again, the ultimate approach taken by Iranian authorities to propagate their narrative is the censorship of all competing versions. While Iran is having some institutional success in applying soft power to building anti-American regime alliances, this is, however, often at the cost of losing the allegiance of the next generation of Arab youth.

Information Revolution

Today, as the world's population has increasing, and varying, access to communication networks, information is power. However, technological advances reducing the cost of processing and transmission of information results in an explosion of content with a tendency to overwhelm networks and recipients. In this "paradox of plenty," attention is becoming a precious resource. Those who can distinguish valuable information, such as editors and cue-givers, are increasingly in demand (Nye, 2004a). While "winning" in traditional power politics depends on might and economy, "politics in an information age may ultimately be about whose story wins" (Nye, 2004a, ¶ 24). In this statement, Nye underlines how, among editors and cue-givers, credibility is fundamental to those wielding soft power to control the information revolution.

Following the 2005 election of Mahmoud Ahmadinejad, Iran's press laws became stricter. Today, Iran may be one of the most repressive Internet-censorship regimes in the world (Reporters without Borders, 2007, pp. 138-139). While theocratic Iranian authorities direct and constrain the regime's communication media and political values, younger generations strive to popularize new scenarios. The Obama administration wields soft power to support the Iranian opposition amidst circumstances of widespread and deliberate misinformation regarding the nature, intention, and degree of American influences within domestic Iranian politics.

In the struggle between competing narratives America cannot win unless the mainstream wins. Soft power is essential for both attracting the mainstream and drying up support for extremists (Nye, 2006, ¶ 8). Delegates of the Alliance of Youth Movements (AYM) describe U.S. Secretary of State Hillary Clinton as "the vanguard of a rising of citizen activists" (Clinton, 2009). One of the most vocal advocates of soft and smart power, Clinton functions as a formidable cue-giver in public diplomacy, able to set the agenda and determine the direction of debate. In a 2010 speech Clinton declared Internet freedom to be a fundamental principle of American foreign policy (Landler, 2010). This echoes her wider strategy:

> "We must use what has been called smart power, the full range of tools at our disposal—diplomatic, economic, military, political, legal, and cultural—picking the right tool or combination of tools for each situation. With smart power, diplomacy will be the vanguard of our foreign policy." (quoted in Etheridge, 2009, ¶ 15)

Proponents of spreading digital technology advocate it as more effective than economic sanctions that seek to curtail Iranian nuclear ambitions. Endeavoring to exploit the Internet's potential for infiltrating and opening up politically repressive societies, the Obama administration has given the green light for technology companies to export free online services to Iran, Cuba, and Sudan (Landler, 2010, ¶ 1). The AYM integrates activism and technology in the joint efforts of leaders from the public and private sectors, NGO community, foundations, and digital movements around the world (Graham-Felsen 2010). Bratich (2009, ¶ 7) refers to these networks as "Genetically Modified Grassroots Organizations," as neither spontaneous expressions of citizen awareness nor the sole invention of external forces "these emergent groups are seeded (and their genetic code altered) to control the direction of the movement," particularly by the American State Department. Youth, 35 and under in Iran, America, and elsewhere, are embracing their roles in soft power—we are told—and organizing according to a narrative of capital democracy, in what Forte (2010, ¶ 12) terms as factual, self-documenting conspiracy. These contemporary scenarios make meaning from partisan cue-givers and environmental signals to shape the trajectories of world events.

While Iran is having some success applying soft power to building anti-American regime alliances, in the precarious bid to win the next generation's support, the nation is losing. The U.S., on the other hand, which has liquidated much of its traditional soft power capacities and credibility, is in a process of re-visioning soft power to accommodate the instability of youth allegiance. Turning to the democratic allure of soft power as empowering a technologically savvy international youth network the Obama administration challenges Iran's public diplomacy without directly jeopardizing foreign negotiation.

Smart power is a long-standing trope of political narratives. Power in our global information age, involves a soft dimension of attraction as well as a hard dimension of coercion and inducement (Nye, 2008, p. 107). Dependent on credibility, self-reflexivity, and the role of civil society, effective soft power must skirt the line of attraction/manipulation without degenerating into propaganda. The current U.S. administration is testing this line, enfolding divisive voices of peripheral and civic trendsetting into the mainstream culture of globalization—as a means to project and translate American directives into future influence.

References

Armitage, R. L., & Nye, J. S., Jr. (2007). *CSIS Commission on Smart Power: A Smarter, More Secure America.* Washington, DC: Center for Strategic and International Studies.
http://csis.org/files/media/csis/pubs/071106_csissmartpowerreport.pdf

Bratich, J. (2009). The Fog Machine: Iran, Social Media, and the Rise of Genetically Modified Grassroots Organizations. *CounterPunch,* June 22.
http://www.counterpunch.org/bratich06222009.html

Chorin, E., & Malka, H. (2008). Iran's Soft Power Creates Hard Realities. *CSIS: Middle East Notes and Comment,* April 15. Washington, DC: Center for Strategic and International Studies.
http://csis.org/files/media/csis/pubs/0408_menc.pdf

Clinton, H. (2009). Secretary Clinton Delivers Video Message for Alliance of Youth Movements Summit. *DIPNOTE: U.S. Department of State Official Blog,* October 16.
http://blogs.state.gov/index.php/archive/entry/secretary_aym_summit

Cohen, R. (2010). Iran in Its Intricacy. *The New York Times,* March 4.
http://www.nytimes.com/2010/03/05/opinion/05iht-edcohen.html

Etheridge, E. (2009). How "Soft Power" Got "Smart." *The New York Times,* January 14.
http://opinionator.blogs.nytimes.com/2009/01/14/how-soft-power-got-smart/

Farrar-Wellman, A. (2009) Iranian Soft Power. *AEI Iran Tracker,* March 1.
http://www.irantracker.org/analysis/iranian-soft-power

Forte, M. (2010). Interviewed on Al Jazeera: Social Media, Soft Power, and American Empire. *Zero Anthropology,* April 20.
http://zeroanthropology.net/2010/04/20/interviewed-today-on-al-jazeera-social-media-soft-power-and-american-empire/

Graham-Felsen, S. (2010). Why I'm Joining the Alliance for Youth Movements. *The Huffington Post,* March 9
http://www.huffingtonpost.com/sam-grahamfelsen/why-im-joining-the-allian_b_491398.html

Johnson, C. (2000). *Blowback: The Costs and Consequences of American Empire.* New York: Holt Paperbacks.

Landler, M. (2010). U.S. Hopes Exports Will Help Open Closed Societies. *The New York Times,* March 7. http://www.nytimes.com/2010/03/08/world/08export.html

Maleki, A. (2007). Soft Power and Its Implications on Iran. (PowerPoint slides). Tehran: Tehran University, Institute for North America & European Studies, May 15.
http://www.caspianstudies.com/Foreignpolicy/my%20new%20article/Soft%20Power.ppt

Matthews, W. (2009). Can Obama Get Results from Soft Power? *Defense News,* January 19.

http://www.defensenews.com/story.php?i=3907876

Nye, J. S., Jr. (1990). *Bound to Lead: The Changing Nature of American Power*. New York: Basic Books.

————. (2002). *The Paradox of American Power: Why the World's Only Superpower Can't Go It Alone*. New York: Oxford University Press.

————. (2004a). The Benefits of Soft Power. *Compass: A Journal of Leadership*, August 2. http://hbswk.hbs.edu/archive/4290.html

————. (2004b). *Soft Power: The Means to Success in World Politics*. Cambridge, MA: Perseus Books.

————. (2006, August 19) In Mideast, the Goal is "Smart" Power. *The Boston Globe*, August 19. http://www.boston.com/news/globe/editorial_opinion/oped/articles/2006/08/19/in_mideast_the_goal_is_smart_power/

————. (2007) Smart Power. *The Huffington Post*, November 29. http://www.huffingtonpost.com/joseph-nye/smart-power_b_74725.html

————. (2008). Public Diplomacy and Soft Power. *Annals of the American Academy of Political and Social Science*, 616, 94-109.

————. (2010). Soft Power and Public Diplomacy in the 21st Century. *British Council Parliamentary Lecture*, January 20. http://www.britishcouncil.org/new/PageFiles/11706/2010%2001%2022%20Joe%20Nye%20Soft%20Power.pdf

Reporters without Borders. (2007). *Freedom of the Press Worldwide in 2007*. Paris: Reporters without Borders. http://www.rsf.org/IMG/pdf/rapport_en_bd-4.pdf

Rugh, W. A. (2009). The Case for Soft Power. In Philip Seib (Ed.), *Toward a New Public Diplomacy: Redirecting U.S. Foreign Policy* (pp. 3-21). New York: Palgrave Macmillan.

CHAPTER THIRTEEN

Soft Power: Ends and Means

Miles Smart

The adjective "soft" does nothing to diminish the intentions of its partner "power." While soft power is a concept employed by numerous players seeking diverse ends, in the context of U.S. foreign policy, soft power is the means to assert dominance politically and economically without the use of coercion. The strategic positioning of the U.S. on the international stage has always employed a certain amount of soft power to attract sympathies and alliances. However, the true strength and source of U.S. power globally was and is achieved through military and economic might, both applied and implied. If power, achieved through either hard or soft means is the end goal, then the discussion of hard versus soft is of little consequence. This analysis seeks to demonstrate that the means to power are of trivial importance when assessing the ends of power. It is the ends of power and a criticism thereof which relegates soft power as a concept to nothing more than neoliberal (in terms of international relations and not economic ideology) propaganda which is hypocritical and offers no real alteration from current relations of power between superpowers such as the U.S. and subordinate polities.

Defining Soft Power

The term soft power was coined by Joseph S. Nye, Jr. and was meant as a real means by which the U.S. could gain enduring influence on the world stage. Nye is a member of the political elite and besides being a leading political academic he has also been employed by the Department of Defense, the State Department, and held positions on numerous non-governmental policy-oriented groups such as the Trilateral Commission (The Trilateral Commission, 2009).

Nye defines soft power as "the ability to get what you want through attraction rather than coercion or payments" (Nye, 2004, p. x). Soft power is composed from various sources but is measured in the attractiveness of a country's culture, political ideals, and policies to other countries (Nye, 2004). Even though the soft power concept arose out of U.S. foreign policy discourse, it is not strictly limited to U.S. concerned discussions. The role of the 2008 Olympic Games in Beijing was one of strategic soft power maneuvering for China as it aimed to assert its leadership and authority upon the world stage (Manzenreiter, 2010). Whether or not it was effective is debatable but the strategy of using soft power is employed to varying degrees by all countries.

Soft power can be defined and applied in many ways and need not be restricted to the context of international relations. Even within international relations, the definition of soft power is flexible and open to contestation. Moreover, that which qualifies as a soft power resource is subject to interpretation. Some see the strategic development of groups which promote the American brand of democracy with its ties to neoliberal economic policies as a soft power tool. Ginden and Weld (2007) cautiously characterize the establishment and support of pro-democracy groups and initiatives in foreign countries as benevolent at best and interventionist at worst. The history of American "democratic intervention" paints a picture of malicious and selfish intent however. While some non-Americans may be attracted to the domestic American political process, the so called spread of democracy, liberty, or freedom, hailed by all U.S. administrations since World War II, is nothing more than hot air used to cover more underhanded means and intentions. When Palestine held democratic elections in 2006 and gave Hamas a mandate, the U.S. under Bush rejected Hamas' legitimacy and implicitly supported Israeli actions which imprisoned or killed many Hamas party members. The acceptance of decidedly undemocratic and oppressive domestic policies in China has no effect on U.S.-Chinese economic cooperation. The U.S. does not execute foreign policy following a central principle, such as liberty is good and oppression is bad. Strategic positioning is of the utmost importance and in the aforementioned instances of hypocrisy, the U.S. was more interested in maintaining a relationship with Israel than supporting a nascent democracy. As such, the attractiveness of U.S. democracy and liberty is severely limited as a resource for soft power when the U.S. operates counter to its own stated ideals.

Soft Power and Hard Power

Soft power is not just a strategy but a set of resources and abilities. Defined as such, soft power does not stand in opposition to hard power but in unison. There are all sorts of possible hard power/soft power configurations and they are not necessarily mutually inclusive. Niall Ferguson (2004) argues that soft power has its uses, but it is hard power or the threat of hard power to which the U.S. owes its status as a superpower. Ferguson sees American popular culture as being most embraced in areas where American power is well established (Europe, Japan, Latin America) and held to ridicule where American hegemony is most contested, like in Iran (Ferguson, 2004, p. 19-21). That said, no one would deny the global penetration of American popular culture and its ability to attract interest in, if not support of, American culture, political life, and relevant foreign policies. However, that attractiveness can easily be labeled superficial when it comes to serious foreign policy decisions and the support they may or may not gather in foreign populations.

Soft power's main proponent, Nye, admits that wielding soft-power resources is slow and cumbersome in comparison to hard power resources (Nye, 2004). But in contrast to Ferguson, Nye sees soft power and not hard power as the legitimizing force in U.S. hegemony. Following this line of thought, hard power can achieve and even maintain dominance, but legitimacy is the ultimate goal. Legitimacy allows the powerful to maintain their position without force but rather through acceptance and localized support. Hard power alone cannot achieve legitimacy in the minds of global citizens and their polities. Because the U.S. operated against the general global consensus when invading Iraq in 2003, they have lost legitimacy, both as an occupying force in Iraq and in general as a world leader.

Soft Power under Bush and Obama

The contrast of American leadership between the foreign policy of the Bush administration and the Obama administration offers an incisive vantage point for a discussion of U.S. soft power. George W. Bush's enthusiastic use of hard power showed a disregard for soft power in both behaviour and rhetoric. Then Secretary of Defense Donald Rumsfeld responded to a question about his opinion of soft power with "I don't know what it means" (Financial Times, 2003). That statement is more than a display of ignorance, it was a policy principle firmly followed. The decline of America's image worldwide during the Bush administration was also a decline in U.S. soft power resources.

Obama's rhetoric is an open avowal of the need for U.S. soft power as a means of enhancing America's place on the world stage. Obama carries within himself huge soft power resources. The architect of the term himself Joseph Nye, commented during the 2008 election that Obama's biography, with his multi-ethnic background and global familial connections, "would do more for America's soft power around the world than anything else" (Traub, 2007, p.50).

Rhetoric and stance aside, the behaviour of the Obama administration is not radically different than that of the previous Bush administration. Obama might be more dove than hawk but only slightly so. The U.S. continues to use the most coercive form of power in Afghanistan and Pakistan in order to maintain strategic dominance and it is reasonable to assume that they do so because the current administration acknowledges the limits of soft power and the necessity of force.

The sympathy for the U.S. immediately after 9/11 combined with diplomatic pressure allowed for the implementation of counter terrorist security measures adopted by U.S. allied nations. Many of these measures have been and continue to be criticized for their infringements on civil liberties. By tying developmental aid and economic partnership to these security measures and demanding cooperation in the "war on terror," the U.S. quickly eroded the soft power benefits of 9/11 sympathy (Fowler & Sen, 2010). Moreover, the hard power tactics of the war on terror tends to create resentment over the U.S.' mess and a view that the U.S. was simply using the war on terror to extend oppressive foreign policies (Fowler & Sen, 2010). This practice has continued under the Obama administration as the U.S. exerts extraordinary influence on the government of Pakistan even while the citizenry is unsupportive and the ruling regime faces stiff domestic opposition.

Idealistic Imperialism

The concept of soft power, as used by its proponents, is a vision of idealistic imperialism. When playing the game of geopolitics, soft power is a tool of enhancement, not necessity. The idealist says that it helps mitigate hard power excesses; the realist knows that those excesses are what get things done. The question of whether political leaders who make real decisions concerning foreign policy should choose to either embrace or disregard soft power ideals is insignificant. The ends of power seeking by both pragmatic soft power and hawkish hard power are the same. Those ends are the dominance of international politics and economics. Any discussion of whether the means of foreign policy are justifiable ought to be preceded by an analysis of whether or not the ends are justifiable or even desirable.

Humanity's current political, economic, and technological complex is a beast of its own. Like any of the diverse human lifestyles that have existed throughout our shared cultural existence, our current pattern has a long history and contains motivating ideologies which tell us what to do and how to do it. Of more importance is the persuasive ability of ideology to entrench our convictions. Conviction causes myopia in our assessment of the complex and restricts deep criticism of the whole. This is not a fault, it's simply a trait of humans that they believe in and defend their lifestyle. This phenomenon allows the whole to sustain itself and follow a path informed by ideology and executed by successive generations.

The current dominant ideology is one of technological and industrial progress and economic expansion, typified by the U.S. Political organization through the global capitalist system motivates competition between nations. The goal of global competition is to attain more power which in turn improves one's economic condition, both domestically and in relation to the competition. Embarking on a path of unprovoked war to achieve domestic prosperity and global dominance brings with it great risks and political actors know this. As such, negotiation and restrained strategy are the preferred mode of operation currently. This may sound silly in the context of U.S. military dominance, but the U.S. restrains its military actions and endorsements to engagements that are believed to pose minimized risk and offer strategic benefit.

For the most part, the U.S. walks softly and carries a big stick, implementing power using various means other then direct military actions. While the U.S. is capable of completely destroying any competitor through military might (5,400 nuclear warheads at last count), it doesn't want to as this would (and as has happened in the case of Iraq and Vietnam) cause blemishes to the global image of the U.S. and hinder international relations (Norris & Kristensen, 2008, p. 50). Soft power is meant to facilitate the reduction of coercive relationships and invite cooperation—but a cooperation that allows for continued U.S. hegemony. Influential supporters of soft power, from Nye to Obama, are interested in perpetuating the status quo. The adoption of a softer approach to foreign policy does nothing to diminish their conviction that the U.S. ought to remain a global superpower by virtue of its political and economic ideals. The means to U.S. hegemony may shift back and forth between brutal and gentle force but the desired end does not.

References

Ferguson, N. (2004). *Colossus: The Rise and Fall of the American Empire.* New York, NY: Penguin Books.

Fowler, A. & Sen, K. (2010). Embedding the War on Terror: State and Civil Society Relations. *Development and Change,* 41(1), 1-27.

Ginden, J. & Weld, K. (2007). Benevolence or Intervention? Spotlighting U.S. Soft Power. *NACLA Report on the Americas,* 40(1), 19-44.

Manzenreiter, W. (2010). The Beijing Games in the Western Imagination of China: The Weak Power of Soft Power. *Journal of Sports and Social Issues,* 34(1), 29-48.

Norris, J. S. & Kristensen, H. M. (2008). U.S. Nuclear Forces, 2008. *Bulletin of the Atomic Scientists,* 64(1), 50-53.

Nye, Joseph S. (2004). *Soft Power: The Means to Success in World Politics.* New York, NY: Public Affairs.

Financial Times. (2003). Old Softie. *Financial Times,* September 30, p.16.

Traub, J. (2007). Is (His) Biography (Our) Destiny. *The New York Times Magazine*, November 4, p. 50.

The Trilateral Commission. (2009). Joseph S. Nye, Jr. *The Trilateral Commission: Membership*. http://www.trilateral.org/membship/bios/jn.htm

CHAPTER FOURTEEN

Soft Drink: Hard Power

Lesley Foster

Former United States President Dwight Eisenhower's powerful and poignant farewell speech on 17 January 1961 carried a tone of caution to the U.S. public and to the country's coming leaders. The basis on which Eisenhower rested his speech was his reflection on the results of his experience, throughout his eight-year term in office and through monumental wars (inheriting the Korean War from President Truman), and how he had developed a very intimate perspective on the rise of the U.S.' military and paramilitary strength at home and abroad. He diplomatically warned of the effects of power-hungry leaders: "America's leadership and prestige depend, not merely upon our unmatched material progress, riches and military strength, but on how we use our power in the interests of world peace and human betterment" and asked for the American people to take this more holistic approach in dealing with their rapid development and called for a "balance between the clearly necessary and the comfortably desirable", but more importantly, "balance between actions of the moment and the national welfare of the future" (Eisenhower, 1961, Section 3). War, environmental disintegration, violence and huge economic disparity—the current layers of today's global instability point to the ignorance of America's foreign policy enforcers and their inability to properly take heed of Eisenhower's cautionary words, especially at that time, a country on the brink entering a Cold War and a technological revolution. Eisenhower aptly commented on the changing face of the American military, the rapid technological changes married to a new global reach, the rise of the "military-industrial complex," with the resulting increased risk of vulnerability to Americans as they came to rely on their military presence as the absolute solution in every, and all policy issues:

> "This conjunction of an immense military establishment and a large arms industry is new in the American experience….We recognize the imperative need for this development. Yet we must not fail to comprehend its grave implications. Our toil,

resources and livelihood are all involved; so is the very structure of our society."
(Eisenhower, 1961, Section 4)

Eisenhower's warnings speak of vested influences becoming the dominant ones, with little interest in diplomacy (possessed of a particular historical and ideological orientation), as they speak of the importance of consciousness in a growing, rapid-paced society, and of the evil to come as "the potential for the disastrous rise of misplaced power exists and will persist" (Eisenhower, 1961, Section 4). At the time of Eisenhower's farewell cautionary speech, "the military industrial complex was already well entrenched in American life and…even Ike never imagined the emergence of a Complex of such great proportions that it would someday almost entirely envelop American culture" (Turse, 2008, p. 15). The manifestation of this specific misplaced power through the Complex in a contemporary context is what I am interested in pursuing in this chapter. I thus explore the ways in which the Complex exerts itself within American foreign policy, globally and at home, through the privatized military industry about which Eisenhower spoke critically, through corporate imperialism, and through the more specific social and cultural implications and consequences that the rise of everyday military presence has on day-to-day life in the heart of the empire.

The New Imperialism: the Many Faces of Consumer Domination and the Endless Profiteering of War-Making

In the Global North, cultural and social practices and values have been reduced to capital and consumption coupled with a "deepening culture of militarism" (Boggs, 2005, p. 125). The "right" to own, to "possess," has been valiantly adopted and enforced through by the military-industrial complex, which has grown monumentally since Eisenhower's cautionary farewell speech in 1961 and even more so post- 9/11. The Complex funds, promotes and is "connected to everything you would expect, from the top arms manufacturers to big oil corporations…the entertainment industry and the world's largest food suppliers and beverage companies" (Turse, 2008, p. 17). Unfortunately the Complex's influence is not limited to consumer products but has enormous influence in "support[ing] the most prestigious universities in America" (Turse, 2008, p. 17) directly infiltrating and shaping knowledge that will undoubtedly have grave ramifications for the development of future minds. The growth of the Complex "will enable or enhance imperial adventures in decades to come; it will lead to lethal new technologies to be wielded against people across the globe; it will feed a superpower arms race of one, only increasing the already vast military asymmetry between the [U.S.] and everyone else" (Turse, 2008, p. 39). This culture of consumption and the notion of entitlement to the "right to own" runs parallel to the increase of the military-industrial complex's presence in everyday society and, with it, heralds the sheer ease of profiteering that survives on American ignorance towards the true implications and realities of war and militarization:

> "Whether or not the nation has become 'addicted' to war (and preparation for war), there can be little doubt that warfare motifs, discourses and priorities increasingly shape all phases of social life impacting everything from language, media representations and popular culture to the workplace, forms of consumption and politics." (Boggs, 2005, p. ix)

Nick Turse (2008) describes this shaping of the military-industrial complex as the Matrix, referencing the 1999 Hollywood film of the same name, where only few people are conscious of the military-industrial complex and its impacts and effects on day-to-day life. In the Matrix—an insular created world, where free thought is an imaginary ideal and the ones plugged into the matrix "are ignorant of the very existence of the artificial reality that they 'live' in"—Turse (2008, p. 16) aptly employs this as an analogy with reference to the dominant orientation in American culture towards the social and cultural dysfunction confronting the global community, illuminating the easy seduction of a populace whose information is ultimately filtered and funded through military means and perspectives. As Carl Boggs (2005) describes it, the modern-day American mentality is shaped by an ideology consisting of, "the contemporary merging of flag-waving patriotism, militarism and imperial hubris [that] furnishes American citizens with a powerful (if no doubt fleeting) sense of national unity and global purpose," and more importantly, the soft (in)visible forms of militarism filtered through the military-industrial complex provide the fuel for the American Empire to expand, exist and dominate (Boggs, 2005, p. ix).

Currently, the legs on which the American Empire stands are perhaps shakier than they were during the Cold War era given the impact of decolonization and anti-imperial politics, but the values continue to be rife with the same domineering will in the name of capital and global expansion. The ways the Empire spreads its corporate and military seed is tied in a dialectical relationship with class exploitation. As Turse (2008) explains, the military-industrial complex is one that is extraordinarily sophisticated, and thrives in attacking weak socio-cultural elements to fuel this enormous military machine. With a "high level of military-civilian interpenetration in a heavily consumer-driven society," what this means is that "almost every American…is, at least, passively, supporting the Complex…" (Turse, 2008, p. 18). Thus, inadvertently through consumer participation (for example, drinking Coca-Cola products, listening to one's iPod), or blatantly due to socio-economic factors (targeted military recruitment campaigns), and wider commercial engagement and direct involvement with the military, the Complex exerts a ubiquitous presence in the culture of consumption, even affecting basic survival in the contemporary era.

Corporate Imperialism and its Paramilitary Arms

Just as the military-industrial complex can, and does, survive through its many different masks, some corporations also thrive through contracting to private paramilitary groups. One of the greatest risks of this faceless, (in)visible militarization is the many ways it works off of economic disparity or conversely, the active development of underdevelopment, and how those covert missions oppressively affect local communities. P.W. Singer's (2002) book, *Corporate Warriors: The Rise of the Privatized Military Industry*, describes this as "the empowerment of private industry" (2002, p. 187). He outlines how private industries, in the past, due to their limited access to the means of physical violence, when compared with the state, held nowhere near the political clout that they do today. In today's neoliberal privatized domination, "multinational corporations and their allied private military firms now have the capability to engage in what they term 'security-led investment'; in which the physical weakness of the local state is irrelevant to their business operations" (Singer, 2002, p. 188). This "security-led investment" is a neocolonial form of imperialism that ensures, and instills an American military presence in any part of the world. This is where borders fade away for the transnational elites and military walls, and their rules, become higher for the economically "unfit" to overcome.

One of the most dominant and widespread of the transnational corporations is the mega-beverage corporation, Coca-Cola, combining strengths in access to the military along with its relationships with neoliberal institutions, in order to project itself globally. Indeed, Coca-Cola supplied to American troops overseas during the Second World War, "became iconic of American presence abroad"—a returning war veteran exclaimed, "the Coca-Cola Company's cooperation with the Army in getting Coca-Cola to the men in the field is the best advertisement that Coca-Cola has ever had" (Rothacher, 2004, p. 69). Through compelling advertising tools Coca-Cola projects a highly desirable image of "communal[ity]: if you drink coke, the ads suggest, that you will belong to a warm, loving, accepting family, singing in perfect harmony" (Rothacher, 2004, p. 70). Coca-Cola projects an image of functionality, of family—a family that is reliable and always there. With Coca-Cola's presence having seeped its way into all walks of life, regardless of culture and society, akin to its brand projection, it has been subject to many global criticisms due to its empire-like and "cultural imperialist" characteristics (Rothacher, 2004, p. 80). Coca-Cola has no doubt employed a global strategy in its profiteering, "the company, which arose out of the Jim Crow South, adhered to traditions and business practices that sprouted from its southern roots" (Gill, 2007, p. 235). The human rights violations that have been filed against the Coca-Cola Company in the latter part of the 20th and 21st century also spans the global terrain from, "draining public groundwater and ruining agriculture in…villages [in India] to aggravat[ing] class divisions among indigenous peoples in the state of Chiapas [Mexico] by granting concessions to religious elders, who distributed Coca-Cola during festivities that once used cane alcohol in ceremonies dedicated to the gods." (Gill, 2007, p. 235)

Coca-Cola, benefitting from neoliberalist restructuring and the subcontracting of violence to private groups, leading to increased militarization, preys on the powerless in the name of capital. In the name of traditional colonial assimilation, it bulldozes tradition. Coca-Cola's actions take on a different form of hard and soft power in regards to the normalized, dominant idea of violence and war and, in doing so deflects the regular public attention that the traditional ideas and forms of violence and war might receive. Corporate war does not carry the same urgent implications that other forms of war carry, such as the current "war on terror," "humanitarian" war, or war associated with genocide, due to the fact that corporate wars are associated with a dominant-globalized system (the military-industrial complex) that is not in opposition, threatening or corrosive to the dominant, to the "free world"—it actually works in conjunction with it, protecting the neoliberal entitlement to own and conquer.

Colombia's plight and fight against "Killer Coke"

South America's relationship with Coca-Cola, like that of many countries outside of the Global North, is highly vulnerable to Coca-Cola's dominance. Headed by Venezuela's president Hugo Chávez, there has been a strategic move in South America against oppressive North American neoliberal policies, specifically in Colombia where the notoriously dysfunctional country "remains an important neoliberal outpost in South America, with its unaccountable security forces that are backed by U.S. military aid and available to repress opposition from a growing number of dispossessed people" (Gill, 2004, p. 235). The U.S.'s is consistently portrayed as a heroic outside force creating economic stability, in its relationship with Colombia, despite the prolific corruption. Since post 9-11 "anti-terrorist" laws have been instituted as masks for the slashing of workers rights and privatization through the International Monetary Fund (IMF) and its "structural adjustment" plans, and due to these forms of intense internal conflict and corruption at the governmental and legal level, Colombia is increasingly vulnerable to imperial conquest and social fragmentation. In particular, the persecution of social justice activists, "under the guise of prosecuting terrorists has also given the Colombian government an excuse to curtail the rights and liberties of unions. Unions are increasingly the subject of legal attack as well as extra-legal killings and threats" (Killer Coke, 2010a), which is clearly one of the ways that "counter-terrorism" has been tied to the suppression of workers' rights. Coca-Cola's presence in Colombia has led to major clashes between the unions that organize the company's labour and the worker's rights that the Coca-Cola Company fails to respect. The human rights violations have been so grave that union solidarity and activist groups in North America have rallied against the Coca-Cola Company to internationalize the struggle and to gain political momentum. Movements such as the "Killer Coke" campaign and its damning documentary, "The Coca-Cola Case – A documentary film about Coke and labor rights in the bottling plants" (2009), produced under the auspices of the National Film Board (NFB) of Canada, specifically targets university campuses across North America where Coca-Cola monopolies are rampant, to spread the word of Coca-Cola's corporate violence in Colombia. As the campaign states:

> "Coca-Cola's employment practices in Colombia, both those within the letter of the law and those in contravention of the law, have had the effect of driving wages, work standards and job security for Coca-Cola workers sharply downward, and simultaneously, of decimating the workers' union, SINALTRAINAL. Both trends are reinforced by the appalling human rights violations that workers have suffered at the hands of paramilitary forces." (Killer Coke, 2010a)

In the 2001 lawsuit filed by the United Steel Workers of America and other trade unionists against Coca-Cola on behalf of SINALTRAINAL, allegations were put forth that the paramilitary offenses against the Colombian trade unionists were being supported by U.S. forces trained at the U.S. Army's School of the Americas "where trainees were encouraged to torture and murder those who do 'union organizing and recruiting;' pass out 'propaganda in favor of workers;' and 'sympathize with demonstrators or strikes'" (Killer Coke, 2010b). The death and kidnapping of trade unionists in Colombia is astonishing and the lack of accountability even more so: "4,000 unionists have been assassinated by the paramilitaries in the last decade, and 192 of them in 2002 alone and no one has ever been prosecuted for it" (Killer Coke, 2010c). Coca-Cola's rebuttals to these human rights violations are equally as shocking as the allegations, "'it is not that the murder and terrorism of trade unionists did not occur,' according to an [International Labor Rights Forum] [(ILRF)] press release" (Baran, 2003, p. 2), Coke's legal representatives explain that, "[Coke] cannot be held liable in a U.S. federal court for events outside the United States. 'Coca-Cola also argues that it does not 'own,' and therefore does not control, the bottling plants in Colombia'" (Baran, 2003, p. 2). Through outsourcing, Coke has found a way to wash their hands of any legal accountability while at the same time successfully spreading the corporate military seed.

Figure 14.1: Poster Protesting Coca-Cola and the Murder of Trade Unionists in Colombia

This poster against Coca-Cola for its killing of unionists in Colombia, was displayed at Fête de l'Humanité in 2006. The text reads: "I don't consume Coca-Cola because it finances war." Source: "Kilobug" at Wikimedia Commons. (Creative Commons License: Share, Remix, Attribution.)

Figure 14.2: Poster Protesting Coca-Cola and the Murder of Trade Unionists in
Colombia

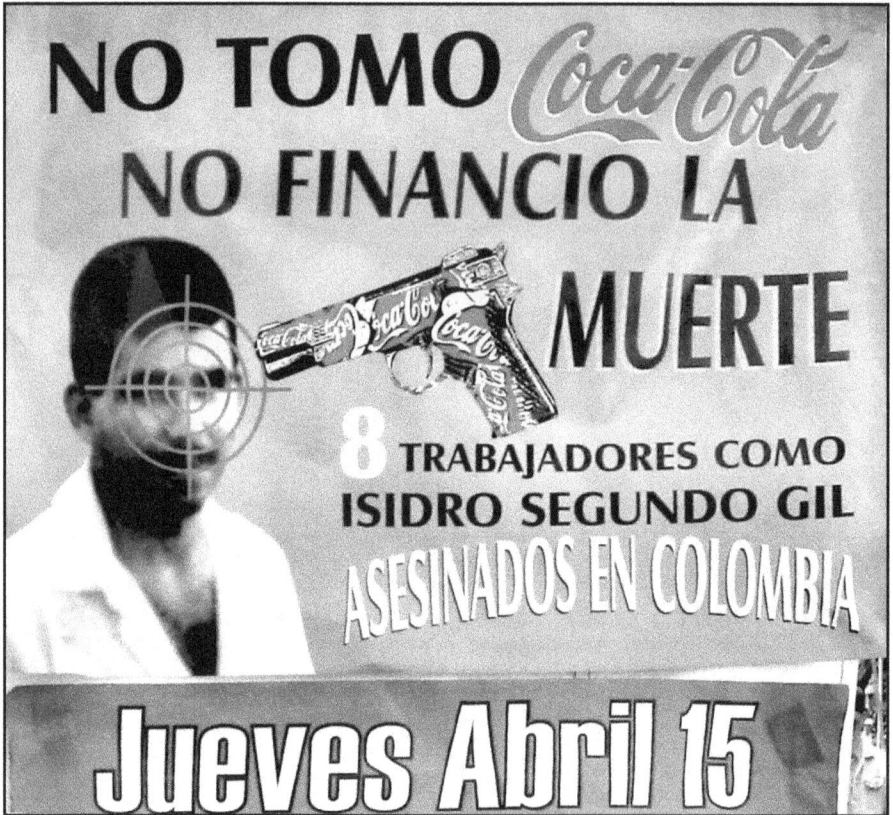

This poster against Coca-Cola for its killing of unionists in Colombia, was displayed at Fête de
l'Humanité in 2006. The text reads: "I do not drink Coca-Cola. I do not finance death. Eight
workers, like Isidro Segundo Gil, assassinated in Colombia." Source: "Kilobug" at Wikimedia
Commons. (Creative Commons License: Share, Remix, Attribution.)

The ways in which the Coca-Cola Company is ingrained in the global cultural fiber poses a tremendous hurdle for the victims of Coke's international
iron fist. To denounce Coca-Cola is to denounce an important and familiar
socio-cultural presence in everyday life. To actively initiate such a denunciation
without any social or cultural point of reference for Coke's (in)visible crimes
seems culturally and socially unviable, and yet, remarkably, in the name of resistance, resolutions have been made towards lessening Coca-Cola's soft/hard
presence in day-to-day life. So what is it that can be done to resist the Coca-
Cola corporate empire? Resistance has taken many different forms: university
campuses across the U.S. and Canada have awakened to Coke's neoliberal-
imperial politics and have ceased contracts with the company at their institutions; letter campaigns have been started; and, teachers have begun to boycott
Coca-Cola products. Solidarity action is taking wind locally and globally towards

raises conscience of the inner workings and effects of the military-industrial complex and specifically corporate imperialism's resolution to first destroy defenseless nations and then internally dispossess the people of their basic human rights. Unfortunately rather than the violent and murderous realities of the company, the dominant perspective and image of well-being, positivity, wholeness and prosperity remains tied to the product. The "creation of need" in today's consumer-culture climate supersedes the lives of dispossessed people at the hands of the social and cultural implantation of the corporate-military complex. The ways the complex has embedded itself raises the question of blowback: Due to this increased militarization what social costs and cultural changes have been set forth at home in the heart of the empire?

Figure 14.3: Protesting Coke on Campus

Canadian university students taking part in the Killer Coke campaign. Here we see students playing dead at the King's College/University of Western Ontario Day of Action, 12 October 2006. (Reproduced with the kind permission of the Killer Coke Campaign, Protest Pics: www.killercoke.org/protestcanada.htm)

TERRORfied: Blowback at Home

"Blowback" as described by Chalmers Johnson (2002) is "a metaphor for the unintended consequences of covert operations against foreign nations and governments" (Johnson, 2002, p. 23) and in the post 9-11 climate of "terror" it can be defined as reactions to the U.S.' power projection and conquest through "the current global economic arrangements mean[ing] more wealth for the 'West' and more misery for the 'rest'" (Johnson, 2002 p. 25). At home, in the heart of Empire, attention is rarely given to the increased militarization and blowback effects at home—the "other" is always the one carrying conflict—and there is a huge inability to look right in one's own backyard. Since the World Trade Center attacks in 2001 there has been a fever of fear that has built up a crisis in fighting and defending "freedom" in the name of democratic ideals and values. The new war has sprouted a military class from the soldiers to the reigning effects of the military-industrial (corporate) complex control. The onset of these new allegedly "defensive" wars against Iraq and Afghanistan has aroused newly patriotic and hegemonic sympathizers through the increased militarization resulting in a myriad of social dysfunction—both inside the military and paramilitary units, as well as the increased governmental focus on military spending resulting in the corroding of other vital institutions. This imperial cost of maintaining a strong military front "is a nation's relying on its armed forces for numerous tasks for which they are unqualified, indeed their particular capabilities almost guaranteeing to make problematic situation[s] worse" (Johnson, 2002, p. 29). In this reliance, we do well to remember Eisenhower's cautionary words when thinking of the tactics used in the name of defense and protection of liberty for one nation-state.

Catherine Lutz (2002) refers to the ways in which increased militarization manifests itself as "structural violence" where the consequences from the increasing militarization are contradictory for it "accentuates both localism (as when [smaller municipalities] and other cities compete for huge military contracts or bases) and federalism (as when the fate of dry cleaning businesses in [smaller municipalities] can hinge on Pentagon regulations on putting starch in uniforms or on sudden deployments of large numbers of soldiers)" (Lutz, 2002, p. 727). With a large number of U.S. residents relying on government dollars in an economically fragile time, "America's New War" is blurring the lines between "policing and soldiering and between the civilian and the military worlds and identities" (Lutz, 2002, p. 732) actively creating an immense gap between the reality of the militarization and its long-term effects. Among the myriad examples of how increased militarization affects the U.S. and creates a disorder of terror and misinformation it is vital to investigate the marriage of the military-industrial complex to the American mass media.

The managing and filtering of information is an epidemic in the U.S. where rapid-fire news and infotainment now intersect, "professional firm[s] ha[ve] been hired to manage information flow and interpretation and the Pentagon's specialists in disinformation have received more funding, new offices, and new names" (Lutz, 2002, p. 731). The social dysfunction that this sort of news filtering creates in the U.S. is massive in creating social misconceptions about the "enemy," the "terrorists" or the "insurgents," while glorifying the military and failing to represent the marginalized. Some of the marginalized exist on the fringes of military discourse, such as women in the military, with their work in a patriotic field accompanied by violence and sexual harassment. The media also neglect the military torture of detainees. While only a few of the local consequences have been touched on in this paper, the complexity and the ways this structured violence, as Lutz labels it, of increased militarization is necessary to examine in contrast with the global effects to highlight the reality that human rights violations, blowback effects, and "structured" violence are not far from home: they are simply masked in the Complex's illusionary tactics and its careful embedding into American day-to-day life.

Conclusion

The military-industrial complex is all around us—it in fact embodies a contemporary time. We identity ourselves through its products and feel secure in owning the power that these products provide, whether it be a bottle of coke or the outpour of financial benefits from a military post in one's hometown. The ignorance of the Complex has created a matrix where Americans have, through their imperial identity complex, indoctrinated themselves into believing that they are the do-gooders, the saviors and healers on a global scale. The blowback effects of the U.S.' harsh militarization abroad and at home is provoking action against imperial expansionism, ranging from resistance against transnational corporations, to the named "terrorist" groups and their acts of violence in the name of retribution. Here, Eisenhower's words continue to ring true in that there needs to be a "balance between actions of the moment and the national welfare of the future" to hope for a way to curtail the outcomes of these viscous imperial ventures and perhaps prevent further social dysfunction resulting in extreme violence and dispossession at home and abroad.

References

Baran, M. (2003). Stop Killer Coke! Death squads have assassinated eight trade union leaders in Coca-Cola bottling plants in Colombia. The Stop Killer Coke campaign holds the beverage giant responsible. *Dollar and Sense Magazine*, 203.
http://www.dollarsandsense.org/archives/2003/1103baran.html

Boggs, C. (2005). *Imperial Delusions: American Militarism and Endless Wars*. Lanham, MD: Rowman and Littlefield Publishers Inc.

Eisenhower, D. D. (1961). Farewell Address to the Nation. Washington, DC, January 17.
http://www.militaryindustrialcomplex.com/eisenhower_farewell_address.asp

Gill, L. (2007). Right There With You: Coca-Cola, Labor Restructuring and Political Violence in Colombia. *Critique of Anthropology*, 27(3), 235-260.

Johnson, C. (2002). American Militarism and Blowback: The Costs and Letting the Pentagon Dominate Foreign Policy. *New Political Science*, 24(1), 21-38.

Killer Coke. (2010a.) NYC Fact-Finding Delegation on Coca-Cola in Colombia, Final Report: An Investigation of Allegations of Murder and Violence In Coca-Cola's Colombian Plants.
http://www.killercoke.org/report.htm

——————. (2010b) Who We Are. *Website of the Killer Coke Campaign*.
http://www.killercoke.org/who.htm

——————. (2010c). Colombian Unionists and Support for the Coca-Cola Boycott. Resolution #R-29, International Longshore and Warehouse Union, 32nd International Convention, San Francisco, California, April 28-May 2. http://www.killercoke.org/pdf/ILWU-resolution.pdf

Lutz, C. (2002). Making War at Home in the United States: Militarization and the Current Crisis. *American Anthropologist*, 104(3), 723-735.

Rothacher, A. (2004). *Corporate Cultures and Global Brands*. Hackensack, NJ: World Scientific Publishing Co.

Singer, P. W. (2002). *Corporate Warriors: The Rise of the Privatized Military Industry*. Ithaca, NY: Cornell University Press.

Turse, N. (2008). *The Complex: How the Military Invades Our Everyday Lives*. New York: Henry Holt and Company.

ΔPPENDICES

Δppendix Δ

Δddress by U.S. President Woodrow Wilson before a Joint Session of Congress (the "Fourteen Points" Speech), 08 Jonuory 1918

Gentlemen of the Congress:

Once more, as repeatedly before, the spokesmen of the Central Empires have indicated their desire to discuss the objects of the war and the possible basis of a general peace. Parleys have been in progress at Brest-Litovsk between Russian representatives and representatives of the Central Powers to which the attention of all the belligerents has been invited for the purpose of ascertaining whether it may be possible to extend these parleys into a general conference with regard to terms of peace and settlement.

The Russian representatives presented not only a perfectly definite statement of the principles upon which they would be willing to conclude peace, but also an equally definite program of the concrete application of those principles. The representatives of the Central Powers, on their part, presented an outline of settlement which, if much less definite, seemed susceptible of liberal interpretation until their specific program of practical terms was added. That program proposed no concessions at all, either to the sovereignty of Russia or to the preferences of the populations with whose fortunes it dealt, but meant, in a word, that the Central Empires were to keep every foot of territory their armed forces had occupied—every province, every city, every point of vantage as a permanent addition to their territories and their power.

It is a reasonable conjecture that the general principles of settlement which they at first suggested originated with the more liberal statesmen of Germany and Austria, the men who have begun to feel the force of their own peoples' thought and purpose, while the concrete terms of actual settlement came from the military leaders who have no thought but to keep what they have got. The negotiations have been broken off. The Russian representatives were sincere and in earnest. They cannot entertain such proposals of conquest and domination.

The whole incident is full of significance. It is also full of perplexity. With whom are the Russian representatives dealing? For whom are the representatives of the Central Empires speaking? Are they speaking for the majorities of their respective parliaments or for the minority parties, that military and imperialistic minority which has so far dominated their whole policy and controlled the affairs of Turkey and of the Balkan States which have felt obliged to become their associates in this war?

The Russian representatives have insisted, very justly, very wisely, and in the true spirit of modern democracy, that the conferences they have been holding with the Teutonic and Turkish statesmen should be held within open, not closed, doors, and all the world lies been audience, as was desired. To whom have we been listening, then? To those who speak the spirit and intention of the resolutions of the German Reichstag of the 9th of July last, the spirit and intention of the liberal leaders and parties of Germany, or to those who resist and defy that spirit and intention and insist upon conquest and subjugation? Or are we listening, in fact, to both, unreconciled and in open and hopeless contradiction? These are very serious and pregnant questions. Upon the answer to them depends the peace of the world.

But whatever the results of the parleys at Brest-Litovsk, whatever the confusions of counsel and of purpose in the utterances of the spokesmen of the Central Empires, they have again attempted to acquaint the world with their objects in the war and have again challenged their adversaries to say what their objects are and what sort of settlement they would deem just and satisfactory. There is no good reason why that challenge should not be responded to, and responded to with the utmost candor. We did not wait for it. Not once, but again and again we have laid our whole thought and purpose before the world, not in general terms only, but each time with sufficient definition to make it clear what sort of definite terms of settlement must necessarily spring out of them. Within the last week Mr. Lloyd George has spoken with admirable candor and in admirable spirit for the people and Government of Great Britain.

There is no confusion of counsel among the adversaries of the Central Powers, no uncertainty of principle, no vagueness of detail. The only secrecy of counsel, the only lack of fearless frankness, the only failure to make definite statement of the objects of the war, lies with Germany and her allies. The issues of life and death hang upon these definitions. No statesman who has the least conception of his responsibility ought for a moment to permit himself to continue this tragical and appalling outpouring of blood and treasure unless he is sure beyond a peradventure that the objects of the vital sacrifice are part and parcel of the very life of society and that the people for whom he speaks think them right and imperative as he does.

There is, moreover, a voice calling for these definitions of principle and of purpose which is, it seems to me, more thrilling and more compelling than any of the many moving voices with which the troubled air of the world is filled. It is the voice of the Russian people. They are prostrate and all but helpless, it would seem, before the grim power of Germany, which has hitherto known no relenting and no pity. Their power, apparently, is shattered. And yet their soul is not subservient. They will not yield either in principle or in action. Their conception of what is right, of what is humane and honorable for them to accept, has been stated with a frankness, a largeness of view, a generosity of spirit, and a universal human sympathy which must challenge the admiration of every friend of mankind; and they have refused to compound their ideals or desert others that they themselves may be safe.

They call to us to say what it is that we desire, in what, if in anything, our purpose and our spirit differ from theirs; and I believe that the people of the United States would wish me to respond, with utter simplicity and frankness. Whether their present leaders believe it or not, it is our heartfelt desire and hope that some way may be opened whereby we may be privileged to assist the people of Russia to attain their utmost hope of liberty and ordered peace.

It will be our wish and purpose that the processes of peace, when they are begun, shall be absolutely open and that they shall involve and permit henceforth no secret understandings of any kind. The day of conquest and aggrandizement is gone by; so is also the day of secret covenants entered into in the interest of particular governments and likely at some unlooked-for moment to upset the peace of the world. It is this happy fact, now clear to the view of every public man whose thoughts do not still linger in an age that is dead and gone, which makes it possible for every nation whose purposes are consistent with justice and the peace of the world to avow now or at any other time the objects it has in view.

We entered this war because violations of right had occurred which touched us to the quick and made the life of our own people impossible unless they were corrected and the world secured once for all against their recurrence.

What we demand in this war, therefore, is nothing peculiar to ourselves. It is that the world be made fit and safe to live in; and particularly that it be made safe for every peace-loving nation which, like our own, wishes to live its own life, determine its own institutions, be assured of justice and fair dealing by the other peoples of the world, as against force and selfish aggression.

All the peoples of the world are in effect partners in this interest, and for our own part we see very clearly that unless justice be done to others it will not be done to us.

The program of the world's peace, therefore, is our program; and that program, the only possible program, all we see it, is this:

1. Open covenants of peace must be arrived at, after which there will surely be no private international action or rulings of any kind, but diplomacy shall proceed always frankly and in the public view.

2. Absolute freedom of navigation upon the seas, outside territorial waters, alike in peace and in war, except as the seas may be closed in whole or in part by international action for the enforcement of international covenants.

3. The removal, so far as possible, of all economic barriers and the establishment of an equality of trade conditions among all the nations consenting to the peace and associating themselves for its maintenance.

4. Adequate guarantees given and taken that national armaments will be reduced to the lowest points consistent with domestic safety.

5. A free, open-minded, and absolutely impartial adjustment of all colonial claims, based upon a strict observance of the principle that in determining all such questions of sovereignty the interests of the population concerned must have equal weight with the equitable claims of the government whose title is to be determined.

6. The evacuation of all Russian territory and such a settlement of all questions affecting Russia as will secure the best and freest cooperation of the other nations of the world in obtaining for her an unhampered and unembarrassed opportunity for the independent determination of her own political development and national policy, and assure her of a sincere welcome into the society of free nations under institutions of her own choosing; and, more than a welcome, assistance also of every kind that she may need and may herself desire. The treatment accorded Russia by her sister nations in the months to come will be the acid test of their good will, of their comprehension of her needs as distinguished from their own interests, and of their intelligent and unselfish sympathy.

7. Belgium, the whole world will agree, must be evacuated and restored, without any attempt to limit the sovereignty which she enjoys in common with all other free nations. No other single act will serve as this will serve to restore confidence among the nations in the laws which they have themselves set and determined for the government of their relations with one another. Without this healing act the whole structure and validity of international law is forever impaired.

8. All French territory should be freed and the invaded portions restored, and the wrong done to France by Prussia in 1871 in the matter of Alsace-Lorraine, which has unsettled the peace of the world for nearly fifty years, should be righted, in order that peace may once more be made secure in the interest of all.

9. A re-adjustment of the frontiers of Italy should be effected along clearly recognizable lines of nationality.

10. The peoples of Austria-Hungary, whose place among the nations we wish to see safeguarded and assured, should be accorded the freest opportunity of autonomous development.

11. Romania, Serbia, and Montenegro should be evacuated; occupied territories restored; Serbia accorded free and secure access to the sea; and the relations of the several Balkan states to one another determined by friendly counsel along historically established lines of allegiance and nationality; and international guarantees of the political and economic independence and territorial integrity of the several Balkan states should be entered into.

12. The Turkish portions of the present Ottoman Empire should be assured a secure sovereignty, but the other nationalities which are now under Turkish rule should be assured an undoubted security of life and an absolutely unmolested opportunity of autonomous development, and the Dardanelles should be permanently opened as a free passage to the ships and commerce of all nations under international guarantees.

13. An independent Polish state should be erected which should include the territories inhabited by indisputably Polish populations, which should be assured a free and secure access to the sea, and whose political and economic independence and territorial integrity should be guaranteed by international covenant.

14. A general association of nations must be formed under specific covenants for the purpose of affording mutual guarantees of political independence and territorial integrity to great and small states alike.

In regard to these essential rectifications of wrong and assertions of right, we feel ourselves to be intimate partners of all the governments and peoples associated together against the imperialists. We cannot be separated in interest or divided in purpose. We stand together until the end.

For such arrangements and covenants we are willing to fight and to continue to fight until they are achieved; but only because we wish the right to prevail and desire a just and stable peace such as can be secured only by removing the chief provocations to war, which this program does remove.

We have no jealousy of German greatness, and there is nothing in this program that impairs it. We grudge her no achievement or distinction of learning or of pacific enterprise such as have made her record very bright and very enviable. We do not wish to injure her or to block in any way her legitimate influence or power. We do not wish to fight her either with arms or with hostile arrangements of trade, if she is willing to associate herself with us and the other peace-loving nations of the world in covenants of justice and law and fair dealing.

We wish her only to accept a place of equality among the peoples of the world—the new world in which we now live—instead of a place of mastery.

Neither do we presume to suggest to her any alteration or modification of her institutions. But it is necessary, we must frankly say, and necessary as a preliminary to any intelligent dealings with her on our part, that we should know whom her spokesmen speak for when they speak to us, whether for the Reichstag majority or for the military party and the men whose creed is imperial domination.

We have spoken now, surely, in terms too concrete to admit of any further doubt or question. An evident principle runs through the whole program I have outlined. It is the principle of justice to all peoples and nationalities, and their right to live on equal terms of liberty and safety with one another, whether they be strong or weak.

Unless this principle be made its foundation, no part of the structure of international justice can stand. The people of the United States could act upon no other principle, and to the vindication of this principle they are ready to devote their lives, their honor, and everything that they possess. The moral climax of this, the culminating and final war for human liberty has come, and they are ready to put their own strength, their own highest purpose, their own integrity and devotion to the test.

President Woodrow Wilson - January 8, 1918

Appendix B

Address by U.S. President George H. W. Bush before a Joint Session of Congress, 11 September, 1990

Mr. President and Mr. Speaker and Members of the United States Congress, distinguished guests, fellow Americans, thank you very much for that warm welcome.

We gather tonight, witness to events in the Persian Gulf as significant as they are tragic. In the early morning hours of August 2nd, following negotiations and promises by Iraq's dictator Saddam Hussein not to use force, a powerful Iraqi army invaded its trusting and much weaker neighbor, Kuwait. Within three days, 120,000 Iraqi troops with 850 tanks had poured into Kuwait and moved south to threaten Saudi Arabia. It was then that I decided to act to check that aggression.

At this moment, our brave servicemen and women stand watch in that distant desert and on distant seas, side by side with the forces of more than 20 other nations. They are some of the finest men and women of the United States of America. And they're doing one terrific job. These valiant Americans were ready at a moment's notice to leave their spouses and their children, to serve on the front line halfway around the world. They remind us who keeps America strong: they do. In the trying circumstances of the Gulf, the morale of our service men and women is excellent. In the face of danger, they're brave, they're well-trained, and dedicated.

A soldier, Private First Class Wade Merritt of Knoxville, Tennessee, now stationed in Saudi Arabia, wrote his parents of his worries, his love of family, and his hope for peace. But Wade also wrote, "I am proud of my country and its firm stance against inhumane aggression. I am proud of my army and its men. I am proud to serve my country." Well, let me just say, Wade, America is proud of you and is grateful to every soldier, sailor, marine, and airman serving the cause of peace in the Persian Gulf. I also want to thank the Chairman of the Joint Chiefs of Staff, General Powell; the Chiefs here tonight; our commander in the Persian Gulf, General Schwartzkopf; and the men and women of the Department of Defense. What a magnificent job you all are doing. And thank you very, very much from a grateful people. I wish I could say that their work is done. But we all know it's not.

So, if there ever was a time to put country before self and patriotism before party, the time is now. And let me thank all Americans, especially those here in this Chamber tonight, for your support for our armed forces and for their mission. That support will be even more important in the days to come. So, tonight I want to talk to you about what's at stake—what we must do together to defend civilized values around the world and maintain our economic strength at home.

Our objectives in the Persian Gulf are clear, our goals defined and familiar: Iraq must withdraw from Kuwait completely, immediately, and without condition. Kuwait's legitimate government must be restored. The security and stability of the Persian Gulf must be assured. And American citizens abroad must be protected. These goals are not ours alone. They've been endorsed by the United Nations Security Council five times in as many weeks. Most countries share our concern for principle. And many have a stake in the stability of the Persian Gulf. This is not, as Saddam Hussein would have it, the United States against Iraq. It is Iraq against the world.

As you know, I've just returned from a very productive meeting with Soviet President Gorbachev. And I am pleased that we are working together to build a new relationship. In Helsinki, our joint statement affirmed to the world our shared resolve to counter Iraq's threat to peace. Let me quote: "We are united in the belief that Iraq's aggression must not be tolerated. No peaceful international order is possible if larger states can devour their smaller neighbors." Clearly, no longer can a dictator count on East-West confrontation to stymie concerted United Nations action against aggression. A new partnership of nations has begun.

We stand today at a unique and extraordinary moment. The crisis in the Persian Gulf, as grave as it is, also offers a rare opportunity to move toward an historic period of cooperation. Out of these troubled times, our fifth objective—a new world order—can emerge: a new era—freer from the threat of terror, stronger in the pursuit of justice, and more secure in the quest for peace. An era in which the nations of the world, East and West, North and South, can prosper and live in harmony. A hundred generations have searched for this elusive path to peace, while a thousand wars raged across the span of human endeavor. Today that new world is struggling to be born, a world quite different from the one we've known. A world where the rule of law supplants the rule of the jungle. A world in which nations recognize the shared responsibility for freedom and justice. A world where the strong respect the rights of the weak. This is the vision that I shared with President Gorbachev in Helsinki. He and other leaders from Europe, the Gulf, and around the world understand that how we manage this crisis today could shape the future for generations to come.

The test we face is great, and so are the stakes. This is the first assault on the new world that we seek, the first test of our mettle. Had we not responded to this first provocation with clarity of purpose, if we do not continue to demonstrate our determination, it would be a signal to actual and potential despots around the world. America and the world must defend common vital interests—and we will. America and the world must support the rule of law—and we will. America and the world must stand up to aggression—and we will. And one thing more: In the pursuit of these goals America will not be intimidated.

Vital issues of principle are at stake. Saddam Hussein is literally trying to wipe a country off the face of the Earth. We do not exaggerate. Nor do we exaggerate when we say Saddam Hussein will fail. Vital economic interests are at risk as well. Iraq itself controls some 10 percent of the world's proven oil reserves. Iraq plus Kuwait controls twice that. An Iraq permitted to swallow Kuwait would have the economic and military power, as well as the arrogance, to intimidate and coerce its neighbors—neighbors who control the lion's share of the world's remaining oil reserves. We cannot permit a resource so vital to be dominated by one so ruthless. And we won't.

Recent events have surely proven that there is no substitute for American leadership. In the face of tyranny, let no one doubt American credibility and reliability. Let no one doubt our staying power. We will stand by our friends. One way or another, the leader of Iraq must learn this fundamental truth. From the outset, acting hand in hand with others, we've sought to fashion the broadest possible international response to Iraq's aggression. The level of world cooperation and condemnation of Iraq is unprecedented. Armed forces from countries spanning four continents are there at the request of King Fahd of Saudi Arabia to deter and, if need be, to defend against attack. Moslems and non-Moslems, Arabs and non-Arabs, soldiers from many nations stand shoulder to shoulder, resolute against Saddam Hussein's ambitions.

We can now point to five United Nations Security Council resolutions that condemn Iraq's aggression. They call for Iraq's immediate and unconditional withdrawal, the restoration of Kuwait's legitimate government, and categorically reject Iraq's cynical and self-serving attempt to annex Kuwait. Finally, the United Nations has demanded the release of all foreign nationals held hostage against their will and in contravention of international law. It is a mockery of human decency to call these people "guests." They are hostages, and the whole world knows it.

Prime Minister Margaret Thatcher, a dependable ally, said it all: "We do not bargain over hostages. We will not stoop to the level of using human beings as bargaining chips ever." Of course, of course, our hearts go out to the hostages and to their families. But our policy cannot change, and it will not change. America and the world will not be blackmailed by this ruthless policy.

We're now in sight of a United Nations that performs as envisioned by its founders. We owe much to the outstanding leadership of Secretary-General Javier Perez de Cuellar. The United Nations is backing up its words with action. The Security Council has imposed mandatory economic sanctions on Iraq, designed to force Iraq to relinquish the spoils of its illegal conquest. The Security Council has also taken the decisive step of authorizing the use of all means necessary to ensure compliance with these sanctions. Together with our friends and allies, ships of the United States Navy are today patrolling Mideast waters. They've already intercepted more than 700 ships to enforce the sanctions. Three regional leaders I spoke with just yesterday told me that these sanctions are working. Iraq is feeling the heat. We continue to hope that Iraq's leaders will recalculate just what their aggression has cost them. They are cut off from world trade, unable to sell their oil. And only a tiny fraction of goods gets through.

The communique with President Gorbachev made mention of what happens when the embargo is so effective that children of Iraq literally need milk or the sick truly need medicine. Then, under strict international supervision that guarantees the proper destination, then food will be permitted.

At home, the material cost of our leadership can be steep. That's why Secretary of State Baker and Treasury Secretary Brady have met with many world leaders to underscore that the burden of this collective effort must be shared. We are prepared to do our share and more to help carry that load; we insist that others do their share as well.

The response of most of our friends and allies has been good. To help defray costs, the leaders of Saudi Arabia, Kuwait, and the UAE—the United Arab Emirates—have pledged to provide our deployed troops with all the food and fuel they need. Generous assistance will also be provided to stalwart front-line nations, such as Turkey and Egypt. I am also heartened to report that this international response extends to the neediest victims of this conflict—those refugees. For our part, we've contributed $28 million for relief efforts. This is but a portion of what is needed. I commend, in particular, Saudi Arabia, Japan, and several European nations who have joined us in this purely humanitarian effort.

There's an energy-related cost to be borne as well. Oil-producing nations are already replacing lost Iraqi and Kuwaiti output. More than half of what was lost has been made up. And we're getting superb cooperation. If producers, including the United States, continue steps to expand oil and gas production, we can stabilize prices and guarantee against hardship. Additionally, we and several of our allies always have the option to extract oil from our strategic petroleum reserves if conditions warrant. As I've pointed out before, conservation efforts are essential to keep our energy needs as low as possible. And we must then take advantage of our energy sources across the board: coal, natural gas, hydro, and nuclear. Our failure to do these things has made us more dependent on foreign oil than ever before. Finally, let no one even contemplate profiteering from this crisis. We will not have it.

I cannot predict just how long it will take to convince Iraq to withdraw from Kuwait. Sanctions will take time to have their full intended effect. We will continue to review all options with our allies, but let it be clear: we will not let this aggression stand.

Our interest, our involvement in the Gulf is not transitory. It predated Saddam Hussein's aggression and will survive it. Long after all our troops come home—and we all hope it's soon, very soon—there will be a lasting role for the United States in assisting the nations of the Persian Gulf. Our role then: to deter future aggression. Our role is to help our friends in their own self-defense. And something else: to curb the proliferation of chemical, biological, ballistic missile and, above all, nuclear technologies.

Let me also make clear that the United States has no quarrel with the Iraqi people. Our quarrel is with Iraq's dictator and with his aggression. Iraq will not be permitted to annex Kuwait. That's not a threat, that's not a boast, that's just the way it's going to be.

Our ability to function effectively as a great power abroad depends on how we conduct ourselves at home. Our economy, our Armed Forces, our energy dependence, and our cohesion all determine whether we can help our friends and stand up to our foes. For America to lead, America must remain strong and vital. Our world leadership and domestic strength are mutual and reinforcing; a woven piece, strongly bound as Old Glory. To revitalize our leadership, our leadership capacity, we must address our budget deficit—not after election day, or next year, but now.

Higher oil prices slow our growth, and higher defense costs would only make our fiscal deficit problem worse. That deficit was already greater than it should have been—a projected $232 billion for the coming year. It must—it will—be reduced.

To my friends in Congress, together we must act this very month—before the next fiscal year begins on October 1st—to get America's economic house in order. The Gulf situation helps us realize we are more economically vulnerable than we ever should be. Americans must never again enter any crisis, economic or military, with an excessive dependence on foreign oil and an excessive burden of Federal debt.

Most Americans are sick and tired of endless battles in the Congress and between the branches over budget matters. It is high time we pulled together and get the job done right. It's up to us to straighten this out. This job has four basic parts. First, the Congress should, this month, within a budget agreement, enact growth-oriented tax measures—to help avoid recession in the short term and to increase savings, investment, productivity, and competitiveness for the longer term. These measures include extending incentives for research and experimentation; expanding the use of IRA's for new homeowners; establishing tax-deferred family savings accounts; creating incentives for the creation of enterprise zones and initiatives to encourage more domestic drilling; and, yes, reducing the tax rate on capital gains.

And second, the Congress should, this month, enact a prudent multiyear defense program, one that reflects not only the improvement in East-West relations but our broader responsibilities to deal with the continuing risks of outlaw action and regional conflict. Even with our obligations in the Gulf, a sound defense budget can have some reduction in real terms; and we're prepared to accept that. But to go beyond such levels, where cutting defense would threaten our vital margin of safety, is something I will never accept. The world is still dangerous. And surely, that is now clear. Stability's not secure. American interests are far reaching. Interdependence has increased. The consequences of regional instability can be global. This is no time to risk America's capacity to protect her vital interests.

And third, the Congress should, this month, enact measures to increase domestic energy production and energy conservation in order to reduce dependence on foreign oil. These measures should include my proposals to increase incentives for domestic oil and gas exploration, fuel-switching, and to accelerate the development of the Alaskan energy resources without damage to wildlife. As you know, when the oil embargo was imposed in the early 1970's, the United States imported almost 6 million barrels of oil a day. This year, before the Iraqi invasion, U.S. imports had risen to nearly 8 million barrels per day. And we'd moved in the wrong direction. And now we must act to correct that trend.

And fourth, the Congress should, this month, enact a 5-year program to reduce the projected debt and deficits by $500 billion—that's by half a trillion dollars. And if, with the Congress, we can develop a satisfactory program by the end of the month, we can avoid the ax of sequester—deep across-the-board cuts that would threaten our military capacity and risk substantial domestic disruption. I want to be able to tell the American people that we have truly solved the deficit problem. And for me to do that, a budget agreement must meet these tests: It must include the measures I've recommended to increase economic growth and reduce dependence on foreign oil. It must be fair. All should contribute, but the burden should not be excessive for any one group of programs or people. It must address the growth of government's hidden liabilities. It must reform the budget process and, further, it must be real.

I urge Congress to provide a comprehensive 5-year deficit reduction program to me as a complete legislative package, with measures to assure that it can be fully enforced. America is tired of phony deficit reduction or promise-now, save-later plans. It is time for a program that is credible and real. And finally, to the extent that the deficit reduction program includes new revenue measures, it must avoid any measure that would threaten economic growth or turn us back toward the days of punishing income tax rates. That is one path we should not head down again.

I have been pleased with recent progress, although it has not always seemed so smooth. But now it's time to produce. I hope we can work out a responsible plan. But with or without agreement from the budget summit, I ask both Houses of the Congress to allow a straight up-or-down vote on a complete $500-billion deficit reduction package not later than September 28. If the Congress cannot get me a budget, then Americans will have to face a tough, mandated sequester. I'm hopeful, in fact, I'm confident that the Congress will do what it should. And I can assure you that we in the executive branch will do our part.

In the final analysis, our ability to meet our responsibilities abroad depends upon political will and consensus at home. This is never easy in democracies, for we govern only with the consent of the governed. And although free people in a free society are bound to have their differences, Americans traditionally come together in times of adversity and challenge.

Once again, Americans have stepped forward to share a tearful goodbye with their families before leaving for a strange and distant shore. At this very moment, they serve together with Arabs, Europeans, Asians, and Africans in defense of principle and the dream of a new world order. That's why they sweat and toil in the sand and the heat and the sun. If they can come together under such adversity, if old adversaries like the Soviet Union and the United States can work in common cause, then surely we who are so fortunate to be in this great Chamber—Democrats, Republicans, liberals, conservatives—can come together to fulfill our responsibilities here.

Thank you. Good night. And God bless the United States of America.

Appendix C

A New Generation Draws the Line, by UK Prime Minister Tony Blair, 19 April, 1999

We have learnt by bitter experience not to appease dictators. We tried it 60 years ago. It didn't work then and it shouldn't be tried now. Milosevic's actions in Kosovo have given rise to scenes of suffering and cruelty people thought were banished from Europe forever.

Europe and the United States must stand firm together. Milosevic's policy of ethnic cleansing must be defeated and reversed. President Clinton has shown exactly the right resolve and determination. Once again, our thanks go to him and to the American people for their support in the cause of what is right.

Of course, we will be subject to the usual barrage of criticism, sometimes from people who, I think, find it hard to come to terms with the fact that there is a new generation of leaders in the United States and in Europe, who were born after World War II, who hail from the progressive side of politics, but who are prepared to be as firm as any of our predecessors right or left in seeing this thing through. See it through, we will.

Some argue we waited too long to act. To them I say it was right to give the negotiations every chance. Others argue we should not have acted at all. Of them I ask, what was the alternative? To do nothing would have been to acquiesce in Milosevic's brutality. It was clear that unless he was stopped, Kosovo would share Bosnia's fate.

The evidence is sobering. The Serbian offensive last year forced over 300,000 people from their homes. Villages were burned, people massacred. Despite all the efforts of the international community, including Russia, Milosevic rejected diplomacy in Paris this year. Within hours, he had let his forces off the leash in Kosovo. Within days, tens of thousands of people had fled their homes.

Milosevic was preparing for ethnic cleansing long before a single NATO bomb ever fell. What has happened was part of a plan to drive hundreds of thousands of ethnic Albanians out of their homes, execute many of their menfolk and torch their villages.

In Bosnia we waited four years before acting decisively. As a result of that conflict, over 200,000 people lost their lives, and 2 million people were made homeless. The duration of the conflict meant that a million of them were never able to return to their homes. NATO has not made the same mistake in Kosovo. Anyone who has seen the pictures of the hundreds of thousands of refugees leaving Kosovo, or who has heard the piteous stories of suffering imposed by the Serbian special police and the paramilitary thugs who work with them, knows why we had to act. Now they want to know that we are going to succeed.

Just as I believe there was no alternative to taking action, I am convinced there is no alternative to continuing until we succeed. On its 50th birthday NATO must prevail. We are fighting for a world where dictators are no longer able to visit horrific punishments on their own peoples in order to stay in power. It is important the people of Serbia know our quarrel is not with them. It is with the architects of Kosovo's ethnic cleansing. Just as after World War II, a war-crimes tribunal will bring those responsible to justice.

Our policy in Kosovo is taking its toll on Milosevic's killing machine. We should not be fooled by his state-controlled television. If he was so confident of his position, why did he suppress the independent media in Serbia? But we need to be patient. As I said, as President Clinton said, as other world leaders said at the outset of this action, he will not be defeated overnight.

We are also right to be cautious of the notion of a ground intervention force. Of course ground forces will be necessary in Kosovo to give the refugees the confidence to return to their homes in safety. But that is very different from fighting our way in. While we keep all options under review at all times, that is not our plan. A land invasion would be a massive undertaking and would take time to assemble. The casualties would potentially be large. And the civilian population would be at Milosevic's mercy. That is why airstrikes remain the sensible option in the present crisis, intensifying them and adding to their impact.

Milosevic knows what he has to do to end NATO's air campaign: a verifiable cessation of all combat activities and killings; the withdrawal of military, police and paramilitary forces from Kosovo; an international security force; the return of all refugees and unimpeded access for humanitarian aid, and a political framework for Kosovo based on Rambouillet.

We will not stop until he agrees to all of these conditions. The world knows too much of Milosevic to fall for any of his ploys. The succession of offers from Belgrade show that he is now looking for a way out. He wants to hang on to the results of his ethnic cleansing while protecting his killing machine. But anything short of what I've listed, and there's nothing doing. The airstrikes go on.

We should start now planning for the longer term, building on the agreement that was reached at Rambouillet, accepted by the KLA, but rejected by Milosevic. After all their suffering, it is clear that the Kosovar Albanians will never trust Milosevic to rule Kosovo again. Any political solution must recognize that fact. Russia has a unique and leading role to play in these efforts.

We need to enter a new millennium where dictators know that they cannot get away with ethnic cleansing or repress their peoples with impunity. In this conflict we are fighting not for territory but for values. For a new internationalism where the brutal repression of whole ethnic groups will no longer be tolerated. For a world where those responsible for such crimes have nowhere to hide.

Appendix D

A Just and Necessary War, by U.S. President William Jefferson Clinton, 23 May, 1999

We are in Kosovo with our allies to stand for a Europe, within our reach for the first time, that is peaceful, undivided and free. And we are there to stand against the greatest remaining threat to that vision: instability in the Balkans, fueled by a vicious campaign of ethnic cleansing.

The problem is not simply ethnic hatred, or even ethnic conflict. The people of the former Yugoslavia have lived together for centuries with greater and lesser degrees of conflict, but not the constant "cleansing" of peoples from their land. Had they experienced nothing but that, their nations would be homogenous today, not endlessly diverse.

The intolerable conditions the region finds itself in today are the result of a decade-long campaign by Slobodan Milosevic to build a greater Serbia by singling out whole peoples for destruction because of their ethnicity and faith. The brutal methods are familiar now. Spreading hate in the media. Killing moderate leaders. Arming paramilitaries and ordering soldiers to conduct planned campaigns of murder and expulsion. Eradicating the culture, the heritage, the very record of the presence of his victims. Refugees are not a byproduct of the fighting he has initiated; the fighting is designed to create refugees. We are haunted by the images of people driven from their homes, pushing the elderly in wheelbarrows, telling stories of relatives murdered.

We saw this for the first time in Croatia and in Bosnia. The international community responded at first with a studied neutrality that equated victims with aggressors; it followed with diplomacy and the deployment of unarmed peacekeepers with the mandate, but not the means, to protect civilians. By the time NATO acted, 250,000 people were dead, more than two million displaced, and many have still not returned. People will look back on Kosovo and say that this time, because we acted soon and forcefully enough, more lives were saved and the refugees all came home. The Balkan conflict that began 10 years ago in Kosovo will have ended in Kosovo.

We cannot respond to such tragedies everywhere, but when ethnic conflict turns into ethnic cleansing where we can make a difference, we must try, and that is clearly the case in Kosovo. Had we faltered, the result would have been a moral and strategic disaster. The Kosovars would have become a people without a homeland, living in difficult conditions in some of the poorest countries in Europe, overwhelming new democracies. The Balkan conflict would have continued indefinitely, posing a risk of a wider war and of continuing tensions with Russia. NATO itself would have been discredited for failing to defend the very values that give it meaning. Those who say Kosovo is too small to be of great importance forget these simple facts.

When the violence in Kosovo began in early 1998, we exhausted every diplomatic avenue for a settlement. Last October, we convinced Mr. Milosevic that he should withdraw some forces from Kosovo and allow an unarmed international presence. That is the solution advocates of compromise propose today. But it failed last fall. Mr. Milosevic broke his promises, poured more troops into Kosovo, poised for an offensive he had been planning for months. When it began, we had to act.

Mr. Milosevic's strategy has been to outlast us by dividing the alliance. He has failed. Instead of disunity in Brussels, there are growing signs of disaffection in Belgrade: Serbian soldiers abandoning their posts, Serbian civilians protesting the policies of their leader, young men avoiding conscription, prominent Serbs calling on Mr. Milosevic to accept NATO's conditions. Meanwhile, our air campaign has destroyed or damaged one-third of Serbia's armored vehicles in Kosovo, half its artillery, most of its ability to produce ammunition, all its capacity to refine fuel and done enormous damage to other sectors of its economy. Though he has driven hundreds of thousands of Kosovar Albanians from their homes, Mr. Milosevic has not eliminated the Kosovar Liberation Army. Indeed, its ranks are swelling, and it has begun to go on the offensive against Serb forces hunkered down to hide from air strikes.

Now Mr. Milosevic faces the certainty of continuing air strikes, the persistence of the K.L.A. and the prospect of having to answer to his people for starting an unwinnable conflict that is bringing military failure and economic ruin. The question now is not whether his ethnic cleansing will be reversed, but when, and how much of his military he is willing to see destroyed along the way.

While I do not rule out other military options, we are pursuing our present strategy for three reasons. First, and most important, it is working and will succeed in meeting NATO's basic conditions of restoring the Kosovars to their homes, with Serb forces out of Kosovo and the deployment of an international security force. This force must have NATO at its core, which means it must have NATO command and control and NATO rules of engagement, with special arrangements for non-NATO countries, just like our force in Bosnia. Our military campaign will continue until these conditions are met, not because we are stubborn or arbitrary, but because these are the only conditions under which the refugees will go home in safety and under which the K.L.A. have any incentive to disarm — the basic requirements of a resolution that will work.

Second, this strategy has broad and deep support in the alliance, and allows us to meet our objectives. While there may be differences in domestic circumstances, cultural ties to the Balkans and ideas on tactics, there is no question about our unity on goals and our will to prevail. I have worked hard to shape our present consensus; 60 days into the air campaign, NATO is more unified on Kosovo than it was at the beginning.

Third, this strategy gives us the best opportunity to meet our goals in a way that strengthens, not weakens, our fundamental interest in a long-term, positive relationship with Russia. Russia is now helping to work out a way for Belgrade to meet our conditions. Russian troops should participate in the force that will keep the peace in Kosovo, turning a source of tension into an opportunity for cooperation, like our joint effort in Bosnia.

Finally, we must remember that the reversal of ethnic cleansing in Kosovo is not sufficient to end ethnic conflict in the Balkans and establish lasting stability. The European Union and the United States must do for southeastern Europe what we did for Western Europe after World War II and for Central Europe after the cold war. Freedom, respect for minority rights, and prosperity are powerful forces for progress. They give people goals to work for; they elevate hope over fear and tomorrow over yesterday.

We can do that by rebuilding struggling economies, encouraging trade and investment and helping the nations of the region join NATO and the European Union.

Already, the region's democracies are responding to the pull of integration by sticking with their reforms, taking in refugees and supporting NATO's campaign. A democratic Serbia that respects the rights of its people and its neighbors can and should join them.

If it does, we will help to restore it to its rightful place as a European state in the Balkans, not a balkanized state at the periphery of Europe.

The Balkans are not fated to be the heart of European darkness, a region of bombed mosques, men and boys shot in the back, young women raped, all traces of group and individual history rewritten or erased. Just as leaders took their people down that road, leaders must take them back to a better tomorrow. Ultimately, we and our allies can help make this happen, if we stick with NATO's campaign and follow through with a strategy to insure that the forces pulling southeastern Europe together are stronger than the forces tearing it apart.

Appendix E

Address by U.S. President George W. Bush before a Joint Session of Congress, 20 September, 2001

Mr. Speaker, Mr. President Pro Tempore, members of Congress, and fellow Americans:

In the normal course of events, Presidents come to this chamber to report on the state of the Union. Tonight, no such report is needed. It has already been delivered by the American people.

We have seen it in the courage of passengers, who rushed terrorists to save others on the ground—passengers like an exceptional man named Todd Beamer. And would you please help me to welcome his wife, Lisa Beamer, here tonight. We have seen the state of our Union in the endurance of rescuers, working past exhaustion. We've seen the unfurling of flags, the lighting of candles, the giving of blood, the saying of prayers—in English, Hebrew, and Arabic. We have seen the decency of a loving and giving people who have made the grief of strangers their own. My fellow citizens, for the last nine days, the entire world has seen for itself the state of our Union—and it is strong.

Tonight we are a country awakened to danger and called to defend freedom. Our grief has turned to anger, and anger to resolution. Whether we bring our enemies to justice, or bring justice to our enemies, justice will be done. I thank the Congress for its leadership at such an important time. All of America was touched on the evening of the tragedy to see Republicans and Democrats joined together on the steps of this Capitol, singing "God Bless America." And you did more than sing; you acted, by delivering 40 billion dollars to rebuild our communities and meet the needs of our military. Speaker Hastert, Minority Leader Gephardt, Majority Leader Daschle, and Senator Lott, I thank you for your friendship, for your leadership, and for your service to our country. And on behalf of the American people, I thank the world for its outpouring of support. America will never forget the sounds of our National Anthem playing at Buckingham Palace, on the streets of Paris, and at Berlin's Brandenburg Gate.

We will not forget South Korean children gathering to pray outside our embassy in Seoul, or the prayers of sympathy offered at a mosque in Cairo. We will not forget moments of silence and days of mourning in Australia and Africa and Latin America. Nor will we forget the citizens of 80 other nations who died with our own: dozens of Pakistanis; more than 130 Israelis; more than 250 citizens of India; men and women from El Salvador, Iran, Mexico, and Japan; and hundreds of British citizens. America has no truer friend than Great Britain. Once again, we are joined together in a great cause—so honored the British Prime Minister has crossed an ocean to show his unity with America. Thank you for coming, friend.

On September the 11th, enemies of freedom committed an act of war against our country. Americans have known wars—but for the past 136 years, they have been wars on foreign soil, except for one Sunday in 1941. Americans have known the casualties of war—but not at the center of a great city on a peaceful morning. Americans have known surprise attacks—but never before on thousands of civilians. All of this was brought upon us in a single day—and night fell on a different world, a world where freedom itself is under attack. Americans have many questions tonight. Americans are asking: Who attacked our country? The evidence we have gathered all points to a collection of loosely affiliated terrorist organizations known as al Qaeda. They are some of the murderers indicted for bombing American embassies in Tanzania and Kenya, and responsible for bombing the USS Cole. Al Qaeda is to terror what the mafia is to crime. But its goal is not making money; its goal is remaking the world—and imposing its radical beliefs on people everywhere.

The terrorists practice a fringe form of Islamic extremism that has been rejected by Muslim scholars and the vast majority of Muslim clerics, a fringe movement that perverts the peaceful teachings of Islam. The terrorists' directive commands them to kill Christians and Jews, to kill all Americans, and make no distinctions among military and civilians, including women and children. This group and its leader—a person named Usama bin Laden—are linked to many other organizations in different countries, including the Egyptian Islamic Jihad and the Islamic Movement of Uzbekistan. There are thousands of these terrorists in more than 60 countries. They are recruited from their own nations and neighborhoods and brought to camps in places like Afghanistan, where they are trained in the tactics of terror. They are sent back to their homes or sent to hide in countries around the world to plot evil and destruction.

The leadership of al Qaeda has great influence in Afghanistan and supports the Taliban regime in controlling most of that country. In Afghanistan, we see al Qaeda's vision for the world. Afghanistan's people have been brutalized; many are starving and many have fled. Women are not allowed to attend school. You can be jailed for owning a television. Religion can be practiced only as their leaders dictate. A man can be jailed in Afghanistan if his beard is not long enough.

The United States respects the people of Afghanistan. After all, we are currently its largest source of humanitarian aid; but we condemn the Taliban regime. It is not only repressing its own people, it is threatening people everywhere by sponsoring and sheltering and supplying terrorists. By aiding and abetting murder, the Taliban regime is committing murder.

And tonight, the United States of America makes the following demands on the Taliban: Deliver to United States authorities all the leaders of al Qaeda who hide in your land. Release all foreign nationals, including American citizens, you have unjustly imprisoned. Protect foreign journalists, diplomats, and aid workers in your country. Close immediately and permanently every terrorist training camp in Afghanistan, and hand over every terrorist, and every person in their support structure, to appropriate authorities. Give the United States full access to terrorist training camps, so we can make sure they are no longer operating. These demands are not open to negotiation or discussion. The Taliban must act, and act immediately. They will hand over the terrorists, or they will share in their fate.

I also want to speak tonight directly to Muslims throughout the world. We respect your faith. It's practiced freely by many millions of Americans, and by millions more in countries that America counts as friends. Its teachings are good and peaceful, and those who commit evil in the name of Allah blaspheme the name of Allah. The terrorists are traitors to their own faith, trying, in effect, to hijack Islam itself. The enemy of America is not our many Muslim friends; it is not our many Arab friends. Our enemy is a radical network of terrorists, and every government that supports them. Our war on terror begins with al Qaeda, but it does not end there. It will not end until every terrorist group of global reach has been found, stopped, and defeated.

Americans are asking, why do they hate us? They hate what they see right here in this chamber—a democratically elected government. Their leaders are self-appointed. They hate our freedoms—our freedom of religion, our freedom of speech, our freedom to vote and assemble and disagree with each other. They want to overthrow existing governments in many Muslim countries, such as Egypt, Saudi Arabia, and Jordan. They want to drive Israel out of the Middle East. They want to drive Christians and Jews out of vast regions of Asia and Africa. These terrorists kill not merely to end lives, but to disrupt and end a way of life. With every atrocity, they hope that America grows fearful, retreating from the world and forsaking our friends. They stand against us, because we stand in their way.

We are not deceived by their pretenses to piety. We have seen their kind before. They are the heirs of all the murderous ideologies of the 20th century. By sacrificing human life to serve their radical visions—by abandoning every value except the will to power—they follow in the path of fascism, Nazism, and totalitarianism. And they will follow that path all the way, to where it ends: in history's unmarked grave of discarded lies. Americans are asking: How will we fight and win this war? We will direct every resource at our command—every means of diplomacy, every tool of intelligence, every instrument of law enforcement, every financial influence, and every necessary weapon of war—to the disruption and to the defeat of the global terror network.

Now this war will not be like the war against Iraq a decade ago, with a decisive liberation of territory and a swift conclusion. It will not look like the air war above Kosovo two years ago, where no ground troops were used and not a single American was lost in combat. Our response involves far more than instant retaliation and isolated strikes. Americans should not expect one battle, but a lengthy campaign, unlike any other we have ever seen. It may include dramatic strikes, visible on TV, and covert operations, secret even in success. We will starve terrorists of funding, turn them one against another, drive them from place to place, until there is no refuge or no rest. And we will pursue nations that provide aid or safe haven to terrorism. Every nation, in every region, now has a decision to make. Either you are with us, or you are with the terrorists. From this day forward, any nation that continues to harbor or support terrorism will be regarded by the United States as a hostile regime.

Our nation has been put on notice: We're not immune from attack. We will take defensive measures against terrorism to protect Americans. Today, dozens of federal departments and agencies, as well as state and local governments, have responsibilities affecting homeland security. These efforts must be coordinated at the highest level. So tonight I announce the creation of a Cabinet-level position reporting directly to me—the Office of Homeland Security. And tonight I also announce a distinguished American to lead this effort, to strengthen American security: a military veteran, an effective governor, a true patriot, a trusted friend—Pennsylvania's Tom Ridge. He will lead, oversee, and coordinate a comprehensive national strategy to safeguard our country against terrorism, and respond to any attacks that may come.

These measures are essential. But the only way to defeat terrorism as a threat to our way of life is to stop it, eliminate it, and destroy it where it grows. Many will be involved in this effort, from FBI agents to intelligence operatives to the reservists we have called to active duty. All deserve our thanks, and all have our prayers. And tonight, a few miles from the damaged Pentagon, I have a message for our military: Be ready. I've called the Armed Forces to alert, and there is a reason. The hour is coming when America will act, and you will make us proud. This is not, however, just America's fight. And what is at stake is not just America's freedom. This is the world's fight. This is civilization's fight. This is the fight of all who believe in progress and pluralism, tolerance and freedom.

We ask every nation to join us. We will ask, and we will need, the help of police forces, intelligence services, and banking systems around the world. The United States is grateful that many nations and many international organizations have already responded—with sympathy and with support. Nations from Latin America, to Asia, to Africa, to Europe, to the Islamic world. Perhaps the NATO Charter reflects best the attitude of the world: An attack on one is an attack on all. The civilized world is rallying to America's side. They understand that if this terror goes unpunished, their own cities, their own citizens may be next. Terror, unanswered, can not only bring down buildings, it can threaten the stability of legitimate governments. And you know what? We're not going to allow it.

Americans are asking: What is expected of us? I ask you to live your lives, and hug your children. I know many citizens have fears tonight, and I ask you to be calm and resolute, even in the face of a continuing threat. I ask you to uphold the values of America, and remember why so many have come here. We are in a fight for our principles, and our first responsibility is to live by them. No one should be singled out for unfair treatment or unkind words because of their ethnic background or religious faith. I ask you to continue to support the victims of this tragedy with your contributions. Those who want to give can go to a central source of information, libertyunites.org, to find the names of groups providing direct help in New York, Pennsylvania, and Virginia.

The thousands of FBI agents who are now at work in this investigation may need your cooperation, and I ask you to give it. I ask for your patience, with the delays and inconveniences that may accompany tighter security; and for your patience in what will be a long struggle. I ask your continued participation and confidence in the American economy. Terrorists attacked a symbol of American prosperity. They did not touch its source. America is successful because of the hard work, and creativity, and enterprise of our people. These were the true strengths of our economy before September 11th, and they are our strengths today. And, finally, please continue praying for the victims of terror and their families, for those in uniform, and for our great country. Prayer has comforted us in sorrow, and will help strengthen us for the journey ahead.

Tonight I thank my fellow Americans for what you have already done and for what you will do. And ladies and gentlemen of the Congress, I thank you, their representatives, for what you have already done and for what we will do together. Tonight, we face new and sudden national challenges. We will come together to improve air safety, to dramatically expand the number of air marshals on domestic flights, and take new measures to prevent hijacking. We will come together to promote stability and keep our airlines flying, with direct assistance during this emergency. We will come together to give law enforcement the additional tools it needs to track down terror here at home. We will come together to strengthen our intelligence capabilities to know the plans of terrorists before they act, and to find them before they strike.

We will come together to take active steps that strengthen America's economy, and put our people back to work. Tonight we welcome two leaders who embody the extraordinary spirit of all New Yorkers: Governor George Pataki, and Mayor Rudolph Giuliani. As a symbol of America's resolve, my administration will work with Congress, and these two leaders, to show the world that we will rebuild New York City.

After all that has just passed—all the lives taken, and all the possibilities and hopes that died with them—it is natural to wonder if America's future is one of fear. Some speak of an age of terror. I know there are struggles ahead, and dangers to face. But this country will define our times, not be defined by them. As long as the United States of America is determined and strong, this will not be an age of terror; this will be an age of liberty, here and across the world.

Great harm has been done to us. We have suffered great loss. And in our grief and anger we have found our mission and our moment. Freedom and fear are at war. The advance of human freedom—the great achievement of our time, and the great hope of every time—now depends on us. Our nation, this generation will lift a dark threat of violence from our people and our future. We will rally the world to this cause by our efforts, by our courage. We will not tire, we will not falter, and we will not fail.

It is my hope that in the months and years ahead, life will return almost to normal. We'll go back to our lives and routines, and that is good. Even grief recedes with time and grace. But our resolve must not pass. Each of us will re-member what happened that day, and to whom it happened. We'll remember the moment the news came—where we were and what we were doing. Some will remember an image of a fire, or a story of rescue. Some will carry memories of a face and a voice gone forever.

And I will carry this: It is the police shield of a man named George How-ard, who died at the World Trade Center trying to save others. It was given to me by his mom, Arlene, as a proud memorial to her son. This is my reminder of lives that ended, and a task that does not end. I will not forget this wound to our country or those who inflicted it. I will not yield; I will not rest; I will not relent in waging this struggle for freedom and security for the American people. The course of this conflict is not known, yet its outcome is certain. Freedom and fear, justice and cruelty, have always been at war, and we know that God is not neutral between them.

Fellow citizens, we'll meet violence with patient justice—assured of the rightness of our cause, and confident of the victories to come. In all that lies before us, may God grant us wisdom, and may He watch over the United States of America. Thank you.

ABOUT THE AUTHORS

Corey Anhorn, at the time of writing, was an undergraduate student in the Honours program in Anthropology at Concordia University in Montréal, Québec, Canada. He is also currently an Officer in the Canadian Forces Infantry Reserves. His research focuses on Military Anthropology, International Development, and Human Rights issues both domestically and abroad.

Ricky Curotte completed his B.A. in History and Anthropology at Concordia University in Montréal, Québec, Canada. He is a Kanienkehaka from a little border town called Hemmingford, Québec. His primary interests in Anthropology are indigenous peoples, transnationalism, identity and legal systems. Ricky is currently pursuing his studies in anthropology at the M.A. level.

Justin De Genova is a fourth year B.A. student in Anthropology at Concordia University, in Montréal, Québec, Canada. He was born and raised in Vancouver, British Columbia. His primary areas of interest in Anthropology are politics and urban regions.

Zoe Dominiak is an Honors B.A. student in Anthropology at Concordia University, in Montréal, Québec, Canada. Originally from British Columbia, she is a researcher and practitioner in Quebec's cultural industries. Her primary area of investigation is the anthropology of art, with an emphasis on cultural mediation and media studies.

Cameron Fenton is an independent journalist and an Anthropology student at Concordia University. Originally from Edmonton, Alberta, he now resides in Montréal, Québec.

Maximilian Forte is an associate professor in anthropology in the Department of Sociology and Anthropology at Concordia University in Montréal, Québec, Canada. He directed the "New Imperialism" seminar, and his own research interests in this area focus on imperialist theory and practice, the militarization of the academy, soft power and social media, and ideologies of empire.

Lesley Foster is an Anthropology Major and Minor in Spanish at Concordia University in Montréal, Québec, Canada and lives periodically in Buenos Aires, Argentina. She is originally from Edmonton, Alberta, Canada. Her primary area of interest is in Latin American Studies.

Thomas Prince is pursuing his B.A. degree at Concordia University in Montréal, Québec, Canada, a double major in Economics and Honours Anthropology. Thomas' academic interests include human rights and alternative development methods. He currently works for the Concordia Volunteer Abroad Program, as the Administrative Assistant.

Kate Roland is completing her undergraduate studies in Sociology at Concordia University in Montréal, Québec, Canada. Far afield from her usual topics, this course has fuelled her interest in balancing military efforts with diplomacy.

Mark Shapiro is a B.A. student pursuing a Joint Specialization in Anthropology and Sociology at Concordia University, in Montréal, Québec, Canada. His primary areas of interest in anthropology are Middle East studies and militarization of the academy.

Nageen Siddiqui is a B.A. student in Sociology Community and Ethnic Studies and Adult Education at Concordia University, in in Montréal, Québec, Canada. She is originally from Pakistan. Her primary areas of interest, in sociology and adult education, are human rights issues and facilitating adult literacy programs.

Miles Smart is an Honours B.A. student at Concordia University, in Montréal, Québec, Canada. He hopes to continue his interests in anarcho-primitivist philosophy and indigeneity in future graduate studies.

Katelyn Spidle is a fourth year student, double majoring in Anthropology and Journalism, at Concordia University, in Montréal, Québec, Canada. She is originally from Brantford, Ontario, and enjoys drifting between her Big City and Small Town homes.

Rosalia T. Stillitano is a B.A. student in Anthropology at Concordia University, in Montréal, Québec, Canada, and she is originally from Montréal.

Her primary areas of interest in anthropology are indigenous peoples, political anthropology, and globalization (trafficking in persons, and human rights).

Elizabeth Vezina is a fourth year B.A. student in the Honours program in Anthropology at Concordia University in Montréal, Québec, Canada. Her fields of study have been as eclectic as her interests in life, which includes contemporary dance, the social construction of the senses, indigenous society and political anthropology. She hopes that these studies will help her to make a contribution to her community in the future.

INDEX

www.ingramcontent.com/pod-product-compliance
Lightning Source LLC
Chambersburg PA
CBHW022104280326
41933CB00007B/250